Canadian Short Stories
FOURTH SERIES

Canadian Short Stories
FOURTH SERIES

Selected by
ROBERT WEAVER

TORONTO
Oxford University Press

Oxford University Press, 70 Wynford Drive, Don Mills, Ontario, M3C 1J9

Toronto   Oxford   New York
Delhi   Bombay   Calcutta   Madras   Karachi
Kuala Lumpur   Singapore   Hong Kong   Tokyo   Nairobi   Dar es Salaam
Cape Town   Melbourne   Auckland

and associated companies in
Berlin   Ibadan

CANADIAN CATALOGUING IN PUBLICATION DATA

Main entry under title:
Canadian short stories, fourth series
ISBN 0-19-540502-1
1. Short stories, Canadian (English) – 20th century.*
I. Weaver, Robert, 1921–
PS8319.C354 1985   C813'.01   C85-099414-4
PR9197.32.C354 1985

Printed in Canada by
Webcom Limited

Contents

Preface

In 1960 Oxford University Press published *Canadian Short Stories*, an anthology I had edited for its World's Classics series. The book was number 573 on the World's Classics list, one in a series of small clothbound reprints, published in London and Toronto and priced at $1.75. Unknown to us at the time, this volume was the beginning of a series.

The first *Canadian Short Stories* was historical in its approach; it opened with three stories from the late nineteenth century and concluded with work by four young writers: James Reaney, Douglas Spettigue, Alice Munro, and Mordecai Richler. Re-issued as an Oxford in Canada Paperback in 1966, it is still in print. It was followed by the Second Series (1968), a collection of short fiction from the late 1950s and early 1960s, and the Third Series (1978), which contains stories from the late 1960s and early 1970s. And now here is a selection of stories from the early 1980s. Two writers appear in all four anthologies: Mavis Gallant and Alice Munro.

Great changes have taken place in the Canadian short story in the quarter-century since the first of these anthologies was published. In the 1950s the short story had seemed at times to be on the verge of disappearing—not only in Canada but in England and the United States as well. In those days a writer who was fortunate enough to have a book of stories appear in print knew that his publisher was doing his cultural duty, not making a hard-headed business decision. In 1960 no one would have predicted that by the 1970s the short story would occupy a central position in Canadian writing; but that is what happened. One of the pleasures of my career as an editor has been to watch Canadian short-story writers develop and mature, with work—realism, fantasy, post-modernism, 'magic realism', autobiographical fiction —that can satisfy almost every literary taste. And more and more of these stories are being published internationally. Through very often local in their origins and concerns (like much short fiction), modern Canadian stories travel well. For example, the imagined life of people in small towns in southwestern Ontario —the world of Alice Munro—has become familiar to readers in the United States, England, Australia, and Sweden. Mavis Gallant and Munro are regular contributors to *The New Yorker*. As I was working on this anthology the Norwegian publisher Gordon Hølmebakk sent me a copy of *Canada Forteller*, a collection of stories he has edited—beginning with Duncan Campbell Scott and Stephen Leacock and ending with Sandra Birdsell and Guy Vanderhaeghe—that is being distributed throughout Scandinavia.

There's a story by Norman Levine, often reprinted, called 'We All Begin in a Little Magazine'. Though written in 1971, its title still applies. Most short-story writers make their first appearance in a 'little magazine' with a tiny but discerning circulation—magazines like *The Fiddlehead* in Fredericton, *Descant* in Toronto, and *Dandelion* in Calgary. But much support for the short story in recent years has been provided by book publishers. Large national houses such as Stoddard, Macmillan, McClelland & Stewart, and Penguin; more specialized literary publishers such as Lester & Orpen Dennis, Oberon Press, Coach House Press, and Talonbooks; and smaller regional firms like Oolichan on Vancouver Island, NeWest in Edmonton, and Turnstone Press in Winnipeg—all have published single-author collections. And of course there are many anthologies. All this book publishing implies a healthy interest in, and readership for, short stories. But despite these satisfactory conditions, the commercial magazine market has actually worsened since the 1950s. The only popular magazine that publishes short fiction consistently—within some fairly rigid editorial limitations—is *Chatelaine*. *Saturday Night* published good stories in the past, but now its concentration on politicians, senior civil servants, and business leaves little space for fiction.

Two recent casualties on the literary scene that touch me personally are the disappearance from CBC Radio at the end of September 1985 of the literary series 'Anthology' and the program of serial readings, 'Book Time'. I worked at the CBC for more than thirty-five years, until my retirement at the end of March 1985. But even before my time, CBC Radio was deeply involved in the literary life of Canada. Today it is obsessed with information programs. Now that 'Anthology' and 'Book Time' are gone, writers are deprived not only of two markets but (a not-insignificant matter) of an important audience for their stories and poems. And think of the deprivation CBC Radio itself, and its listeners, will suffer.

I want to end on a more cheerful note. Oxford University Press Canada has been my publisher for more than thirty years, through the publication of seven anthologies of one kind or another. There have been far too many people at Oxford who have been friendly and helpful to even begin to name them and I want to thank them all. One person I will name, however, is William Toye, who has been my editor at Oxford since 1962; and who was an editor with me on *The Tamarack Review* (one of those 'little magazines') for twenty-five years, from its first issue to its last. We have been in the trenches together for a long time. I think he would agree with me that it has not been the worst of times to be an editor in this country.

ROBERT WEAVER

Toronto
September 1985

Acknowledgements

'The Salt Garden' from *Bluebeard's Egg* by Margaret Atwood. Used by permission of the Canadian Publishers, McClelland and Stewart Limited, Toronto.

'Niagara Falls' by Sandra Birdsell was first published in *Ladies of the House* (Turnstone Press, 1984) and is reprinted by permission of Turnstone Press.

'There Are a Lot of Ways to Die' from *Digging Up the Mountain* by Neil Bissoondath. Reprinted by permission of Macmillan of Canada, A Division of Canada Publishing Corporation.

'The Black Queen' from *The Black Queen Stories* by Barry Callaghan, © 1982. Reprinted by permission of Lester & Orpen Dennys Publishers, Ltd., Canada.

'The Sins of Tomas Benares' from *Café Le Dog* by Matt Cohen. Used by permission of The Canadian Publishers, McClelland and Stewart Limited, Toronto.

'The Chosen Husband' © 1985 by Mavis Gallant. Appeared originally in *The New Yorker* (April 1985). Reprinted by permission of Georges Borchardt, Inc. and Mavis Gallant.

'The Dragon' from *Fables of Brunswick Avenue* by Katherine Govier © copyright Katherine Govier 1985. Reprinted by permission of Penguin Books Canada Limited.

'The Thrill of the Grass' from *The Thrill of the Grass* by W.P. Kinsella © copyright W.P. Kinsella 1984. Reprinted by permission of Penguin Books Canada Limited.

'Django, Karfunkelstein, & Roses' reprinted by permission of Norman Levine.

'My Refugee' reprinted by permission of Joyce Marshall.

'Miles City, Montana' © 1985 Alice Munro. All rights reserved. Appeared originally in *The New Yorker* (January 1985). Reprinted by permission of Virginia Barber Literary Agency, Inc.

'A Bolt of White Cloth' from *A Bolt of White Cloth* by Leon Rooke. Reprinted by permission of Stoddart Publishing Co. Limited, Toronto, Canada.

'Mrs Turner Cutting the Grass' from *Various Miracles* by Carol Shields. Reprinted by permission of Stoddart Publishing Co. Limited, Toronto, Canada.

'Madonna' © by Elizabeth Spencer. All rights reserved. Reprinted by permission of Virginia Barber Literary Agency, Inc.

'Crossing the Rubicon' from *Real Mothers: Short Stories by Audrey Thomas.* Reprinted by permission of Audrey Thomas.

'A Matter of Balance' reprinted by permission of W.D. Valgardson.

'Man Descending' from *Man Descending* by Guy Vanderhaeghe. Reprinted by permission of Macmillan of Canada, A Division of Canada Publishing Corporation.

'What Happened to Ravel's Bolero?' reprinted by permission of Helen Weinzweig.

MARGARET ATWOOD

The Salt Garden

Alma turns up the heat, stirs the clear water in the red enamel pot, adds more salt, stirs, adds. She's making a supersaturated solution: re-making it. She made it already, at lunchtime, with Carol, but she didn't remember that you had to boil the water and she just used hot water from the tap. Nothing happened, though Alma had promised that a salt tree would form on the thread they hung down into the water, suspending it from a spoon laid crossways on the top of the glass.

'It takes time,' Alma said. 'It'll be here when you come home,' and Carol went trustingly back to school, while Alma tried to figure out what she'd done wrong.

This experiment thing is new. Alma isn't sure where Carol picked it up. Surely not from school: she's only in grade two. But they're doing everything younger and younger. It upsets Alma to see them trying on her high heels and putting lipstick on their little mouths, even though she knows it's just a game. They wiggle their hips, imitating something they've seen on television. Maybe the experiments come from television too.

Alma has racked her brains, as she always does when Carol expresses interest in anything, searching for information she ought to possess but usually doesn't. These days, Alma encourages anything that will involve the two of them in an activity that will block out questions about the way they're living; about the whereabouts of Mort, for instance. She's tried trips to the zoo, sewing dolls' dresses, movies on Saturdays. They all work, but only for a short time.

When the experiments came up, she remembered about putting vinegar into baking soda, to make it fizz; that was a success. Then other things started coming back to her. Now she can recall having been given a small chemistry set as a child, at the age of ten or so it must have been, by her father, who had theories in advance of his time. He thought girls should be brought up more like boys, possibly because he had no sons: Alma is an only child. Also he wanted her to do better than he himself had done. He had a job beneath his capabilities, in the post office, and he felt thwarted by that. He didn't want Alma to feel thwarted: that was how he'd attempted to warn Alma away from an early marriage, from leaving university to put Mort through architectural school by working as a secretary for a food-packaging company. 'You'll wake up one day and you'll feel thwarted,' he told her. Alma sometimes wonders whether this word describes what she feels, but usually decides that it doesn't.

Long before that period, though, he'd tried to interest Alma in chess and mathematics and stamp collecting, among other things. Not much of this rubbed off on Alma, at least not to her knowledge; at the predictable age she became disappointingly obsessed with make-up and clothes, and her algebra marks took a downturn. But she does retain a clear image of the chemistry set, with its miniature test tubes and the wire holder for them, the candle for heating them, and the tiny corked bottles, so appealingly like doll's-house glassware, with the mysterious substances in them: crystals, powders, solutions, potions. Some of these things had undoubtedly been poisonous; probably you could not buy such chemistry sets for children now. Alma is glad not to have missed out on it, because it was alchemy, after all, and that was how the instruction book presented it: magic. *Astonish your friends. Turn water to milk. Turn water to blood.* She remembers terminology, too, though the meanings have grown hazy with time. *Precipitate. Sublimation.*

There was a section on how to do tricks with ordinary household objects, such as how to make a hard-boiled egg go into a milk bottle, back in the days when there were milk bottles. (Alma thinks about them and sees the cream floating on the top, tastes the cardboard tops she used to beg to be allowed to lick off, smells the horse droppings from the wagons: she's getting old.) How to turn milk sour in an instant. How to make invisible writing with lemon juice. How to stop cut apples from turning brown. It's from this part of the instruction book (the best section, because who could resist the thought of mysterious powers hidden in the ordinary things around you?) that she's called back the supersaturated solution and the thread: *How to make a magical salt garden*. It was one of her favourites.

Alma's mother had complained about the way Alma was using up the salt, but her father said it was a cheap price to pay for the development of Alma's scientific curiosity. He thought Alma was learning about the spaces between molecules, but it was no such thing, as Alma and her mother both silently knew. Her mother was Irish, in dark contrast to her father's clipped and cheerfully bitter Englishness; she read tea-leaves for the neighbour women, which only they regarded as a harmless amusement. Maybe it's from her that Alma has inherited her bad days, her stretches of fatalism. Her mother didn't agree with her father's theories about Alma, and emptied out her experiments whenever possible. For her mother, Alma's fiddling in the kitchen was merely an excuse to avoid work, but Alma wasn't thinking even of that. She just liked the snowfall in miniature, the enclosed, protected world in the glass, the crystals forming on the thread, like the pictures of the Snow Queen's palace in the Hans Christian Andersen book at school. She can't remember ever having astonished any of her friends with tricks from the instruction book. Astonishing herself was enough.

The water in the pot is boiling again; it's still clear. Alma adds more salt, stirs while it dissolves, adds more. When salt gathers at the bottom of the pot, swirling instead of vanishing, she turns off the heat. She puts another spoon into the glass before pouring the hot water into it: otherwise the glass might break. She knows about this from having broken several of her mother's drinking glasses in this way.

She picks up the spoon with the thread tied to it and begins to lower the thread into the glass. While she is doing this, there is a sudden white flash, and the kitchen is blotted out with light. Her hand goes blank, then appears before her again, black, like an after-image on the retina. The outline of the window remains, framing her hand, which is still suspended above the glass. Then the window itself crumples inward, in fragments, like the candy-crystal of a shatter-proof windshield. The wall will be next, curving in towards her like the side of an inflating balloon. In an instant Alma will realize that the enormous sound has come and gone and burst her eardrums so that she is deaf, and then a wind will blow her away.

Alma closes her eyes. She can go on with this, or she can try to stop, hold herself upright, get the kitchen back. This isn't an unfamiliar experience. It's happened to her now on the average of once a week, for three months or more; but though she can predict the frequency she never knows when. It can be at any moment, when she's run the bathtub full of water and is about to step in, when she's sliding her arms into the sleeves of her coat, when she's making love, with Mort or Theo, it could be either of them and it has been. It's always when she's thinking about something else.

It isn't speculation: it's more like a hallucination. She's never had hallucinations before, except a long time ago when she was a student and dropped acid a couple of times. Everyone was doing it then, and she hadn't taken much. There had been moving lights and geometric patterns, which she'd watched in a detached way. Afterwards she'd wondered what all the talk about cosmic profundity had been about, though she hadn't wanted to say anything. People were very competitive about the meaningfulness of their drug trips in those days.

But none of it had been like this. It's occurred to her that maybe these things are acid flashes, though why should she be getting them now, fifteen years later, with none in between? At first she was so badly frightened that she'd considered going to see someone about it: a doctor, a psychiatrist. Maybe she's borderline epileptic. Maybe she's becoming schizophrenic or otherwise going mad. But there don't seem to be any other symptoms: just the flash and the sound, and being blown through the air, and the moment when she hits and falls into darkness.

The first time, she ended up lying on the floor. She'd been with Mort then, having dinner in a restaurant, during one of their interminable conversations about how things could be arranged better. Mort loves the word *arrange*, which is not one of Alma's favourites. Alma is a romantic: if you love someone, what needs arranging? And if you don't, why put in the effort? Mort, on the other hand, has been reading books about Japan; also he thinks they should draw up a marriage contract. On that occasion, Alma pointed out that they were already married. She wasn't sure where Japan fitted in: if he wanted her to scrub his back, that was all right, but she didn't want to be Wife Number One, not if it implied a lot of other numbers, either in sequence or simultaneously.

Mort has a girl friend, or that's how Alma refers to her. Terminology is becoming difficult these days: *mistress* is no longer suitable, conjuring up as it does peach-coloured negligées trimmed in fur, and mules, which nobody wears any more; nobody, that is, like Mort's girl friend, who is a squarely built young woman with a blunt-cut pageboy and freckles. And *lover* doesn't seem to go with the emotions Mort appears to feel towards this woman, whose name is Fran. Fran isn't the name of a mistress or a lover; more of a wife, but Alma is the wife. Maybe it's the name that's confusing Mort. Maybe that's why he feels, not passion or tenderness or devotion towards this woman, but a mixture of anxiety, guilt, and resentment, or this is what he tells Alma. He sneaks out on Fran to see Alma and calls Alma from telephone booths, and Fran doesn't know about it, which is the reverse of the way things used to be. Alma feels sorry for Fran, which is probably a defence.

It's not Fran that Alma objects to, as such. It's the rationalization of Fran. It's Mort proclaiming that there's a justifiable and even moral reason for doing what he does, that it falls into subsections, that men are polygamous by nature and so forth. That's what Alma can't stand. She herself does what she does because it's what she does, but she doesn't preach about it.

The dinner was more difficult for Alma than she'd anticipated, and because of this she had an extra drink. She stood up to go to the bathroom, and then it happened. She came to covered with wine and part of the tablecloth. Mort told her she'd fainted. He didn't say so, but she knew he put it down to hysteria, brought on by her problems with him, which to this day neither of them has precisely defined but which he thinks of as her problems, not his. She also knew that he thought she did it on purpose, to draw attention to herself, to collect sympathy and concern from him, to get him to listen to her. He was irritated. 'If you were feeling dizzy,' he said, 'you should have gone outside.'

Theo, on the other hand, was flattered when she passed out in his arms. He put it down to an excess of sexual passion, brought on by his technique, although again he didn't say so. He was quite pleased with her, and rubbed her hands and brought her a glass of water.

Theo is Alma's lover: no doubt about the terminology there. She met him at a party. He introduced himself by asking if she'd like another drink. (Mort, on the other hand, introduced himself by asking if she knew that if you cut the whiskers off cats they would no longer be able to walk along fences, which should have been a warning of some kind to Alma, but was not.) She was in a tangle with Mort, and Theo appeared to be in a similar sort of tangle with his wife, so they seemed to each other comparatively simple. That was before they had begun to accumulate history, and before Theo had moved out of his house. At that time they had been clutchers, specialists in hallways and vestibules, kissing among the hung-up coats and the rows of puddling rubbers.

Theo is a dentist, though not Alma's dentist. If he were her dentist, Alma doubts that she ever would have ended up having what she still doesn't think of as an affair with him. She feels that the inside of her mouth, and especially the insides of her teeth, are intimate in an anti-sexual way; surely a man would be put off by such evidences of bodily imperfection, of rot. (Alma doesn't have bad teeth; still, even a look inside with that little mirror, even the terminology, *orifice, cavity, mandible, molar.* . . .)

Dentistry, for Theo, is hardly a vocation. He hadn't felt called by teeth; he's told her he picked dentistry because he didn't know what else to do; he had good fine-motor coordination, and it was a living, to put it mildly.

'You could have been a gigolo,' Alma said to him on that occasion. 'You would have got extra in tips.' Theo, who does not have a rambunctious sense of humour and is fastidious about clean underwear, was on the verge of being shocked, which Alma enjoyed. She likes making him feel more sexual than he is, which in turn makes him more sexual. She indulges him.

So, when she found herself lying on Theo's broadloom, with Theo bending over her, gratified and solicitous, saying, 'Sorry, was I too rough?' she did nothing to correct his impression.

'It was like a nuclear explosion,' she said, and he thought she was using a simile. Theo and Mort have one thing in common: they've both elected themselves as the cause of these little manifestations of hers. That, or female body chemistry: another good reason why women shouldn't be allowed to be airplane pilots, a sentiment Alma once caught Theo expressing.

The content of Alma's hallucinations doesn't surprise her. She suspects that other people are having similar or perhaps identical experiences, just as, during the Middle Ages, many people saw (for instance) the Virgin Mary, or witnessed miracles: flows of blood that stopped at the touch of a bone, pictures that spoke, statues that bled. As for now, you could get hundreds of people to swear they've been on spaceships and talked with extraterrestrial beings. These kinds of delusions go in waves, Alma thinks, in epidemics. Her lightshows, her blackouts, are no doubt as common as measles, only people aren't admitting to them. Most likely they're doing what she should do, trotting off to their doctors and getting themselves renewable prescriptions for Valium or some other pill that will smooth out the brain. They don't want anyone to think they're unstable, because although most would agree that what she's afraid of is something it's right to be afraid of, there's a consensus about how much. Too much fear is not normal.

Mort, for instance, thinks everyone should sign petitions and go on marches. He signs petitions himself, and brings them for Alma to sign, on occasions when he's visiting her legitimately. If she signed them during one of his sneak trips, Fran would know and put two and two together, and by now not even Alma wants that. She likes Mort better now that she sees less of him. Let Fran do his laundry, for a change. The marches he goes to with Fran, however, as they are more like social occasions. It's for this reason that Alma herself doesn't attend the marches: she doesn't want to make things awkward for Fran, who is touchy enough already on the subject of Alma. There are certain things, like parent-teacher conferences, that Mort is allowed to attend with Alma, and other things that he isn't. Mort is sheepish about these restrictions, since one of his avowed reasons for leaving Alma was that he felt too tied down.

Alma agrees with Mort about the marches and petitions, out loud that is. It's reasonable to suppose that if only everyone in the world would sign the petitions and go on the marches, the catastrophe itself would not occur. Now is the time to stand up and be counted, to throw your body in front of the juggernaut, as Mort himself does in the form of donations to peace groups and letters to politicians, for which he receives tax receipts and neatly typed form letters in response. Alma knows that Mort's way makes sense, or as much sense as anything; but she has never been a truly sensible person. This was one of her father's chief complaints about her. She could never bring herself to squeeze in her two hands the birds that flew into their plate-glass window and injured themselves, as her father taught her to do, in order to collapse their lungs. Instead she wanted to keep them in boxes filled with cotton wool and feed them with an eyedropper, thus causing them—according to her father—to die a lingering and painful death. So he would collapse their lungs himself, and Alma would refuse to look and grieve afterwards.

Marrying Mort was not sensible. Getting involved with Theo was not sensible, Alma's clothes are not and never have been sensible, especially the shoes. Alma knows that if a fire ever broke out in her house, the place would burn to the ground before she could make up her mind about what to do, even though she's in full possession of all the possibilities (extinguisher, fire department's number, wet cloth to put over the nose). So, in the face of Mort's hearty optimism, Alma shrugs inwardly. She tries hard to believe, but she's an infidel and not proud of it. The sad truth is that there are probably more people in the world like her than like Mort. Anyway, there's a lot of money tied up in those bombs. She doesn't interfere with him or say anything negative, however. The petitions are as constructive a hobby as any, and the marches keep him active and happy. He's a muscular man with a reddish face, who's inclined to overweight and who needs to work off energy to avoid the chance of a heart attack, or that's what the doctor says. It's all a good enough way to pass the time.

Theo, on the other hand, deals wth the question by not dealing with it at all. He lives his life as if it isn't there, a talent for obliviousness that Alma envies. He just goes on filling teeth, filling teeth, as if all the tiny adjustments he's making to people's mouths are still going to matter in ten years, or five, or even two. Maybe, Alma thinks in her more cynical moments, they can use his dental records for identification when they're sorting out the corpses, if there are any left to sort; if sorting will be a priority, which she very much doubts. Alma has tried to talk about it, once or twice, but Theo has said he doesn't see any percentage in negative thinking. It will happen or it won't, and if it doesn't the main worry will be the economy. Theo makes investments. Theo is planning his retirement. Theo has tunnel vision and Alma doesn't. She has no faith in people's ability to pull themselves out of this hole, and no sand to stick her head into. The thing is there, standing in one corner of whatever room she happens to be in, like a stranger whose face you know you could see clearly if you were only to turn your head. Alma doesn't turn her head. She doesn't want to look. She goes about her business, most of the time; except for these minor lapses.

Sometimes she tells herself that this isn't the first time people have thought they were coming to the end of the world. It's happened before, during the Black Death for instance, which Alma remembers as having been one of the high points of second-year university. The world hadn't come to an end, of course, but believing it was going to had much the same effect.

Some of them decided it was their fault and went around flagellating themselves, or each other, or anyone else handy. Or they prayed a lot, which was easier then because you had some idea of who you were supposed to be talking to. Alma doesn't think this is a dependable habit of mind any more, since there's an even chance that the button will be pushed by some American religious maniac who wants to play God and help Revelations along, someone who really believes that he and a few others will be raised up incorruptible afterwards, and therefore everyone else can rot. Mort says this is a mistake unlikely to be made by the Russians, who've done away with the afterlife and have to be serious about this one. Mort says the Russians are better chess players, which isn't much consolation to Alma. Her father's attempts to teach her chess had not been too successful, as Alma had a way of endowing the pieces with personalities and crying when her Queen got killed.

Or you could wall yourself up, throw the corpses outside, carry around oranges stuck with cloves. Dig shelters. Issue instructional handbooks.

Or you could steal things from the empty houses, strip the necklaces from the bodies.

Or you could do what Mort was doing. Or you could do what Theo was doing. Or you could do what Alma was doing.

Alma thinks of herself as doing nothing. She goes to bed at night, she gets up in the morning, she takes care of Carol, they eat, they talk, sometimes they laugh, she sees Mort, she sees Theo, she looks for a better job, though not in a way that convinces her. She thinks about going back to school and finishing her degree: Mort says he will pay, they've both agreed he owes her that, though when it comes right down to it she isn't sure she wants to. She has emotions: she loves people, she feels anger, she is happy, she gets depressed. But somehow she can't treat these emotions with as much solemnity as she once did. Never before has her life felt so effortless, as if all responsibility has been lifted from her. She floats. There's a commercial on television, for milk she thinks, that shows a man riding at the top of a wave on a surfboard: moving, yet suspended, as if there is no time. This is how Alma feels: removed from time. Time presupposes a future. Sometimes she experiences this state as apathy, other times as exhilaration. She can do what she likes. But what does she like?

She remembers something else they did during the Black Death: they indulged themselves. They pigged out on their winter supplies, they stole food and gorged, they danced in the streets, they copulated indiscriminately with whoever was available. Is this where she's heading, on top of her wave?

Alma rests the spoon on the two edges of the glass. Now the water is cooling and the salt is coming out of solution. It forms small transparent islands on the surface that thicken as the crystals build up, then break and drift down through the water, like snow. She can see a faint white fuzz of salt gathering on the thread. She kneels so that her eyes are level with the glass, rests her chin and hands on the table, watches. It's still magic. By the time Carol comes home from school, there will be a whole winter in the glass. The thread will be like a tree after a sleet storm. She can't believe how beautiful this is.

After a while she gets up and walks through her house, through the whitish living room which Mort considers Japanese in the less-is-more tradition but which has always reminded her of a paint-by-numbers page only a quarter filled in, past the naked-wood end wall, up the staircase from which Mort removed the banisters. He also took out too many walls, omitted too many doors; maybe that's what went wrong with the marriage. The house is in Cabbagetown, one of the larger ones. Mort, who specializes in renovations, did it over and likes to bring people there to display it to them. He views it, still, as the equivalent of an advertising brochure. Alma, who is getting tired of going to the door in her second-best dressing gown with her hair in a towel and finding four men in suits standing outside it, headed by Mort, is thinking about getting the locks changed. But that would be too definitive. Mort still thinks of the house as his, and he thinks of her as part of the house. Anyway, with the slump in house-building that's going on, and considering who pays the bills, she ought to be glad to do her bit to help out; which Mort has narrowly avoided saying.

She reaches the white-on-white bathroom, turns on the taps, fills the tub with water which she colours blue with a capful of German bath gel, climbs in, sighs. She has some friends who go to isolation tanks and float in total darkness, for hours on end, claiming that this is relaxing and also brings you in touch with your deepest self. Alma had decided to give this experience a pass. Nevertheless, the bathtub is where she feels safest (she's never passed out in the bathtub) and at the same time most vulnerable (what if she were to pass out in the bathtub? She might drown).

When Mort still lived with her and Carol was younger, she used to lock herself into the bathroom, chiefly because it had a door that closed, and do what she called 'spending time with herself', which amounted to daydreaming. She's retained the habit.

At one period, long ago it seems now, though it's really just a couple of months, Alma indulged from time to time in a relatively pleasant fantasy. In this fantasy she and Carol were living on a farm, on the Bruce Peninsula. She'd gone on a vacation there once, with Mort, back before Carol was born, when the marriage was still behaving as though it worked. They'd driven up the Bruce and crossed over onto Manitoulin Island in Lake Huron. She'd noticed the farms then, how meagre they were, how marginal, how many rocks had been pulled out of the fields and piled into cairns and rows. It was one of these farms she chose for her fantasy, on the theory that nobody else would want it.

She and Carol heard about the coming strike on the radio, as they were doing the dishes in the farm kitchen after lunch. (Improbable in itself, she now realizes: it would be too fast for that, too fast to reach a radio show.) Luckily, they raised all their own vegetables, so they had lots around. Initially Alma was vague about what these would be. She'd included celery, erroneously, she knows now: you could never grow celery in soil like that.

Alma's fantasies are big on details. She roughs them in first, then goes back over them, putting in the buttons and zippers. For this one she needed to make a purchase of appropriate seeds, and to ask for advice from the man in the hardware store. 'Celery?' he said. (A balding, fatherly small-town retailer, wearing braces on his pants, a ring of sweat under each arm of his white shirt. Still, the friendliness was tricky. Probably he had contempt for her. Probably he told stories about her to his cronies in the beer parlour, a single woman with a child, living by herself out there on that farm. The cronies would cruise by on her sideroad in their big second-hand cars, staring at her house. She would think twice about going outside in shorts, bending over to pull out weeds. If she got raped, everyone would know who did it but none of them would tell. This man would not be the one but he would say after a few beers that she had it coming. This is a facet of rural life Alma must consider seriously before taking it up.)

'Celery?' he said. 'Up here? Lady, you must be joking.' So Alma did away with the celery, which wouldn't have kept well anyway.

But there were beets and carrots and potatoes, things that could be stored. They'd dug a large root cellar into the side of a hill; it was entered by a door that slanted and that somehow had several feet of dirt stuck onto the outside of it. But the root cellar was much more than a root cellar: it had several rooms, for instance, and electric lights (with power coming from where? It was details like this that when closely examined helped to cause the eventual collapse of the fantasy, though for the electricity Alma filled in with a small generator worked by runoff from the pond).

Anyway, when they heard the news on the radio, she and Carol did not panic. They walked, they did not run, sedately to the root cellar, where they went inside and shut the door behind them. They did not forget the radio, which was a transistor, though of course it was no use after the initial strike, in which all the stations were presumably vaporized. On the shelves built neatly into one wall were rows and rows of bottled water. There they stayed, eating carrots and playing cards and reading entertaining books, until it was safe to come out, into a world in which the worst had already happened so no longer needed to be feared.

This fantasy is no longer functional. For one thing, it could not be maintained for very long in the concrete detail Alma finds necessary before practical questions with no answers began to intrude (ventilation?). In addition, Alma had only an approximate idea of how long they would have to stay in there before the danger would be over. And then there was the problem of refugees, marauders, who would somehow find out about the potatoes and carrots and come with (guns? sticks?). Since it was only her and Carol, the weapons were hardly needed. Alma began to equip herself with a rifle, then rifles, to fend off these raiders, but she was always outnumbered and outgunned.

The major flaw, however, was that even when things worked and escape and survival were possible, Alma found that she couldn't just go off like that and leave other people behind. She wanted to include Mort, even though he'd behaved badly and they weren't exactly together, and if she let him come she could hardly neglect Theo. But Theo could not come, of course, without his wife and children, and then there was Mort's girl friend Fran, whom it would not be fair to exclude.

This arrangement worked for a while, without the quarrelling Alma would have expected. The prospect of imminent death is sobering, and Alma basked for a time in the gratitude her generosity inspired. She had intimate chats with the two other women about their respective men, and found out several things she didn't know; the three of them were on the verge of becoming really good friends. In the evenings they sat around the kitchen table which had appeared in the root cellar, peeling carrots together in a companionable way and reminiscing about what it had been like when they all lived in the city and didn't know each other, except obliquely through the men. Mort and Theo sat at the other end, drinking the Scotch they'd brought with them, mixed with bottled water. The children got on surprisingly well together.

But the root cellar was too small really, and there was no way to enlarge it without opening the door. Then there was the question of who would sleep with whom and at what times. Concealment was hardly possible in such a confined space, and there were three women but only two men. This was all too close to real life for Alma, but without the benefit of separate dwellings.

After the wife and the girl friend started to insist on having their parents and aunts and uncles included (and why had Alma left hers out?), the fantasy became overpopulated and, very quickly, uninhabitable. Alma could not choose, that was her difficulty. It's been her difficulty all her life. She can't draw the line. Who is she to decide, to judge people like that, to say who must die and who is to be given a chance at life?

The hill of the root cellar, honeycombed with tunnels, too thoroughly mined, fell in upon itself, and all perished.

When Alma has dried herself off and is rubbing body lotion on herself, the telephone rings.

'Hi, what are you up to?' the voice says.

'Who is this?' Alma says, then realizes that it's Mort. She's embarrassed not to have recognized his voice. 'Oh, it's you,' she says. 'Hi. Are you in a phone booth?'

'I thought I might drop by,' says Mort, conspiratorially. ''That is, if you'll be there.'

'With or without a committee?' Alma says.

'Without,' says Mort. What this means is clear enough. 'I thought we could make some decisions.' He means to be gently persuasive, but comes through as slightly badgering.

Alma doesn't say that he doesn't need her to help him make decisions, since he seems to make them swiftly enough on his own. 'What kind of decisions?' she says warily. 'I thought we were having a moratorium on decisions. That was your last decision.'

'I miss you,' Mort says, letting the words float, his voice shifting to a minor key that is supposed to indicate yearning.

'I miss you too,' says Alma, hedging her bets. 'But this afternoon I promised Carol I'd buy her a pink gym suit. How about tonight?'

'Tonight isn't an option,' says Mort.

'You mean you aren't allowed out to play?' says Alma.

'Don't be snarky,' Mort says a little stiffly.

'Sorry,' says Alma, who isn't. 'Carol wants you to come on Sunday to watch "Fraggle Rock" with her.'

'I want to see you alone,' Mort says. But he books himself in for Sunday anyway, saying he'll double-check it and call her back. Alma says good-bye and hangs up, with a sense of relief that is very different from the feelings she's had about saying good-bye to Mort on the telephone in the past; which were, sequentially, love and desire, transaction of daily business, frustration because things weren't being said that ought to be, despair and grief, anger and a sense of being fucked over. She continues on with the body lotion, with special attention to the knees and elbows. That's where it shows up first, when you start to look like a four-legged chicken. Despite the approach of the end of the world, Alma likes to keep in shape.

She decides to take the streetcar. She has a car and knows how to drive, she can drive perfectly well, but lately she's been doing it less and less. Right now she prefers modes of transportation that do not require any conscious decisions on her part. She'd rather be pulled along, on a track if possible, and let someone else do the steering.

The streetcar stop is outside a health-food store, the window of which is filled with displays of dried apricots and carob-covered raisins, magical foods that will preserve you from death. Alma too has had her macrobiotic phase: she knows what elements of superstitious hope the consumption of such talismans involves. It would have been just as effective to have strung the raisins on a thread and worn them around her neck, to ward off vampires. On the brick wall of the store, between the window and the door, someone has written in spray paint: JESUS HATES YOU.

The streetcar comes and Alma gets on. She's going to the subway station, where she will get off and swiftly buy a pink gym suit and two pairs of summer socks for Carol and go down the stairs and get onto a subway train going north, using the transfer she's just stuck into her purse. You aren't supposed to use transfers for stopovers but Alma feels reckless.

The car is a little crowded. She stands near the back door, looking out the window, thinking about nothing in particular. It's a sunny day, one of the first, and warm; things are too bright.

All at once some people near the back door begin to shout: *Stop! Stop!* Alma doesn't hear them at first, or she hears them at the level of non-comprehension: she knows there is noise, but she thinks it's just some teenagers fooling around, being too loud, the way they do. The streetcar conductor must think this too, because he keeps on going, at a fast clip, spinning along, while more and more people are shouting and then screaming, *Stop! Stop! Stop!* Then Alma begins to shout too, for she sees what is wrong: there's a girl's arm caught in the back door, and the girl herself is outside, being dragged along it must be; Alma can't see her but she knows she's there.

Alma finds herself jumping up and down, like a frustrated child, and screaming '*Stop! Stop!*' with the rest of them, and still the man drives on, oblivious. Alma wants someone to throw something or hit him, why is no one moving? They're packed in too close, and the ones at the front don't know, can't see. This goes on for hours which are really minutes, and finally he slows down and stops. He gets out, walks around to the back.

Luckily there's an ambulance right beside them, so the girl is put into it. Alma can't see her face or how badly injured she is, though she cranes her neck, but she can hear the noises she's making: not crying, not whimpering, something more animal and abandoned, more terrified. The most frightening thing must have been not the pain but the sense that no one could see or hear her.

Now that the streetcar has stopped and the crisis is over, people around Alma begin muttering to one another. The driver should be removed, they say. He should lose his licence, or whatever it is they have. He should be arrested. But he comes back and pushes something at the front and the doors open. They will all have to get off the streetcar, he says. He sounds angry, as if the girl caught in the door and the shouting have been someone else's fault.

They aren't far from the subway stop and the store where Alma intends to do her furtive shopping: Alma can walk. At the next stoplight she looks back. The driver is standing beside the streetcar, hands in his pockets, talking with a policeman. The ambulance is gone. Alma notices that her heart is pounding. This is how it is in riots, she thinks, or fires: someone begins to shout and then you're in the middle of it, without knowing what is happening. It goes too fast, and you shut out the cries for help. If people had shouted 'help' instead of 'stop', would the driver have heard them sooner? But the people did shout, and he did stop, eventually.

Alma can't find a pink gym suit in Carol's size, so she buys a mauve one instead. There will be repercussions about that. She makes it onto the subway train, using her spurious transfer, and begins her short journey through the darkness she can see outside the window, watching her own face floating on the glass that seals it out. She sits with her hands clasped around the package on her lap, and begins looking at the hands of the people across from her. She's found herself doing this quite often lately: noticing what the hands are like, how they are almost luminous, even the hands of old people, knobby hands with blue veins and mottles. These symptoms of age don't frighten her as a foretaste of her own future, the way they once did; they no longer revolt her. Male or female, it doesn't matter; the hands she's looking at right now belong to a middle-aged woman of no distinction, they're lumpy and blunt, with chipped orange nail polish, they're clutching a brown leather purse.

Sometimes she has to restrain an impulse to get up, cross the aisle, sit down, take hold of these alien hands. It would be misunderstood. She can remember feeling this way once, a long time ago, when she was on a plane, going to join Mort at a conference in Montreal. They were planning to take a mini-vacation together after it. Alma was excited by the prospect of the hotel room, the aroma of luxury and illicit sex that would surround them. She looked forward to being able to use the bath towels and drop them on the floor without having to think about who was going to wash them. But the plane had started to lurch around in the air, and Alma was frightened. When it took a dip, like an elevator going down, she'd actually grabbed the hand of the man sitting next to her; not that it would make any difference whose hand you were holding if there really was a crash. Still, it made her feel safer. Then, of course, he'd tried to pick her up. He was fairly nice in the end: he sold real estate, he said.

Sometimes she studies Theo's hands, finger by finger, nail by nail. She rubs them over her body, puts the fingers in her mouth, curling her tongue around them. He thinks it's merely eroticism. He thinks he's the only person whose hands she thinks about in this way.

Theo lives in a two-bedroom apartment in a high-rise not far from his office. Or at least Alma thinks he lives there. Though it makes her feel, not unpleasantly, a little like a call girl, it's where she meets him, because he doesn't like coming to her house. He still considers it Mort's territory. He doesn't think of Alma as Mort's territory, only the house, just as his own house, where his wife lives with their three children, is still his territory. That's how he speaks of it: 'my house'. He goes there on weekends, just as Mort goes to Alma's house. Alma suspects he and his wife sneak into bed, just as she and Mort do, feeling like students in a fifties dorm, swearing each other to secrecy. They tell themselves that it would never do for Fran to find out. Alma hasn't been explicit about Theo to Mort, though she's hinted that there's someone. That made him perk up. 'I guess I have no right to complain,' he said.

'I guess you don't,' said Alma. It's ridiculous the way the five of them carry on, but it would seem just as ridiculous to Alma not to go to bed with Mort. After all, he is her husband. It's something she's always done. Also, the current arrangement has done wonders for their sex life. Being a forbidden fruit suits her. She's never been one before.

But if Theo is still sleeping with his wife, Alma doesn't want to know about it. He has every right, in a way, but she would be jealous. Oddly enough, she doesn't much care any more what goes on between Mort and Fran. Mort is thoroughly hers already; she knows every hair on his body, every wrinkle, every rhythm. She can relax into him with scarcely a thought, and she doesn't have to make much conscious effort to please him. It's Theo who's the unexplored territory, it's with Theo that she has to stay alert, go carefully, not allow herself to be lulled into a false sense of security: Theo, who at first glance appears so much gentler, more considerate, more tentative. For Alma, he's a swamp to Mort's forest: she steps lightly, ready to draw back. Yet it's his body—shorter, slighter, more sinewy than Mort's— she's possessive about. She doesn't want another woman touching it, especially one who's had more time to know it than she's had. The last time she saw Theo (here, in this apartment building, the impersonal white lobby of which she's now entering), he said he wanted to show her some recent snapshots of his family. Alma excused herself and went into the bathroom. She didn't want to see a picture of Theo's wife, but also she felt that even to look would be a violation of both of them; the use, by Theo, of two women to cancel each other out. It's occurred to her that she is to Theo's wife as Mort's girl friend is to her: the usurper, in a way, but also the one to be pitied because of what is not being admitted.

She knows that the present balance of power can't last. Sooner or later, pressures will be brought to bear. The men will not be allowed to drift back and forth between their women, their houses. Barriers will be erected, signs will go up: STAY PUT OR

GET OUT. Rightly so; but none of these pressures will come from Alma. She likes things the way they are. She's decided that she prefers having two men rather than one: it keeps things even. She loves both of them, she wants both of them; which means, some days, that she loves neither and wants neither. It makes her less anxious and less vulnerable, and suggests multiple futures. Theo may go back to his wife, or wish to move in with Alma. (Recently he asked her an ominous question—'What do you want?'—which Alma dodged.) Mort may want to return, or he may decide to start over with Fran. Or Alma could lose both of them and be left alone with Carol. This thought, which would once have given rise to panic and depression not unconnected with questions of money, doesn't worry her much at the moment. She wants it to go on the way it is forever.

Alma steps into the elevator and is carried up. Weightlessness encloses her. It's a luxury; her whole life is a luxury. Theo, opening the door for her, is a luxury, especially his skin, which is smooth and well-fed and darker than hers, which comes of his being part Greek, a generation or two back, and which smells of brisk sweetish chemicals. Theo amazes her, she loves him so much she can barely see him. Love burns her out; it burns out Theo's features so that all she can see in the dimmed apartment is an outline, shining. She's not on the wave, she's in it, warm and fluid. This is what she wants. They don't get as far as the bedroom, but collapse onto the living-room rug, where Theo makes love to her as if he's running for a train he's never going to catch.

Time passes, and Theo's details reappear, a mole here, a freckle there. Alma strokes the back of his neck, lifting her hand to look surreptitiously at her watch: she has to be back in time for Carol. She must not forget the gym suit, cast aside in its plastic bag at the door, along with her purse and shoes.

'That was magnificent,' says Alma. It's true.

Theo smiles, kisses the inside of her wrist, holds it for a few seconds as if listening for the pulse, picks up her half-slip from the floor, hands it to her with tenderness and deference, as if presenting her with a bouquet of flowers. As if she's a lady on a chocolate box. As if she's dying, and only he knows it and wants to keep it from her.

'I hope,' he says pleasantly, 'that when this is all over we won't be enemies.'

Alma freezes, the half-slip half on. Then air goes into her, a silent gasp, a scream in reverse, because she's noticed at once: he didn't say 'if', he said 'when'. Inside his head there's a schedule. All this time during which she's been denying time, he's been checking off the days, doing a little countdown. He believes in predestination. He believes in doom. She should have known that, being such a neat person, he would not be able to stand anarchy forever. They must leave the water, then, and emerge onto dry land. She will need more clothes, because it will be colder there.

'Don't be silly,' Alma says, pulling imitation satin up to her waist like a bedsheet. 'Why would we?'

'It happens,' says Theo.

'Have I ever done or said anything to make you feel it would happen to us?' Alma says. Maybe he's going back to his wife. Maybe he isn't, but has decided anyway that she will not do, not on a daily basis, not for the rest of his life. He still believes there will be one. So does she, or why would she be this upset?

'No,' says Theo, scratching his leg, 'but it's the kind of thing that happens.' He stops scratching, looks at her, that look she used to consider sincere. 'I just want you to know I like you too well for that.'

Like. That finishes it, or does it? As often with Theo, she's unsure of what is being said. Is he expressing devotion, or has it ended already, without her having been aware of it? She's become used to thinking that in a relationship like theirs everything is given and nothing is demanded, but perhaps it's the other way around. Nothing is given. Nothing is even *a given*. Alma feels suddenly too visible, too blatant. Perhaps she should return to Mort and become once more unseen.

'I like you too,' she says. She finishes dressing, while he continues to lie on the floor, gazing at her fondly, like someone waving to a departing ship, who nevertheless looks forward to the moment when he can go and have his dinner. He doesn't care what she's going to do next.

'Day after tomorrow?' he says, and Alma, who wants to have been wrong, smiles back.

'Beg and plead,' she says.

'I'm not good at it,' he says. 'You know how I feel.'

Once, Alma would not even have paused at this; she would have been secure in the belief that he felt the same way she did. Now she decides that it's a matter of polite form with him to pretend she understands him. Or maybe it's an excuse, come to think of it, so he will never have to come right out on the table and affirm anything or explain himself.

'Same time?' she says.

The last of her buttons is done up. She'll pick up her shoes at the door. She kneels, leans over to kiss him good-bye. Then there is an obliterating flash of light, and Alma slides to the floor.

When she comes to, she's lying on Theo's bed. Theo is dressed (in case he had to call an ambulance, she thinks), and sitting beside her, holding her hand. This time he isn't pleased. 'I think you have low blood pressure,' he says, being unable to ascribe it to sexual excitement. 'You should have it checked out.'

'I thought maybe it was the real thing, this time,' Alma whispers. She's relieved; she's so relieved the bed feels weightless beneath her, as if she's floating on water.

Theo misunderstands her. 'You're telling me it's over?' he says, with resignation or eagerness, she can't tell.

'It's not over,' Alma says. She closes her eyes; in a minute, she'll feel less dizzy, she'll get up, she'll talk, she'll walk. Right now the salt drifts down behind her eyes, falling like snow, down through the ocean, past the dead coral, gathering on the branches of the salt tree that rises from the white crystal dunes below it. Scattered on the underwater sand are the bones of many small fish. It is so beautiful. Nothing can kill it. After everything is over, she thinks, there will still be salt.

SANDRA BIRDSELL

Niagara Falls

In January, Henry J. Zacharias had his first stroke.

It was late afternoon, around four o'clock, when Elizabeth began the eleven-mile drive from the hospital in Reinfeld to their farm, a trip she would make over and over. 'I keep a close watch on that heart of mine,' Johnny Cash sang as she travelled down the long stretch of road that connected the town with the highway. She switched off the radio. Music didn't seem right at a time like this. She drove cautiously, holding onto the wheel too tightly, fearing an accident. It was at times like these, when your nerves were stretched too tight, that things went wrong. She passed by the feed mill and slowed down as she approached Ellis's Greenhouses. Should she stop and let him know about Henry, that she wouldn't be able to come in for the seeding? No. He would wonder how she could even think about such things.

The thump of tires against the pavement felt rhythmic and sure, but the point at which she aimed seemed fixed and un-reachable as the horizon which sometimes in winter disappeared so that she couldn't tell, where was sky, where was land? She was vaguely aware of a cluster of brown trees in the middle of a field, huddled together in a bank of snow like old women at a funeral, long shadows, their skirts blotting out the wash of pastel sky-colours reflected all about in the hard snow. Minutes later (how many, five, fifteen?) she passed by her lane, past the buildings all yellow with green trim that distinguished Henry J.

Zacharias's farm from the others; from Henry P. Zacharias (no relation), who was called Hank by his neighbours and whose farm was twice the size of theirs and stretched all the way to Roland.

Realizing her error, she braked quickly, felt the wheels skid on ice. She held her breath to contain her rising panic, steering into the skid instinctively, thinking, already I have gotten myself into trouble, felt the vehicle swing out of the slide, pass centre and fishtail sharply. Today she couldn't go off the road, not today because then Hank P. would have to come with his tractor to pull her out and (one thing for certain) she didn't want to have to ask him for anything, but the wheels caught at buried gravel and the car steadied. She breathed a prayer of relief. She backed the car slowly toward the lane. The driveway had disappeared. She searched through the windshield for some sign of it, a track that would guide her safely into the yard, but the combination of waning light and fresh snow had erased all traces of it. The house itself appeared abandoned, the windows dark mirrors reflecting the setting sun. She was cut off from her house. She got out of the car and walked down the lane. The fluffy snow, ankle-deep, bit at her bare skin. She hadn't stopped to put boots on this morning when she saw Henry fall. She'd run from the house not thinking, just oh God, oh God. One minute he was walking, strong, and the next, like a bird crashing into the window, he faltered, his arms flailing, looking for something to hold on to, and he was down, a brilliant red plaid heap in the snow. Fresh snow covered the spot near the mailbox where he'd fallen. She walked back to the car and followed her footprints into the lane, passed them by, and then braver, drove by faith into the circle of her yard.

She waited in the car until she'd stopped shaking and then went into the house. She stamped snow from her feet and walked across the kitchen, her steps sluggish, as though she waded through water, to the calendar which hung beside the telephone. 'Arrive Niagara Falls, 8 am,' she'd written on it that morning.

Only a week away from their first vacation, an anniversary present from their only son, John, and his wife, Sharon. She picked up the pencil and wrote, 'Henry goes to the hospital.' Her spidery, odd-shaped letters ran off the square into the next date. Henry was there in Reinfeld in the hospital and she was here, at the farm. The floor cracked suddenly as though someone just entered the room. Phone John's place, she told herself, see if they're back from the city yet. But she didn't pick up the receiver. She knew too much. She'd seen the doctor thump hard with the heel of his palm against Henry's breastbone to try to rouse him. She knew his illness would take up many squares on the calendar. Inside his head, a large field had been marked off. She'd stood beside his bed and watched him fall deeper into sleep. Where are you? she'd asked him silently, and then, where am I? Was she the one who had fallen asleep today?

'I'll give the money for the train tickets back to John,' she'd told Henry at the hospital. She meant to say, don't you worry now. She was surprised when he responded. He moved his hand across the blanket towards her own.

'Seed,' he said. 'John should be spending money for seed, not trips.' His voice came from a great distance. And she thought again, it is a dream. I'll open my eyes and be in my room upstairs.

She held his curled fingers lightly between her large hands. 'I'll tell him you said so.' Their son wasn't a farmer. He owned a large implement dealership in Reinfeld. Henry was confused, or was he saying, tell John to look after things?

'John spends entirely too much money,' Henry said, and Elizabeth thought that maybe his illness wasn't so bad after all, if he could still think to speak out against John. But several hours later, Henry grew too weak to talk and he sank into sleep.

Elizabeth turned from the telephone. The bad news would keep for a while. She read the words she'd written on the calendar. She picked up the pencil which dangled from its string and in tiny, controlled letters she wrote, 'All day it snowed.' She would train herself to live alone.

She switched on the stove and filled the kettle with water. The mantle clock in the dining room chimed the hour. She went into the room and turned on the light as though that would lessen the effect of the clock's counting. All around the walls on varnished shelves was her collection of china plates. She didn't like china, but it was what other women did. John and Sharon were delighted. They never knew what to buy for her and so they bought a plate from each place they visited. She had a plate with a picture of the Niagara Falls on it. When she'd seen John's slides of the falls, they made her feel like the bonging of the clock made her feel, off balance and clutching the air about her. 'Horseshoe Falls', the plate was inscribed, '160 feet high, 2,950 feet wide, 500,000 tons of water a minute', which to her was the same as saying, 'every second a baby is born'. It was unfathomable.

But it wasn't these plates she'd come searching for, but for something older, something that came from a different time. She found it on the shelf in the china cupboard, the porcelain cup and saucer that had come from Russia. Her mother had brought it with her and had written down that she was to have it when she married. She felt its smoothness against the thick calluses of her palms and took the cup into the kitchen. She filled it with hot water and sat down at the table and pressed its fluted edge to her lips. She looked out the window. The moon had risen and beneath it stretched the winter-blue curve of Henry's fields. Before she'd begun to work in the greenhouses, she'd preferred winter. She'd never been able to face the stark bleakness of Henry's fields without feeling numbed by the ugliness. She hated how she'd battled daily the wind that swept in under windowsills, covering everything with gritty black silt. Her headaches used to come with those high winds. She preferred the depression that the immense stillness of winter carried because in winter, it was clean. She massaged her chest where an odd ache had begun to form and thought about who she should telephone. She should really try to get hold of John just in case he had come home from the city a day earlier than expected and heard about his father. And then she realized that if that happened, he would call her. She didn't have the energy to call John and face the questions he would ask, not letting her finish saying what she'd formed in her mind. Should she call Mika? No, her sister seemed to enjoy hearing bad news and would grab hold of the information and make it seem worse than it really was. Irma. Irma worked in the greenhouses with her. Better to call Irma because Irma understood. She was married to a cranky, bitter man who had lost his legs. And she, eyelids heavy with the thought of it, was married to Henry who today had entered his own place. She had lost his mind.

Elizabeth opened her eyes, realized it was morning and was amazed that she'd slept so soundly. The first thing she saw was Henry's boots on the carpet across the room, beside his bed, and she remembered a week ago, Henry walking three miles to Hank P.'s place. To keep him talking in the barn long enough until the polls closed to prevent Hank P., who was Liberal, from casting his vote. What did you talk about for such a long time? she'd asked, her heart doing its familiar flip flop each time he'd come back from talking with Hank P. We talked about God, and what He means to me, Henry said.

Everything is lawful, Henry often said, but not everything is good and so they were one of few left in the farming area around Reinfeld who didn't have the tell-tale television antenna on top of their roof. Occasionally, she drove into town and watched Ed Sullivan at Irma's place. She had never been able to match Henry's goodness, she thought, as her eyes met his Bible lying on the table beside his bed. She went into what used to be John's bedroom, her sewing room, and stood looking for a moment at the dress pattern spread across the worktable, pieces cut in half lengthwise so that she could add tissue, enlarge the pattern to fit. Yes, that's how it is, she told herself, eating and drinking and never thinking that tomorrow it could all end. She felt guilty immediately. I'm beginning to sound more and more like Mika, she chastened herself, it's a stroke, he could come out of it yet. Above her worktable, the window where she'd been standing when it had happened. She dressed and went downstairs and erased the vacation plans from the calendar. She didn't allow herself to ask how she felt about this. What had happened had happened. It wasn't Henry's fault that she would never get to see the falls. She had nothing to complain about when it came to Henry. She often said to Irma with a clear heart that she had no complaints at all.

Except for the farm, Irma reminded her when she'd said, Henry is all right, I have no complaints. Henry was seventy-two, she forty-seven. Most men his age had already built their retirement houses in Reinfeld, erected fake windmills in their back yards, wishing wells in the front yards, constructed sturdy fences and died. But neither one of them had wanted that. Henry secretly hoped that John would still take up the farm and she, when Mr. Ellis had confided in her his intention to sell, that they would sell the farm and buy the greenhouses. And so when Irma reminded her, 'except for the farm,' the frustration and desperation of past years was as fresh and tart as an unripe apple. The farm wasn't hers to sell. Do, don't ask, Irma said once. Just tell. Irma's husband had no legs, she didn't need to ask for anything, she thought, as she plaited her long auburn hair. She watched herself do this, saw her awkward fingers fumbling with the tiny pins, her face, rounder; she'd been gaining weight. The mirror told her what she still didn't feel completely: you are here, real, alive, and Henry is the one asleep.

Before she telephoned John, she called the hospital and asked, how is he? The same, the nurse said. He spent a quiet night. Henry was too quiet. His falling was like a feather resting among feathers. She telephoned John and gave him the news and arranged to meet him at the hospital. When she hung up some of the tension that had gathered in her shoulder blades fled. She picked up the pencil and wrote, 'My first day alone' and beneath that, 'Phone Mr. Ellis soon'.

In mid-February, as Elizabeth turned off from the highway onto the road that led to Reinfeld, the sun sparkled on crusty snow and on rooftops and she thought Reinfeld looked like a Christmas card picture of Bethlehem shining with the blue tinge of a pointing star, making it special, set apart, unlike the other towns that hugged the American border. The highway didn't pass through Reinfeld's centre, splitting it in two. It wasn't necessary to string gaudy lights above the street or to have a sign that said, 'Welcome to Reinfeld'. Its borders were symmetrical, the streets, predictable, and the sameness in the decoration of the houses made her feel that nothing would ever change. She drove towards the hospital thinking that despite everything, she was content.

She walked into Henry's room. He looked at her, blinked several times and said, 'Chicks. Have you ordered the chicks yet?'

'What?' Elizabeth asked, startled. Her own dream-like state had diminished and she had reconciled herself to his, that it was permanent. His place had become real. The walls were green. His cubicle had a tall, narrow window that looked out over the town of Reinfeld. A brass radiator beneath it. Beside his bed, a wooden one-drawer chest, painted brown. Above it, a mirror. Henry, in a wheelchair, staring down at the curled fingers in his lap, a towel tied beneath his arms to hold him upright. Henry's white legs, thinner, dangling uselessly as the attendant lifted him in and out of bed. Because she was strong and healthy, Henry's place seemed confined. But she knew the effort it took for him just to breathe and so she knew that for him, it was the right size. But now, his voice a whisper, but his voice, saying to her, 'Chicks, have you ordered the chicks yet?'

She'd called Mr. Ellis and had gone back to work transplanting tomatoes and her life had become routine. She was confident enough to try variations to the old pattern, sleeping in past seven o'clock, staying up later at night, continuing the nightly ritual of drinking hot water from the porcelain cup that had come from Russia.

'He spoke to me,' Elizabeth said to the nurse. She'd run from the room, grabbed hold of the first person she came upon.

'Oh, he speaks often,' the nurse said. 'Especially during the night. He talks about an accident. We feel that he hears things.'

'Things, what things?' Accident and chicks. Her face grew flushed.

'Oh, the other patients, their radios.'

They should have told her. Prepared her for the time when he would begin to ask questions. How did it happen? Did I fall? And then, what about Hank P.? How did that one happen?

'And that's not all,' the nurse said as she followed Elizabeth back into Henry's room. 'We have a surprise for you. Show your wife what you can do,' she said to Henry and for the first time, Elizabeth noticed the metal bar hanging above his bed.

Henry reached up, his whole arm trembling, and curled his fingers about the bar. He began to pull himself upright.

Elizabeth slapped her hands against her cheeks in astonishment. 'Isn't that wonderful?' the nurse said.

Yes, but it's only an arm, she told herself later as she sat beside his bed knitting a sweater which she planned to send to her sister for the youngest baby. It's only an arm. When she considered how far he was from walking and even then they weren't sure about his right side. 'Henry,' she said loudly several moments later as he lay panting from exertion. His hearing has not been affected, the doctor had told her, there was no need to yell, but she couldn't help it. It seemed that because he couldn't talk above a whisper, he couldn't hear either. 'I have been wanting to talk to you about the farm.' Her metal needles clicked out a frantic pace. 'I was thinking, the way prices are that now would be a good time to sell.'

He didn't respond. She set the knitting aside and went over to his bed. He stared at the ceiling. She sat down on the edge of the

bed. Spittle ran from one corner of his drooping mouth. She
snatched up a tissue, began to dab at it. 'Think of it,' she said
gently. 'Everything considered, we should get rid of the land.'

He pulled away. 'No,' he said, and then louder, 'I forbid you
to do that.' He began to thrash his head from side to side on the
pillow. She held his cheeks between her hands, felt the faint
flutter of his muscles as he tried to free himself. She felt ashamed,
unworthy.

'Henry, please, be still.' His head was fragile, as fragile as an
ancient porcelain cup that would shatter if you flicked it hard
with your knuckle.

'It's all right,' she said. 'We don't need to talk about it yet.'
She had dreamt of him one night, that she carried him out and
away from the hospital. I'll care for you, she'd said. I'll look
after you, make you well. And here she was, upsetting him. He
grew still. She patted him lightly on the cheek and felt that peculiar ache rise in her chest. The farm, it wasn't hers to sell.
She took up her knitting once again. 'The way your exercises
are going,' she said, 'you will be up and around the yard by
spring.'

He blinked rapidly. 'Phone Hank P.,' he said harshly. 'Tell
him I'll lease the land. One year only.'

Elizabeth dropped a stitch, squinted and raced to pick it up
before the whole sweater unravelled. 'I'll tell him,' she said.

'He's not being very realistic,' John said. 'Expecting anyone
would even want to lease the land for one year. Especially a guy
like Hank P.'

Especially Hank P., Elizabeth thought. He would be the one
to do it. 'You're a fine one to talk about being realistic,' she said
and laughed. When he was small he would butt his head against
her stomach, his crib, the walls, in order to make things happen. In the early grades in school, teachers said that he threw
himself on the floor and banged his head when he didn't make
one hundred percent on a test.

'But he's not thinking,' John said, choosing to ignore her gentle teasing.

Elizabeth shushed him. 'He's your father.' And John was his son. There were indelible marks other than his short stocky frame, his bullishness. John was deeply religious like Henry, in an unbending, fierce way that made her feel defensive and inadequate. And yet, father and son had never worked well together.

'You have to realize why your father wants to hang on. What has he got?' A bed, a chair, a window in a shoebox of a room.

John got up from the kitchen table and put his arm around her shoulders. 'And what about you?' he asked. 'Shouldn't we be thinking about you as well?' If she stood up, she would be a foot taller than he. All his caresses came when she was sitting. She leaned back in the chair and let her head rest against his chest. For the first time since Henry had fallen in the snow, she felt like weeping. He kneaded her shoulders, demonstrative in a way she'd taught him. The way Henry might have been if someone had shown him how. She'd kept house for Henry a full year without realizing that he cared for her. Not until he fired the hired man for making jokes about her size.

'This has been hard on you, we know,' John said. 'Sharon and I don't know how you've managed to keep everything up.'

'It's all right,' she said. 'I'm all right.' She wanted to tell him about her desire. About the greenhouse. When she worked in the greenhouse, the sun's light diffused through the sloping glass roof and its steady warmth on her broad shoulders made her feel secure. The smell of the young moist plants in their flats of peat moss filled her with energy and she walked faster, moved more quickly. She enjoyed reading through all the seed catalogues and meeting the people who came to buy bedding plants.

'It's not all right,' John said. 'Sharon and I have been thinking —even if Father doesn't get well, you should go away for awhile. Take that trip to Niagara Falls.'

'Oh no,' she said. 'Not without Father.' If she went to the falls alone, she might never come back. She'd be swept away by the thundering water. She'd be a speck going over the brink, tumbling in the mist, never stopping. With no one to hold her back, she would lean over the railing with all those other people in yellow rubber raincoats, she would lean just so far and be gone.

'I shouldn't be thinking about trips,' Elizabeth said, 'but what I'll do if worse comes to worst. And I've been thinking, if something happens to your father, I would like to sell the farm and live in town.'

He smiled a quick anxious smile, sat down beside her and took her hands in his. 'Great,' he said. 'I'm glad to hear you say that. Sharon and I were hoping that's what you'd want. We've made plans and I wanted to talk to you about them. It makes it easier that you want to live in town.'

She thought he would say they were going to start a family and wanted her close by.

'We've decided to open another dealership. A bigger one. This time, in Morden.'

She hid her disappointment. 'Why go to Morden? I thought—isn't business good here?'

She saw the look of annoyance pass across his face. 'I'd keep the business in Reinfeld as well,' he said. 'And open another one in Morden. Because business is good. Now's the time to do it.'

'Father always said you spend too much money.' She pulled her hands free and began to clear away the dishes.

She expected an outburst, but John got up and began to help her. He scraped food from plates. Sharon had taken a day to go shopping in the city and he'd come for supper.

'We're positive we should do this,' John said quietly as he set dishes down into the sink. 'We've prayed long and hard and we're sure that this is what God wants us to do, too.'

'Well then, that's good. Do it.' She was conscious of her voice sounding tight and strained.

He cleared his throat noisily and spit phlegm into the garbage can, just as Henry used to do. 'I'll need money to do it,' he said.

'I've got too much tied up in machinery right now to go to the bank.'

'How much money?' Henry had five thousand dollars in their savings account. She had a little from working in the greenhouse.

'Twenty-five thousand.'

'So much? I don't have that much money.'

'I know,' John said and she knew now the reason for his quietness. He was worried. She felt the knot of braids pull at the back of her head. She ran water into the sink, began stacking dishes down into the soapy water.

'What then?' she asked, fearful, her old sickness bumping there beneath her breastbone, dreading his answer.

'Sharon's father has agreed to lend us part of it. I could sell Dad's machinery,' he said. 'I could get a good price for it.'

Henry's acreage was small, a little over one section, that was all. What kind of a price would she get without the machinery?

'Mama,' John said, using his old name for her, a form of endearment. 'He'll never work again. I thought you realized that.'

It was true. And Mr. Ellis could up and sell the greenhouse before Henry realized it. 'And what would I do?' she asked. 'If something happened to your father, what would I do in town? Work in the shop?'

'You wouldn't need to work,' he said. 'If things go as well as they have so far, you wouldn't need to work anymore. Sharon and I would see to that. I think it's a good investment for you. We'd be partners, the three of us, you, me and the Lord.'

'How could you refuse such a generous offer?' Irma asked the following day. They carried wooden flats in from the yard and stacked them against the wall in the greenhouse. The time was right to begin transplanting, culling the spindly seedlings and transferring the stronger ones to the flats where they would grow thick and straight. Now is the time to do it, John had said. Now is the time, she repeated over and over while she worked.

'What do you mean?' Elizabeth asked, offended by Irma's tone of voice. Irma Muller is an old woman who tries to look young, John had once said, because the woman coloured her hair blonde and used cosmetics. Elizabeth had not reminded him that she and Irma were the same age.

'Well kid, how could you refuse a partnership with God, tell me? He's got you over a barrel, that one. Smart.'

Elizabeth knew what it must look like to Irma, but she was certain John was sincere. 'He's my son,' she said. 'If a son can't come to his mother, then who should he go to?' She said this to slight Irma, who let her only daughter Marlene run free like a stray dog.

Irma let a bundle of flats drop to the ground with a great clatter. 'Why doesn't he go to his father?' she asked. 'No, he knows better,' she said and lifted her little finger. 'He's got you right there.'

Elizabeth was hanging her overalls in the back porch after work when she saw Hank P.'s truck pull into the yard. She was about to call into the house, Henry, you'd better come, Hank P. is here, and then quickly step out of sight, but . . . She folded her arms across her chest. She would speak to him on her own. Had Henry somehow gotten a message to him?

Hank stood with the door open neither inside nor out. He seemed uncertain whether he should enter. 'How is Mr. Zacharias today?' he asked. His red sideburns grew thick and curly halfway down the sides of his face, making it seem broader than it was. She noticed a button missing from his shirt and his bare stomach, curly fine hairs. So he didn't wear an undershirt in winter either, not like Henry who wore one summer and winter, day and night. Her eyes met his. He was almost as tall as she was. It made her uneasy to stand eye to eye with a man.

'He's the same,' she said.

'I'm sorry to hear that,' he said, as nice and polite as if someone listened behind the door. He stood turning his cap in his hands, which were sprinkled with cinnamon-coloured freckles (young-looking hands cupping a large white breast). His hair, red, against her own dark hair. That old man, he can't be of much use for you. Was he truly sorry? For her, or for Henry?

She knew what he'd gone through when his Anna died with cancer.

'I've come to see you about the cultivator,' Hank said. 'Mr. Zacharias said last fall, if I fixed it I could use it.'

She nodded.

'So, I thought you should know. I'll be working in the machine shed until it's done.' He turned in the doorway and put his cap back on.

He was being so polite. 'Wait, Henry wanted me to . . . ,' Elizabeth began.

He removed his cap once again and waited.

'Henry said to, he sends regards,' she said and looked away. Blood rushed to her face, I have never made love to anyone other than my husband, she'd told Irma, so that she could taste the memory of him rushing against her. She had written on the calendar, 'Today while I was digging among the garbage heap for mushrooms, I found a leper in lovely clothes of hard knotted flesh.' Henry had read it, asked her what it meant. It's just an idea that came to me, she said. That's all. Did Hank think she was remembering that afternoon half-way between Winnipeg and Reinfeld? The day she'd gone to get the chicks. 'I'm not here most afternoons,' she said to cover her confusion. 'But feel free to come in and help yourself to coffee. I'll leave it on the stove.'

He stared at her longer than was necessary to thank her. He closed the door behind him and she stood rooted, confused and angry with herself because she had not given him Henry's message, because she had blushed so readily and now, after all these years, what did he think?

In March, the doctor intercepted Elizabeth as she was about to enter Henry's room. 'I'm sorry,' he said flatly, 'but Mr. Zacharias has contracted pneumonia.' It seemed like a strange way of putting it, as though Henry had an obligation to take on this new disease.

Her chest ached as she watched Henry's straining to breathe. Tubes dripped medicine into his veins. A nurse came in and pushed a rubber hose into his throat, switched on a machine and sucked up his mucus. Elizabeth gagged. But when it was over, Henry could breathe easier and so she was grateful to the nurse and smiled at her, stepping out of her path quickly to show she was anxious not to be a nuisance.

Today, she would have told him about the snowstorm, how Hank P. had ploughed their lane so she could come to the hospital. 'Snow as high as my waist in the lane,' she had written. But such news was of no use to poor Henry. He struggled to speak. 'What is it?' she asked, dreading some message, some final command, some last question about chicks and accidents.

'Ruining the land,' Henry said.

Her heart constricted. 'Who is ruining the land?' Had he heard somehow that she hadn't leased it yet?

His mouth, encrusted with fever blisters, moved painfully slow. 'Communists.'

Her shoulders sagged with immense relief. She watched the slow drip, drip of medicine into the glass tube for several minutes and then left.

Elizabeth felt the sides of March press in on her as she listened daily to Henry's feverish ranting. The septic tank froze and she didn't call John. John was too busy with his own life and besides, she really was undecided about the money. She hated to picture them praying every day, or the thought that she really might be the answer to their money problems. She called a company in town to come with their heat lamps and torches to thaw out the septic tank, but they weren't in any rush and so in the meantime, she squatted amid the trees beside the granaries and threw her dishwater onto the yard and bathed at Irma's house in town until it was fixed.

Henry seemed never better, never worse. They took away his exercise bar. He was gaunt and appeared bitter over this new setback. She felt responsible. As though she'd caused it to happen by talking of selling off the land. Since she'd decided not to carry Henry's message to Hank P., she couldn't look fully into her husband's eyes, brilliant with the remnant of his fever, but off to one side. The evasion and the sameness of her life depressed her. March weighed heavily and it was on such a day that she arrived for work to find the 'For Sale' sign pushed down into the ground beside the greenhouse. She stared at it, telling herself, this is what you get. This is what happens when you even think such selfish things. She backed the car out and drove home.

When she opened the back door, she saw rubber boots on the mat. She reached up to hang her coveralls and saw Hank's parka. She felt the strangeness of its presence pass through her hands as she hung her clothes beside his. When she stepped into the kitchen he was working with his tools at the sink. The faucet lay in pieces on the counter.

'I thought seeing as how I had my tools with me, I might as well fix it,' he said without turning around.

That was what he'd said that summer, pulling alongside her car, offering to fix the tire. 'You needn't have gone to so much trouble. John would have fixed it for me.' Then knowing she sounded ungrateful, she thanked him, feeling the blood rushing to her face once again.

There was nothing she could do without coming too close to him and so she poured a cup of coffee and watched him work. He was across the room and yet it seemed as though he was there beside her. Bending his red head across her chest, his hand cupping her breast, tongue circling her nipple. Soon he was finished and washing his hands, and she was lying across the seat in the car, thinking, so this is what it's like with another man. She had to tell herself over and over to remember that she'd been disappointed that it hadn't been all that different. He wiped his hands on her good dishtowel and squatted to pack his tools into the toolbox. She noticed the straining of the muscles in his thighs against the fabric of his pants. She stared down at the bottom of the porcelain cup. She used to imagine what it would be like with another man and when she'd glanced down at him poised above her, she'd been amazed at how similar he was to Henry, she thought he'd be bigger, stronger looking. Maybe if she had let herself go more it would have been different, she told herself. Let him touch her all over and smell her the way he wanted to. He stood beside the door ready to leave.

'It's fixed,' he said.

'Thank you.' She smiled.

'I've also finished work on the cultivator today,' he said. 'Tell Mr. Zacharias it's working.'

'I will.' He acted as though someone were looking over his shoulder.

He hesitated. His expression changed. He seemed to be nourishing a cunning thought. 'Has Mr. Zacharias ever said what he plans to do?' He spoke with a gesture, indicating with his freckled, sure hands (between her legs forcing them open) the wide expanse of Henry's fields. 'We, some of the neighbours, would do the seeding for him. If that's his wish.'

'I plan to sell,' Elizabeth said.

His thick eyebrows shot up, he recovered and his face became expressionless.

'Would you be interested?' she asked.

Again their eyes met and she saw something else flicker in his eyes, a look of unsureness. She was surprised and then faintly exhilarated by the thought, I have made him feel uneasy.

'I might be.'

As the door closed behind him, Elizabeth lifted the cup and pressed its edge against her teeth. Her breath was hot inside the cup and moisture clung to the fine dark hairs above her lip. She watched Hank's truck turn the corner at the end of the lane. I plan to sell, she'd said, as though it was her farm to sell. And saying it made it seem real. I am tired of carrying people around on my back, she'll tell Irma, who will crow and say, well it's about time. She got up from the table and wrote on the calendar, 'Make an appointment with the hairdresser.'

In the middle of April, Henry had another stroke. 'Henry has another bout, quite bad,' Elizabeth wrote, her terse calmness of the words denying the turmoil inside. She stayed with him all day now, leaving only to get a bite to eat at a restaurant in town. She stood at the narrow, tall window beside his bed and noticed it was finally spring. Moist warm air rushed into the room overtop the gentle hiss of the radiator. Below in the parking lot, people arriving to visit, wearing light coats, sweaters, and also below, Hank P.'s truck.

She emptied the basin of water into the sink beside Henry's bed with shaking hands and turned to face Hank, who had come into the room without making a sound. He nodded to her. His eyes took in Henry's shell-like body, the tubes in his nose, the bag at the foot of the bed that collected his wastes.

'I heard he was worse. I'm sorry,' Hank said in a kind way that made her remember that his wife had suffered. Hank was different than the Hank who had laughed while she'd rammed her car into his car, because he wouldn't let her pass, making her angry in a way she never thought anyone could. She was about to thank him but saw that his voice had lied. The same smug expression was there, uncovered, and his desire for her, controlled, he would wait until she couldn't wait. He was passing his lust for her across the inert form of her Henry.

'If you need anything at all,' he said. 'I'll come.'

She nodded. 'John can come, too.'

Henry sighed deeply and they were diverted to him, to the bed. His chest moved gently up and down and the blankets with it. His sternness was pinched out like a candle; had it ever been real, or had it been a covering? she wondered. Henry hadn't asked her for anything and he had shared all with her. He was a feather now, falling among feathers.

Hours later as Elizabeth came back from eating lunch, the nurse met her at the door of the hospital and said, 'Mr. Zacharias has just died.' Then they took her to his room and left her alone with him. She pulled out the drawer and dropped his comb and brush into the plastic net bag she carried in her purse. She collected his partial plate from the cardboard container. She thought she might cry. It was the time for it. She looked around the cubicle for one last time. Henry's final giving out had already been absorbed by the breath of others. She imagined the lane, his residue fading even now beneath the melting snow. It was all done now: his slippers, housecoat, the partial plate. She set the bag down. There was one last thing she wanted to do. She gathered Henry in her arms and carried him over to the window. He was lighter than a child. 'See, out there,' she said. 'It's spring.'

When she passed through the large glass doors, she was surprised to discover that it had been raining. 'First rain today,' she would write on the calendar. She'd signed the papers to release Henry's body to the undertakers with a steady hand. No, she'd said, I don't need to wait for my son to come. But I'll wait. She walked towards his car on the parking lot. A door slammed shut as Sharon came running towards her. It's all right, she'll tell them. I'm all right. She would go to see the falls. She would hold onto the railing or she would let herself go. Whatever she did, she would do willingly.

NEIL BISSOONDATH

There Are a Lot of Ways to Die

It was still drizzling when Joseph clicked the final padlocks on the door. The name-plate, home-painted with squared gold letters on a black background and glazed all over with transparent varnish to lend a professional tint, was flecked with water and dirt. He took a crumpled handkerchief from his back pocket and carefully wiped the lettering clean: JOSEPH HEAVEN: CARPET AND RUG INSTALLATIONS. The colon had been his idea and he had put it in over his wife's objections. He felt that it provided a natural flow from his name, that it showed a certain reliability. His wife, in the scornful voice she reserved for piercing his pretensions, had said, 'That's all very well and good for Toronto, but you think people here care about that kind of thing?' But she was the one people accused of having airs, not him. As far as he was concerned, the colon was merely good business; and as the main beneficiary of the profits, she should learn to keep her mouth shut.

He had forgotten to pick up his umbrella from just inside the door where he had put it that morning. Gingerly, he extended his upturned palm, feeling the droplets, warm and wet, like newly spilled blood. He decided they were too light to justify reopening the shop, always something of an event because of the many locks and chains. This was another thing she didn't like, his obsession, as she called it, with security. She wanted a more open store-front, with windows and showcases and well-dressed mannequins smiling blankly at the street. She said, 'It look just like every other store around here, just a wall and a door. It have nothing to catch the eye.' He replied, 'You want windows and showcases? What we going to show? My tools? The tacks? The cutter?' Besides, the locks were good for business, not a week went by without a robbery in the area. Displaying the tools would be a blatant invitation, and a recurrent nightmare had developed in which one of his cutters was stolen and used in a murder.

Across the glistening street, so narrow after the generosity of those he had known for six years, the clothes merchants were standing disconsolately in front of their darkened stores, hands in pockets, whistling and occasionally examining the grey skies for the brightening that would signal the end of the rain and the appearance of shoppers. They stared blankly at him. One half-heartedly jabbed his finger at a stalactitic line of umbrellas and dusty raincoats, inviting a purchase. Joseph showed no interest. The merchant shrugged and resumed his tuneless whistling, a plaintive sound from between clenched front teeth.

Joseph had forgotten how sticky the island could be when it rained. The heat, it seemed, never really disappeared during the night. Instead, it retreated just a few inches underground, only to emerge with the morning rain, condensing, filling the atmosphere with steam. It put the lie to so much he had told his Canadian friends about the island. The morning rain wasn't as refreshing as he'd recalled it and the steam had left his memory altogether. How could he have sworn that the island experienced no humidity? Why had he, in all honesty, recalled tender tropical breezes when the truth, as it now enveloped him, was the exact, stifling opposite? Climate was not so drastically altered, only memory.

He walked to the end of the street, his shirt now clinging to his shoulders. The sidewalk, dark and pitted, seemed to glide by under his feet, as if it were itself moving. He squinted, feeling the folds of flesh bunching up at the corner of his eyes, and found he could fuzzily picture himself on Bloor Street, walking past the stores and the bakeries and the delicatessens pungent with Eastern European flavors, the hazy tops of buildings at Bloor and Yonge far away in the distance. He could even conjure up the sounds of a Toronto summer: the cars, the voices, the rumble of the subway under the feet as it swiftly glided towards downtown.

Joseph shook himself and opened his eyes, not without disappointment. He was having this hallucination too often, for too long. He was ashamed of it and couldn't confess it even to his wife. And he mistrusted it, too: might not even this more recent memory also be fooling him, as the other had done? Was it really possible to see the tops of buildings at Yonge from Bathurst? He wanted to ask his wife, pretending it was merely a matter of memory, but she would see through this to his longing and puncture him once more with that voice. She would call him a fool and not be far wrong. Were not two dislocations enough in one man's lifetime? Would not yet a third prove him a fool?

Their return had been jubilant. Friends and relatives treated it as a victory, seeking affirmation of the correctness of their cloistered life on the island, the return a defeat for life abroad. The first weeks were hectic, parties, dinners, get-togethers. Joseph felt like a curiosity, an object not of reverence but of silent ridicule, his the defeat, theirs the victory. The island seemed to close in around him.

They bought a house in the island's capital. The town was not large. Located at the extreme north-western edge of the island, having hardly expanded from the settlement originally established by Spanish adventurers as a depot in their quest for mythic gold, the town looked forever to the sea, preserving its aura of a way-station, a point at which to pause in brief respite from the larger search.

At first, Joseph had tried to deny this aspect of the town, for the town was the island and, if the island were no more than a way-station, a stopover from which nothing important ever emerged, then to accept this life was to accept second place. A man who had tasted of first could accept second only with delusion: his wife had taken on airs, he had painted his black-and-gold sign.

Then the hallucinations started, recreating Bloor Street, vividly recalling the minute details of daily life. He caught himself reliving the simple things: buying milk, removing a newspaper from the box, slipping a subway token into the slot, sitting in a park. A chill would run through him when he realized they were remembrances of things past, possibly lost forever. The recollected civility of life in Toronto disturbed him, it seemed so distant. He remembered what a curious feeling of well-being had surged through him whenever he'd given directions to a stranger. Each time was like an affirmation of stability. Here, in an island so small that two leisurely hours in a car would reveal all, no one asked for directions, no one was a stranger. You couldn't claim the island: it claimed you.

The street on which their house stood used to be known all over the island. It was viewed with a twinge of admired notoriety and was thought of with the same fondness with which the islanders regarded the government ministers and civil servants who had fled the island with pilfered cash: an awed admiration, a flawed love. The cause of this attention was a house, a mansion in those days, erected, in the popular lore, by a Venezuelan general who, for reasons unknown, had exiled himself to a life of darkly rumored obscurity on the island. As far as Joseph knew, no one had ever actually seen the general: even his name, Pacheco, had been assumed. Or so it was claimed; no one had ever bothered to check.

Eventually the house became known as Pacheco House, and the street as Pacheco Street. It was said that the house, deserted for as long as anyone could remember and now falling into neglect, had been mentioned passingly in a book by an Englishman who had been looking into famous houses of the region. It was the island's first mention in a book other than a history text, the island's first mention outside the context of slavery.

The house had become the butt of schoolboys' frustration. On their way home after school, Joseph and his friends would detour to throw stones at the windows. In his memory, the spitting clank of shattering glass sounded distant and opaque. They had named each window for a teacher, thus adding thrust and enthusiasm to their aim. The largest window, high on the third floor—the attic, he now knew, in an island which had no attics —they named LeNoir, after the priest who was the terror of all students unblessed by fair skin or athletic ability. They were more disturbed by the fact that the priest himself was black; this seemed a greater sin than his choice of vocation. They had never succeeded in breaking the LeNoir window. Joseph might have put this down to divine protection had he not lost his sense of religion early on. It was a simple event: the priest at his last try at communion had showered him with sour breath the moment the flesh of Christ slipped onto Joseph's tongue. Joseph, from then on, equated the wafer with decaying flesh.

The LeNoir window went unscathed for many years and was still intact when, after the final exams, Joseph left the island for what he believed to be forever.

The raindrops grew larger, making a plopping sound on the sidewalk. A drop landed on his temple and cascaded down his cheek. He rubbed at it, feeling the prickly stubble he hadn't bothered to shave that morning.

Pacheco House was just up ahead, the lower floors obscured by a jungle of trees and bush, the garden overgrown and thickening to impenetrability. Above the treeline, the walls—a faded pink, pockmarked by the assault of stones and mangoes—had begun disintegrating, the thin plaster falling away in massive chunks to reveal ordinary grey brick underneath. The remaining plaster was criss-crossed by cracks and fissures created by age and humidity.

During his schooldays, the grounds had been maintained by

the government. The house had been considered a tourist attraction and was displayed in brochures and on posters. An island-wide essay competition had been held, 'The Mystery of Pacheco House', and the winning essay, of breathless prose linked by words like *tropical* and *verdant* and *lush* and *exotic*, was used as the text of a special brochure. But no tourists came. The mystery withered away to embarrassment. The government quietly gave the house up. The Jaycees, young businessmen who bustled about in the heat with the added burden of jackets and ties, offered to provide funds for the upkeep. The offer was refused with a shrug by the Ministry of Tourism, with inexplicable murmurings of 'colonial horrors' by the Ministry of Culture. The house was left to its ghosts.

From the street Joseph could see the LeNoir window, still intact and dirt-streaked. He was surprised that it still seemed to mock him.

Joseph had asked his nephew, a precocious boy who enjoyed exhibiting his scattered knowledge of French and Spanish and who laughed at Joseph's clumsy attempts to resurrect the bits of language he had learnt in the same classes, often from the same teachers, if the boys still threw stones at Pacheco House. No, his nephew had informed him, after school they went to the sex movies or, in the case of the older boys, to the whorehouses. Joseph, stunned, had asked no more questions.

The rain turned perceptibly to deluge, the thick, warm drops penetrating his clothes and running in rivulets down his back and face. The wild trees and plants of the Pacheco garden nodded and drooped, leaves glistening dully in the half-light. The pink walls darkened as the water soaked into them, eating at the plaster. The LeNoir window was black; he remembered some claimed to have seen a white-faced figure in army uniform standing there at night. The story had provided mystery back then, a real haunted house, and on a rainy afternoon schoolboys could feel their spines tingle as they aimed their stones.

On impulse Joseph searched the ground for a stone. He saw only pebbles; the gravel verge had long been paved over. Already the sidewalk had cracked in spots and little shoots of grass had fought their way out, like wedges splitting a boulder.

He continued walking, oblivious of the rain.

Several cars were parked in the driveway of his house. His wife's friends were visiting. They were probably in the living room drinking coffee and eating pastries from Marcel's and looking through *Vogue* pattern books, Joseph made for the garage so he could enter, unnoticed, through the kitchen door. Then he thought, 'Why the hell?' He put his hands into his pockets—his money was soaked and the movement of his fingers ripped the edge off a bill—and calmly walked in through the open front door.

His wife was standing in front of the fake fireplace she had insisted on bringing from Toronto. The dancing lights cast multicoloured hues on her caftan. She almost dropped her coffee cup when she saw him. Her friends, perturbed, stared at him from their chairs which they had had grouped around the fireplace.

His wife said impatiently, 'Joseph, what are you doing here?'

He said, 'I live here.'

She said, 'And work?'

He said, 'None of the boys show up this morning.'

'So you just drop everything?'

'I postponed today's jobs. I couldn't do all the work by myself.'

She put her cup down on the mantelpiece. 'Go dry yourself off. You wetting the floor.'

Her friend Arlene said, 'Better than the bed.'

They all laughed. His wife said, 'He used to do that when he was a little boy, not so, Joseph?'

She looked at her friends and said, 'You know, we having so much trouble finding good workers. Joseph already fire three men. Looks like we're going to have to fire all these now.'

Arlene said, 'Good help so hard to find these days.'

His wife said, 'These people like that, you know, girl. Work is the last thing they want to do.'

Arlene said, 'They 'fraid they going to melt if rain touch their skin.'

His wife turned to him. 'You mean not one out of twelve turned up this morning?'

'Not one.'

Arlene, dark and plump, sucked her teeth and moved her tongue around, pushing at her cheeks and making a plopping sound.

Joseph said, 'Stop that. You look like a monkey.'

His wife and Arlene stared at him in amazement. The others sipped their coffee or gazed blankly at the fireplace.

Arlene said witheringly, 'I don't suffer fools gladly, Joseph.'

He said, 'Too bad. You must hate being alone.'

His wife said, 'Joseph!'

He said, 'I better go dry off.' Still dripping, he headed for the bedroom. At the door he paused and added, 'People should be careful when they talking about other people. You know, glass houses . . .' He was suddenly exhausted: what was the point? They all knew Arlene's story. She had once been a maid whose career was rendered transient by rain and imagined illness; she had been no different from his employees. Her fortune had improved only because her husband—who was referred to behind his back as a 'sometimes worker' because sometimes he worked and sometimes he didn't—had been appointed a minister without portfolio in the government. He had lost the nickname because now he never worked, but he had gained a regular cheque, a car and a chauffeur, and the tainted respectability of political appointment.

Joseph slammed the bedroom door and put his ear to the keyhole: there was a lot of throat-clearing; pages of a *Vogue* pattern book rustled. Finally his wife said, 'Come look at this pattern.' Voices oohed and ahhed and cooed. Arlene said, 'Look at this one.' He kicked the door and threw his wet shirt on the bed.

The rain had stopped and the sky had cleared a little. His wife and her friends were still in the living room. It was not yet midday. His clothes had left a damp patch on the bed, on his side, and he knew it would still be wet at bedtime. He put on a clean set of clothes and sat on the bed, rubbing the dampness, as if this would make it disappear. He reached up and drew the curtains open: grey, drifting sky, vegetation drooping and wet, like wash on a line; the very top of Pacheco house, galvanized iron rusted through, so thin in parts that a single drop of rain might cause a great chunk to go crashing into the silence of the house. Except maybe for the bats, disintegration was probably the only sound now to be heard in Pacheco House. The house was like a dying man who could hear his heart ticking to a stop.

Joseph sensed that something was missing. The rainflies, delicate ant-like creatures with brown wings but no sting. Defenceless, wings attached to their bodies by the most fragile of links, they fell apart at the merest touch. After a particularly heavy rainfall, detached wings, almost transparent, would litter the ground and cling to moist feet like lint to wool. As a child, he used to pull the wings off and place the crippled insect on a table, where he could observe it crawling desperately around, trying to gain the air. Sometimes he would gingerly tie the insect to one end of a length of thread, release it, and control its flight. In all this he saw no cruelty. His friends enjoyed crushing them, or setting them on fire, or sizzling them with the burning end of a cigarette. Joseph had only toyed with the insects; he could never bring himself to kill one.

There was not a rainfly in sight. The only movement was that of the clouds and dripping water. In the town, the insects had long, and casually, been eradicated. He felt the loss.

He heard his wife call her friends to lunch. He half expected to hear his name but she ignored him: he might have not been there. He waited a few more minutes until he was sure they had all gone into the dining room, then slipped out the front door.

Water was gurgling in the drains, rushing furiously through the iron gratings into the sewers. In the street, belly up, fur wet and clinging, lay a dead dog, a common sight. Drivers no longer even bothered to squeal their tires.

Joseph walked without direction, across streets and through different neighbourhoods, passing people and being passed by cars. He took in none of it. His thoughts were thousands of miles away, on Bloor Street, on Yonge Street, among the stalls of Kensington Market.

He was at National Square when the rain once more began to pound down. He found a dry spot under the eaves of a store and stood, arms folded, watching the rain and the umbrellas and the raincoats. A man hurried past him, a handkerchief tied securely to his head the only protection from the rain. It was a useless gesture, and reminded Joseph of his grandmother's warnings to him never to go out at night without a hat to cover his head, 'because of the dew'.

National Square was the busiest part of town. Cars constantly sped by, horns blaring, water splashing. After a few minutes a donkey cart loaded with fresh coconuts trundled by on its way to the Savannah, a wide, flat park just north of the town where the horse races were held at Christmas. A line of impatient cars crept along behind the donkey cart, the leaders bobbing in and out of line in search of an opportunity to pass.

Joseph glanced at his watch. It was almost twelve-thirty. He decided to have something to eat. Just around the corner was a cheap restaurant frequented by office workers from the government buildings and foreign banks which enclosed the square. Holding his hands over his head, Joseph dashed through the rain to the restaurant.

Inside was shadowed, despite the cobwebby fluorescent lighting. The walls were lined with soft-drink advertisements and travel posters. One of the posters showed an interminable stretch of bleached beach overhung with languid coconut-tree branches.

Large, cursive letters read: Welcome To The Sunny Caribbean. The words were like a blow to the nerves. Joseph felt like ripping the poster up.

A row of green metal tables stretched along one wall of the rectangular room. A few customers sat in loosened ties and shirtsleeves, sipping beer and smoking and conversing in low tones. At the far end, at a table crowded with empty bottles and an overflowing ashtray, Joseph noticed a familiar face. It was lined and more drawn than when he'd known it, and the eyes had lost their sparkle of intelligence; but he was certain he was not mistaken. He went up to the man. He said, 'Frankie?'

Frankie looked up slowly, unwillingly, emerging from a daydream. He said, 'Yes?' Then he brightened. 'Joseph? Joseph!' He sprang to his feet, knocking his chair back. He grasped Joseph's hand. 'How you doing, man? It's been years and years. How you doing?' He pushed Joseph into a chair and loudly ordered two beers. He lit a cigarette. His hand shook.

Joseph said, 'You smoking now, Frankie?'

'For years, man. You?'

Joseph shook his head.

Frankie said, 'But you didn't go to Canada? I thought somebody tell me . . . '

'Went and came back. One of those things. How about you? How the years treat you?'

'I work in a bank. Loan officer.'

'Good job?'

'Not bad.'

Joseph sipped his beer. The situation wasn't right. There should have been so much to say, so much to hear. Frankie used to be his best friend. He was the most intelligent person Joseph had ever known. This was the last place he would have expected to find him. Frankie had dreamt of university and professorship, and it had seemed, back then, that university and professorship awaited him.

Frankie took a long pull on his cigarette, causing the tube to crinkle and flatten. He said, 'What was Canada like?' Before Joseph could answer, he added, 'You shouldn't have come back. Why did you come back? A big mistake.' He considered the cigarette.

The lack of emotion in Frankie's voice distressed Joseph. It was the voice of a depleted man. He said, 'It was time.'

Frankie leaned back in his chair and slowly blew smoke rings at Joseph. He seemed to be contemplating the answer. He said, 'What were you doing up there?'

'I had business. Installing carpets and rugs. Is a good little business. My partner looking after it now.'

Frankie looked away, towards the door. He said nothing.

Joseph said, 'You ever see anybody from school?'

Frankie waved his cigarette. 'Here and there. You know, Raffique dead. And Jonesy and Dell.'

Joseph recalled the faces: boys, in school uniform. Death was not an event he could associate with them. 'How?'

'Raffique in a car accident. Jonesy slit his wrists over a woman. Dell . . . who knows? There are a lot of ways to die. They found him dead in the washroom of a cinema. A girl was with him. Naked. She wasn't dead. She's in the madhouse now.'

'And the others?' Joseph couldn't contemplate the death roll. It seemed to snuff out a little bit of his own life.

'The others? Some doing something, some doing nothing. It don't matter.'

Joseph said, 'You didn't go to university.'

Frankie laughed. 'No, I didn't.'

Joseph waited for an explanation. Frankie offered none.

Frankie said, 'Why the hell you come back from Canada? And none of this "It was time" crap.'

Joseph rubbed his face, feeling the stubble, tracing the fullness of his chin. 'I had some kind of crazy idea about starting a business, creating jobs, helping my people.'

Frankie laughed mockingly.

Joseph said, 'I should have known better. We had a party

before we left. A friend asked me the same question, why go back. I told him the same thing. He said it was bullshit and that I just wanted to make a lot of money and live life like a holiday. We quarrelled and I threw him out. The next morning he called to apologize. He was crying. He said he was just jealous.' Joseph sipped the beer, lukewarm and sweating. 'Damn fool.'

Frankie laughed again. 'I don't believe this. You mean to tell me you had the courage to leave *and* the stupidity to come back?' He slapped the table, rocking it and causing an empty beer bottle to fall over. 'You always used to be the idealist, Joseph. I was more realistic. And less courageous. That's why I never left.'

'Nobody's called me an idealist for years.' The word seemed more mocking than Frankie's laugh.

Frankie said, 'And now you're stuck back here for good.' He shook his head vigorously, drunkenly. 'A big, idealistic mistake, Joseph.'

'I'm not stuck here.' He was surprised at how much relief the thought brought him. 'I can go back any time I want.'

'Well, go then.' Frankie's voice was slurred, and it held more than a hint of aggressiveness.

Joseph shook his head. He glanced at his watch. He said, 'It's almost one. Don't you have to get back to work?'

Frankie called for another beer. 'The bank won't fall down if I'm not there.'

'We used to think the world would fall down if not for us.'

'That was a long time ago. We were stupid.' Frankie lit another cigarette. His hand shook badly. 'In this place, is nonsense to think the world, the world out there, have room for you.'

Joseph said, 'You could have been a historian. History was your best subject, not so?'

'Yeah.'

'You still interested in history?'

'Off and on. I tried to write a book. Nobody wanted to publish it.'

'Why not?'

'Because our history doesn't lead anywhere. It's just a big, black hole. Nobody's interested in a book about a hole.'

'You know anything about Pacheco House?'

'Pacheco House? A little.'

'What?'

'The man wasn't a Venezuelan general. He was just a crazy old man from Argentina. He was rich. I don't know why he came here. He lived in the house for a short time and then he died there, alone. They found his body about two weeks later, rotting and stinking. They say he covered himself with old cocoa bags, even his head. I think he knew he was going to die and after all that time alone he couldn't stand the thought of anyone seeing him. Crazy, probably. They buried him in the garden and put up a little sign. And his name wasn't really Pacheco either, people just called him that. They got it from a cowboy film. I've forgot what his real name was but it don't matter. Pacheco's as good as any other.'

'That's all? What about the house itself?'

'That's all. The house is just a house. Nothing special.' Frankie popped the half-finished cigarette into his beer bottle, it sizzled briefly. He added, 'R.I.P. Pacheco, his house and every damn thing else.' He put another cigarette between his lips, allowing it to droop to his chin, pushing his upper lip up and out, as if his teeth were deformed. His hands shook so badly he couldn't strike the match. His eyes met Joseph's.

Joseph couldn't hold the gaze. He was chilled. He said, 'I have to go.'

Frankie waved him away.

Joseph pushed back his chair. Frankie looked past him with bloodshot eyes, already lost in the confusion of his mind.

Joseph, indicating the travel poster, offered the barman five dollars for it. The man, fat, with an unhealthy greasiness, said, 'No way.'

Joseph offered ten dollars.

The barman refused.

Joseph understood: it was part of the necessary lie.

Grey clouds hung low and heavy in the sky. The hills to the north, their lower half crowded with the multicolored roofs of shacks, poverty plain from even so great a distance, were shrouded in mist, as if an inferno had recently burned out and the smoke not yet cleared away.

Some of his workers lived there, in tiny, crowded one-room shacks, with water sometimes a quarter-mile away at a mossy stand-pipe. There was a time when the sight of these shacks could move Joseph to pity. They were, he believed, his main reason for returning to the island. He really had said, 'I want to help my people.' Now the sentence, with its pomposity, its naivety, was just an embarrassing memory, like the early life of the minister's wife.

But he knew that wasn't all. He had expected a kind of fame, a continual welcome, the prodigal son having made good, having acquired skills, returning home to share the wealth, to spread the knowledge. He had anticipated a certain uniqueness but this had been thwarted. Everyone knew someone else who had returned from abroad—from England, from Canada, from the States. He grew to hate the stock phrases people dragged out: 'No place like home, this island is a true Paradise, life's best here.' The little lies of self-doubt and fear.

The gate to Pacheco House was chained but there was no lock: a casual locking-up, an abandonment. The chain, thick and rusted, slipped easily to the ground, leaving a trace of gritty oxide on his fingertips. He couldn't push the gate far; clumps of grass, stems long and tapering to a lancet point, blocked it at the base. He squeezed through the narrow opening, the concrete pillar rough and tight on his back, the iron gate leaving a slash of rust on his shirt. Inside, wild grass, wet and glistening, enveloped his legs up to his knees. The trees were further back, thick and ponderous, unmoving, lending the garden the heavy stillness of jungle.

Walking, pushing through the grass, took a little effort. The vegetation sought not so much to prevent intrusion as to hinder it, to encumber it with a kind of tropical lassitude. Joseph raised his legs high, free of the tangle of vines and roots and thorns, and brought his boots crashing down with each step, crushing leaves into juicy blobs of green and brown, startling underground colonies of ants into frenzied scrambling. Ahead of him, butter-flies, looking like edges of an artist's canvas, fluttered away, and crickets, their wings beating like pieces of stiff silk one against the other, buzzed from tall stalk to tall stalk, narrowly avoiding the grasshoppers which also sought escape. A locust, as long as his hand and as fat, sank its claws into his shirt, just grazing the surface of his skin. He flicked a finger powerfully at it, knocking off its head; the rest of the body simply relaxed and fell off.

Once past the trees, Joseph found himself at the house. The stone foundation, he noticed, was covered in green slime and the wall, the monotony of which was broken only by a large cavity which must once have been a window, stripped of all color. He made his way to the cavity and peered through it into the half-darkness of a large room. He carefully put one leg through, feeling for the floor. The boards creaked badly but held.

The room was a disappointment. He didn't know what he had expected—he hadn't really thought about it—but its empti-ness engendered an atmosphere of uncommon despair. He felt it was a room that had always been empty, a room that had never been peopled with emotion or sound, like a dried-up old spin-ster abandoned at the edge of life. He could smell the pungency of recently disturbed vegetation but he didn't know whether it came from him or through the gaping window.

He made his way to another room, the floorboards creaking under the wary tread of his feet; just another empty space, characterless, almost shapeless in its desertion. A flight of stairs led upwards, to the second floor and yet another empty room, massive, dusty, cobwebs tracing crazy geometric patterns on the walls and the ceiling. In the corners the floorboards had begun to warp. He wondered why all the doors had been removed and by whom. Or had the house ever had doors? Might it not have been always a big, open, empty house, with rooms destined to no purpose, with a façade that promised mystery but an interior that took away all hope?

He had hoped to find something of Pacheco's, the merest testament to his having existed, a bed maybe, or a portrait, or even one line of graffiti. But were it not for the structure itself, a vacuous shell falling steadily to ruin, the smudges of erroneous public fantasy fading like the outer edges of a dream, Pacheco might never have existed. Whatever relics might have been preserved by the government had long been carted away, probably by the last workmen, those who had so cavalierly slipped the chain around the gate, putting a period to a life.

Joseph walked around the room, his footsteps echoing like drumbeats. Each wall had a window of shattered glass and he examined the view from each. Jumbled vegetation, the jungle taking hold in this one plot of earth in the middle of the town: it was the kind of view that would have been described in the travel brochures as *lush* and *tropical*, two words he had grown to hate. Looking through the windows, recalling the manicured grounds of his youth, he felt confined, isolated, a man in an island on an island. He wondered why anyone would pay a lot of money to visit such a place. The answer came to him: for the tourist, a life was not to be constructed here. The tourist sought no more than an approximation of adventure; there was safety in a return ticket and a foreign passport.

There was no way to get to the attic, where the LeNoir window was. Another disappointment: the object of all that youthful energy was nothing more than an aperture to a boxed-in room, airless and musty with age and probably dank with bat mess.

He made his way back down the stairs and out the gaping front door. The air was hot and sticky and the smell of vegetation, acrid in the humidity, was almost overpowering.

Frankie had said that Pacheco was buried in the garden and that a marker had been erected. Joseph knew there was no hope of finding it. Everything was overgrown: the garden, the flowers, the driveway that had once existed, Pacheco's grave, Pacheco himself, the mysterious South American whose last act was to lose his name and his life in sterile isolation.

Joseph began making his way back to the gate. Over to the left he could see the path he had made when going in, the grass flat and twisted, twigs broken and limp, still dripping from the morning rain. He felt clammy, and steamy perspiration broke out on his skin.

At the gate, he stopped and turned around for a last look at the house: he saw it for what it was, a deceptive shell that played on the mind. He looked around for something to throw. The base of the gate-pillars was cracked and broken and moss had begun eating its way to the centre. He broke off a piece of the concrete and flung it at the LeNoir window. The glass shattered, scattering thousands of slivers into the attic and onto the ground below.

His wife wasn't home when he returned. The house was dark and silent. Coffee cups and plates with half-eaten pastries lay on the side-tables. The false fireplace had been switched off. On the mantelpiece, propped against his wife's lipstick-stained cup, was a notepad with a message: 'Have gone out for the evening with Arlene. We have the chauffeur and the limo coz Brian's busy in a cabinet meeting. Don't know what time I'll be back.' She hadn't bothered to sign it.

He ripped the page from the notepad: he hated the word 'coz' and the word 'limo' and he felt a special revulsion for 'Arlene' and 'Brian', fictitious names assumed with the mantle of social status. As a transient domestic, Arlene had been called Thelma, the name scribbled on her birth certificate, and Brian's real name was Balthazar. Joseph avoided the entire issue by simply referring to them as the Minister and the Minister's Wife. The sarcasm was never noticed.

He took the notepad and a pencil and sat down. He wrote *Dear* then crossed it out. He threw the page away and started again. He drew a circle, then a triangle, then a square: the last disappointment, it was the most difficult act. Finally, in big square letters, he wrote, *I am going back*. He put the pad back on the mantelpiece, switched on the fireplace lights, and sat staring into their synchronized dance.

BARRY CALLAGHAN

The Black Queen

Hughes and McCrae were fastidious men who took pride in their old colonial house, the clean simple lines and stucco walls and the painted pale blue picket fence. They were surrounded by houses converted into small warehouses, trucking yards where houses had been torn down, and along the street, a school filled with foreign children, but they didn't mind. It gave them an embattled sense of holding on to something important, a tattered remnant of good taste in an area of waste overrun by rootless olive-skinned children.

McCrae wore his hair a little too long now that he was going grey, and while Hughes with his clipped moustache seemed to be a serious man intent only on his work, which was costume design, McCrae wore Cuban heels and lacquered his nails. When they'd met ten years ago Hughes had said, 'You keep walking around like that and you'll need a body to keep you from getting poked in the eye.' McCrae did all the cooking and drove the car.

But they were not getting along these days. Hughes blamed his bursitis but they were both silently unsettled by how old they had suddenly become, how loose in the thighs, and their feet, when they were showering in the morning, seemed bonier, the toes longer, the nails yellow and hard, and what they wanted was tenderness, to be able to yield almost tearfully, full of a pity for themselves that would not be belittled or laughed at, and when they stood alone in their separate bedrooms they wanted that tenderness from each other, but when they were having their bedtime tea in the kitchen, as they had done for years using lovely green and white Limoges cups, if one touched the other's hand then suddenly they both withdrew into an unspoken, smiling aloofness, as if some line of privacy had been crossed. Neither could bear their thinning wrists and the little pouches of darkening flesh under the chin. They spoke of being with younger people and even joked slyly about bringing a young man home, but that seemed such a betrayal of everything that they had believed had set them apart from others, everything they believed had kept them together, that they sulked and nettled away at each other, and though nothing had apparently changed in their lives, they were always on edge, Hughes more than McCrae.

One of their pleasures was collecting stamps, rare and mint-perfect, with no creases or smudges on the gum. Their collection, carefully mounted in a leatherbound blue book with seven little plastic windows per page, was worth several thousand dollars. They had passed many pleasant evenings together on the Directoire settee arranging the old ochre- and carmine-coloured stamps. They agreed there was something almost sensual about holding a perfectly preserved piece of the past, unsullied, as if everything didn't have to change, didn't have to end up swamped by decline and decay. They disapproved of the new stamps and dismissed them as crude and wouldn't have them in their book. The pages for the recent years remained empty and they liked that; the emptiness was their statement about themselves and their values, and Hughes, holding a stamp up into the light between his tweezers, would say, 'None of that rough trade for us.'

One afternoon they went down to the philatelic shops around Adelaide and Richmond streets and saw a stamp they had been after for a long time, a large and elegant black stamp of Queen Victoria in her widow's weeds. It was rare and expensive, a dead-letter stamp from the turn of the century. They stood side by side over the glass counter-case, admiring it, their hands

spread on the glass, but when McCrae, the overhead fluorescent light catching his lacquered nails, said, 'Well, I certainly
would like that little black sweetheart,' the owner, who had sold
stamps to them for several years, looked up and smirked, and
Hughes suddenly snorted, 'You old queen, I mean why don't
you just quit wearing those goddamn Cuban heels, eh? I mean
why not?' He walked out leaving McCrae embarrassed and hurt
and when the owner said, 'So what was wrong?' McCrae cried,
'Screw you,' and strutted out.

Through the rest of the week they were deferential around
the house, offering each other every consideration, trying to
avoid any squabble before Mother's Day at the end of the week
when they were going to hold their annual supper for friends,
three other male couples. Over the years it had always been an
elegant, slightly mocking evening that often ended bitter-sweetly
and left them feeling close, comforting each other.

McCrae, wearing a white linen shirt with starch in the cuffs
and mother-of-pearl cuff links, worked all Sunday afternoon in
the kitchen and through the window he could see the crab-apple
tree in bloom and he thought how in previous years he would
have begun planning to put down some jelly in the old pressed
glass jars they kept in the cellar, but instead, head down, he
went on stuffing and tying the pork loin roast. Then in the early
evening he heard Hughes at the door, and there was laughter
from the front room and someone cried out, 'What do you do
with an elephant who has three balls on him . . . you don't know,
silly, well you walk him and pitch to the giraffe,' and there were
howls of laughter and the clinking of glasses. It had been the
same every year, eight men sitting down to a fine supper with
expensive wines, the table set with their best silver under the
antique carved wooden candelabra.

Having prepared all the raw vegetables, the cauliflower and
carrots, the avocados and finger-sized miniature corns-on-the-
cob, and placed porcelain bowls of homemade dip in the centre
of a pewter tray, McCrae stared at his reflection for a moment

in the window over the kitchen sink and then he took a plastic slipcase out of the knives-and-forks drawer. The case contained the dead-letter stamp. He licked it all over and pasted it on his forehead and then slipped on the jacket of his charcoal-brown crushed velvet suit, took hold of the tray, and stepped out into the front room.

The other men, sitting in a circle around the coffee table, looked up and one of them giggled. Hughes cried, 'Oh my God.' McCrae, as if nothing were the matter, said, 'My dears, time for the crudités.' He was in his silk stocking feet, and as he passed the tray he winked at Hughes who sat staring at the black queen.

MATT COHEN

The Sins of Tomas Benares

A narrow, three storey house near College Street had been the home of the Benares family since they arrived in Toronto in 1936. Beside the front door, bolted to the brick, was a brass name-plate that was kept polished and bright: DR TOMAS BENARES.

Benares had brought the name-plate—and little else—with him when he and his wife fled Spain just before the Civil War. For twenty years it had resided on the brick beside the doorway. And then, after various happinesses and tragedies—the tragedies being unfortunately more numerous—it had been replaced triumphantly by a new name-plate: DR ABRAHAM BENARES. This son, Abraham, was the only child to have survived those twenty years.

Abraham had lost not only his siblings, but also his mother. The day his name-plate was proudly mounted Tomas could at last say to himself that perhaps his string of bad fortune had finally been cut, for despite everything he now had a son who was a doctor, like himself, and who was married with two children.

By 1960, the Benares household was wealthy in many ways. True, the family had not moved to the north of the city like many other immigrants who had made money, but during the era of the DR ABRAHAM BENARES name-plate the adjoining house was purchased to give space for an expanded office and to provide an investment for Abraham Benares' swelling income as a famous internist. The back yards of both houses were combined into one elegant lawn that was tended twice a week by a professional gardener, an old Russian Jew who Tomas Benares had met first in his office, then at the synagogue. He spent most of his time drinking tea and muttering about the injustices that had been brought upon his people, while Tomas himself, by this time retired, toothless, and bent of back, crawled through the flower beds on his knees, wearing the discarded rubber dishwashing gloves of his son's extraordinarily beautiful wife.

Bella was her name. On anyone else, such a name would have been a joke; but Bella's full figure and dark, Mediterranean face glowed with such animal heat that from the first day he met her Tomas felt like an old man in her presence. Of this Bella seemed entirely unaware. After moving into the house she cooked for Tomas, pressed her scorching lips to his on family occasions, even hovered over him during meals, her fruity breath like a hot caress against his neck. After her children were born she began to refer to Tomas as grandfather, and sometimes while the infants played on the living room floor she would stand beside Tomas with the full weight of her fleshy hand sinking into his arm. 'Look at us,' she said to Tomas once, 'three generations.'

A few years after the birth of his daughter, Abraham Benares was walking with her down to College Street, as he did every Saturday, to buy a newspaper and a bag of apples, when a black Ford car left the street and continued its uncontrolled progress along the sidewalk where Abraham was walking. Instinctively, Abraham scooped Margaret into his arms, but the car was upon him before he could move. Abraham Benares, forty-one years old and the former holder of the city intercollegiate record for the one hundred yard dash, had time only to throw his daughter onto the adjacent lawn while the car mowed him down.

The next year, 1961, the name-plate on the door changed again: DR TOMAS BENARES reappeared. There had been no insurance policy and the old man, now seventy-four years of age but still a licensed physician, recommended the practice of medicine. He got the complaining gardener to redivide the yard with a new fence, sold the house next door to pay his son's debts, and took over the task of providing for his daughter-in-law and his two grandchildren.

Before reopening his practice, Tomas Benares got new false teeth and two new suits. He spent six months reading his old medical textbooks and walked several miles every morning to sweep the cobwebs out of his brain. He also, while walking, made it a point of honour never to look over his shoulder.

On the eve of his ninety-fourth birthday Tomas Benares was sixty-two inches tall and weighed one hundred and twelve pounds. These facts he noted carefully in a small diary. Each year, sitting in his third floor bedroom-study, Tomas Benares entered his height and weight into the pages of this diary. He also summarized any medical problems he had experienced during the year past, and made his prognosis for the year to come. There had once been an essay-like annual entry in which he confessed his outstanding sins and moral omissions from the previous year and outlined how he could correct or at least repent them in the year to follow. These essays had begun when Tomas was a medical student, and had continued well past the year in which his wife died. But when he had retired the first time from practising medicine and had the time to read over the fifty years of entries, he had noticed that his sins grew progressively more boring with age. And so, after that, he simply recorded the number of times he had enjoyed sexual intercourse that year.

Now, almost ninety-four, Tomas Benares couldn't help seeing that even this simple statistic had been absent for almost a decade. His diary was getting shorter while his life was getting longer. His last statistic had been when he was eighty-six—one time; the year before—none at all. But in his eighty-fourth year there had been a dozen transgressions. Transgressions! They should have been marked as victories. Tomas brushed back at the wisps of white hair that still adorned his skull. He couldn't remember feeling guilty or triumphant, couldn't remember any detail at all of the supposed events. Perhaps he had been lying. According to the entry, his height during that erotic year had been sixty-four inches, and his weight exactly twice that—one hundred and twenty-eight pounds. In 1956, when he had begun compiling the statistics, there had been only one admission of intercourse, but his height had been sixty-five inches and his weight one hundred and forty.

Suddenly, Tomas had a vision of himself as an old-fashioned movie. In each frame he was a different size, lived a different life. Only accelerating the reel could make the crowd into one person.

He was sitting in an old blue armchair that had been in the living room when Marguerita was still alive. There he used to read aloud in English to her, trying to get his accent right, while in the adjacent kitchen she washed up the dinner dishes and called out his mistakes. Now he imagined pulling himself out of the armchair, walking to the window to see if his grandson Joseph's car was parked on the street below. He hooked his fingers, permanently curved, into the arms of his chair. And then he pulled. But the chair was a vacuum sucking him down with the gravity of age. Beside him was a glass of raspberry wine. He brought it to his lips, wet the tip of his tongue. He was on that daily two-hour voyage between the departure of his day nurse and the arrival of Joseph. Eventually, perhaps soon, before his weight and height had entirely shrunk away and there were no statistics at all to enter into his diary, he would die. He wanted to die with the house empty. That was the last wish of Tomas Benares.

But even while his ninety-fourth birthday approached, Tomas Benares was not worrying about dying. To be sure he had become smaller with each year, and the prospect of worthwhile sin had almost disappeared; but despite the day nurse and the iron gravity of his chair, Tomas Benares was no invalid. Every morning this whole summer—save the week he had the flu— his nurse, whose name was Elizabeth Rankin, had helped him down the stairs and into the yard where, on his knees, he tended his gardens. While the front of the house had been let go by his careless grandson, Joseph, the back was preserved in the splendour it had known for almost fifty years. Bordering the carefully painted picket fence that surrounded the small yard were banks of flowers, the old strawberry patch, and in one corner a small stand of raspberry canes that were covered by netting to keep away the plague of thieving sparrows.

This morning, too, the morning of his birthday, Elizabeth Rankin helped him down the stairs. Elizabeth Rankin had strong arms, but although he could hardly walk down the three flights of stairs by himself—let alone climb back up—he could think of his own father, who had lived to be one hundred and twenty-three and of his grandfather Benares, who had lived to the same age. There was, in fact, no doubt that this enormous number was fate's stamp on the brow of the Benares men, though even fate could not *always* cope with automobiles.

But, as his own father had told Tomas, the Benares were to consider themselves blessed because fate seemed to pick them out more frequently than other people. For example, Tomas' father, who was born in 1820, had waited through two wives to have children, and when one was finally born, a boy, he had died of an unknown disease that winter brought to the Jewish quarter of Kiev. So frightened had he been by this show of God's spite that Tomas' father had sold the family lumbering business and rushed his wife back to Spain, the cradle of his ancestors, where she bore Tomas in 1884. Tomas' grandfather had, of course, been hale and hearty at the time: one hundred and four years old, he had lived on the top floor of the house just as Tomas now lived on the top floor of his own grandson's house.

That old man, Tomas' grandfather, had been a round, brown apple baked dry by the sun and surrounded by a creamy white fringe of beard. He had been born in 1780 and Tomas, bemoaning the emptiness of his diary on the occasion of his oncoming ninety-fourth, realized suddenly that he was holding two hundrcd years in his mind. His father had warned him: the Benares men were long-lived relics whose minds sent arrows back into the swamp of the past, so deep into the swamp that the lives they recalled were clamped together in a formless gasping mass, waiting to be shaped by those who remembered. The women were more peripheral: stately and beautiful they were easily extinguished; perhaps they were bored to death by the small, round-headed stubborn men who made up the Benares tribe.

'We were always Spaniards,' the old man told Tomas, 'stubborn as donkeys.' *Stubborn as a donkey*, the child Tomas had whispered. Had his mother not already screamed this at him? And he imagined ancient Spain: a vast, sandy expanse where the Jews had been persecuted and in revenge had hidden their religion under prayer shawls and been stubborn as donkeys.

And they hadn't changed, Tomas thought gleefully, they hadn't changed at all; filled with sudden enthusiasm and the image of himself as a white-haired, virile donkey, he pulled himself easily out of his chair and crossed the room to the window where he looked down for Joseph's car. The room was huge: the whole third floor of the house save for an alcove walled off as a bathroom. Yet even in the afternoon the room was dark as a cave, shadowed by its clutter of objects that included everything from his marriage bed to the stand-up scale with the weights and sliding rule that he used to assess himself for his yearly entry.

From the window he saw that his grandson's car had yet to arrive. On the sidewalk instead were children travelling back and forth on tricycles, shouting to each other in a fractured mixture of Portuguese and English. As always, when he saw children on the sidewalk, he had to resist opening the window and warning them to watch out for cars. It had been Margaret, only four years old, who had run back to the house to say that 'Papa is sick,' then had insisted on returning down the street with Tomas.

Two hundred years: would Margaret live long enough to sit frozen in a chair and feel her mind groping from one century to

the next? Last year, on his birthday, she had given him the bottle of raspberry wine he was now drinking. 'Every raspberry is
a blessing,' she had said. She had a flowery tongue, like her
brother, and when she played music Tomas could sense her passion whirling like a dark ghost through the room. What would
she remember? Her mother who had run away; her grandmother
whom she had never known; her father, covered by a sheet by
the time she and Tomas had arrived, blood from his crushed
skull seeping into the white linen.

They had come a long way, the Benares: from the new Jeru-
salem in Toledo to two centuries in Kiev, only to be frightened
back to Spain before fleeing again, this time to a prosperous
city in the New World. But nothing had changed, Tomas thought,
even the bitterness over his son's death still knifed through him
exactly as it had when he saw Margaret's eyes at the door, when
Joseph, at the funeral, broke into a long, keening howl.

Stubborn as a donkey. Tomas straightened his back and walked
easily from the window towards his chair. He would soon be
ninety-four years old; and if fate was to be trusted, which it
wasn't, there were to be thirty more years of anniversaries. During the next year, he thought, he had better put some effort into
improving his statistics.

He picked up his diary again, flipped the pages backward,
fell into a doze before he could start reading.

On his ninety-fourth birthday Tomas slept in. This meant not
waking until after eight o'clock; and then lying in bed and thinking
about his dreams. In the extra hours of sleep Tomas dreamed
that he was a young man again, that he was married, living in
Madrid, and that at noon the bright sun was warm as he walked
the streets from his office to the *café* where he took lunch with
his cronies. But in this dream he was not a doctor but a philoso-
pher; for some strange reason it had been given to him to spend
his entire life thinking about oak trees, and while strolling the
broad, leafy streets it was precisely this subject that held his

mind. He had also the duty, of course, of supervising various graduate students, all of whom were writing learned dissertations on the wonders of the oak; and it often, in this dream, pleased him to spend the afternoon with these bright and beautiful young people, drinking wine and saying what needed to be said.

In the bathroom, Tomas shaved himself with the electric razor that had been a gift from Joseph. Even on his own birthday he no longer trusted his hand with the straight razor that still hung, with its leather strop, from a nail in the wall. This, he suddenly thought, was the kind of detail that should also be noted in his annual diary—the texture of his shrinking world. Soon everything would be forbidden to him, and he would be left with only the space his own huddled skeleton could occupy. After shaving, Tomas washed his face, noting the exertion that was necessary just to open and close the cold water tap, and then he went back to the main room where he began slowly to dress.

It was true, he was willing to admit, that these days he often thought about his own death; but such thoughts did not disturb him. In fact, during those hours when he felt weak and sat in his chair breathing slowly, as if each weak breath might be his last, he often felt Death sitting with him. A quiet friend, Death; one who was frightening at first, but now was a familiar companion, an invisible brother waiting for him to come home.

But home, for Tomas Benares, was still the world of the living. When Elizabeth Rankin came to check on him, she found Tomas dressed and brushed. And a few minutes later he was sitting in his own garden, drinking espresso coffee and listening to the birds fuss in the flowering hedges that surrounded his patio. There Tomas, at peace, let the hot sun soak into his face. Death was with him in the garden, in the seductive buzz of insects, the comforting sound of water running in the nearby kitchen. The unaccustomed long sleep only gave Tomas the taste for more. He could feel himself drifting off, noted with interest that he had no desire to resist, felt Death pull his chair closer, his breath disguised as raspberries and mimosa.

At seventy-four years of age, also on his birthday, Tomas Benares had gone out to his front steps, unscrewed his son's name-plate and reaffixed his own. In the previous weeks he had restored the house to the arrangement it had known before his original retirement.

The front hall was the waiting room. On either side were long wooden benches, the varnished oak polished by a generation of patients. This front hall opened into a small parlour that looked onto the street. In that room was a desk, more chairs for waiting, and the doctor's files. At first his wife ran that parlour; after her death, Tomas had hired a nurse.

Behind the parlour was the smallest room of all. It had space for an examination table, a glass cabinet with a few books and several drawers of instruments, and a single uncomfortable chair. On the ceiling was a fluorescent light, and the window was protected by venetian blinds made of heavy plastic.

After Abraham's death his widow, Bella, and the children had stayed on in the Benares household, and so on the morning of the reopening Tomas had gone into the kitchen to find Bella making coffee and feeding breakfast to Joseph and Margaret. He sat down wordlessly at the kitchen table while Bella brought him coffee and toast, and he was still reading the front section of the morning paper when the doorbell rang. Joseph leapt from the table and ran down the hall. Tomas was examining the advertisement he had placed to announce the recommencement of his practice.

'Finish your coffee,' said Bella. 'Let her wait. She's the one who needs the job.'

But Tomas was already on his feet. Slowly he walked down the hall to the front parlour. He could hear Joseph chatting with the woman, and was conscious of trying to keep his back straight. He was wearing, for his new practice, a suit newly tailored. His old tailor had died, but his son had measured Tomas with the cloth tape, letting his glasses slide down to rest on the tip of his nose exactly like his father had. Now in his new blue suit, a matching tie, and one of the white linen shirts that Marguerita had made for him, Tomas stood in his front parlour.

'Doctor Benares, I am Elizabeth Rankin; I answered your advertisement for a nurse.'

'I am pleased to meet you, Mrs. Rankin.'

'Miss Rankin.' Elizabeth Rankin was then a young woman entering middle age. She had brown hair parted in the middle and then pulled back in a bun behind her neck, eyes of a darker brown in which Tomas saw a mixture of fear and sympathy. She was wearing a skirt and a jacket, but had with her a small suitcase in case it was necessary for her to start work right away.

'Would you like to see my papers, Doctor Benares?'

'Yes, if you like. Please sit down.'

Joseph was still in the room and Tomas let him watch as Elizabeth Rankin pulled out a diploma stating that she had graduated from McGill University in the biological sciences, and another diploma showing that she had received her RN from the same university.

'I have letters of reference, Doctor Benares.'

'Joseph, please get a cup of coffee for Miss Rankin. Do you—'

'Just black, Joseph.'

They sat in silence until Joseph arrived with the coffee, and then Tomas asked him to leave and closed the door behind him.

'I'm sorry,' Elizabeth Rankin said. 'I saw the advertisement and . . .'

She trailed off. It was six months since Tomas had seen her, but he recognized her right away; she was the woman who had been driving the car that had killed his son. At the scene of the accident she had shivered in shock until the ambulance arrived. Tomas had even offered her some sleeping pills. Then she had reappeared to hover on the edge of the mourners at Abraham's funeral.

'You're a very brave woman, Miss Rankin.'

'No, I . . . ' Her eyes clouded over. Tomas, behind the desk, watched her struggle. When he had seen her in the hall, his first reaction had been anger.

'I thought I should do something,' she said. 'I don't need a salary, of course, and I *am* a qualified nurse.'

'I see that,' Tomas said dryly.

'You must hate me,' Elizabeth Rankin said.

Tomas shrugged. Joseph came back into the room and stood beside Elizabeth Rankin. She put her hand on his shoulder and the boy leaned against her.

'You mustn't bother Miss Rankin,' Tomas said, but even as he spoke he could see Elizabeth's hand tightening on the boy's shoulder.

'Call Margaret,' Tomas said to Joseph, and then asked himself why, indeed, he should forgive this woman. No reason came to mind, and while Joseph ran through the house, searching for his sister, Tomas sat in his reception room and looked carefully at the face of Elizabeth Rankin. The skin below her eyes was dark, perhaps she had trouble sleeping; and though her expression was maternal she had a tightly drawn quality that was just below the surface, as though the softness were a costume.

He remembered a friend, who had been beaten by a gang of Franco's men, saying he felt sorry for them. When Tomas' turn came, he had felt no pity for his assailants. And although what Elizabeth Rankin had done was an accident, not a malicious act, she was still the guilty party. Tomas wondered if she knew what he was thinking, wondered how she could not. She was sitting with one leg crossed over the other, her eyes on the door through which the sounds of the children's feet now came. And when Margaret, shy, sidled into the room, Tomas made a formal introduction. He was thinking, as he watched Margaret's face, how strange it was that the victims must always console their oppressors.

Margaret, four years old, curtsied and then held out her hand.

There was no horrified scream, no flicker of recognition.

'Miss Rankin will be coming every morning,' Tomas announced. 'She will help me in my office.'

'You are very kind, Doctor Benares.'

'We will see,' Tomas said. It was then that he had an extraordinary thought, or at least a thought that was extraordinary for him. It occurred to him that Elizabeth Rankin didn't simply want to atone, or to be consoled. She wanted to be taken advantage of.

Tomas waited until the children had left the room, then closed the door. He stood in front of Elizabeth Rankin until she, too, got to her feet.

'Pig,' Tomas Benares hissed; and he spat at her face. The saliva missed its target and landed, instead, on the skin covering her right collarbone. There it glistened, surrounded by tiny beads, before gliding down the open V of her blouse.

The eyes of Elizabeth Rankin contracted briefly. Then their expression returned to a flat calm. Tomas, enraged, turned on his heel and walked quickly out of the room. When he came back fifteen minutes later, Elizabeth Rankin had changed into her white uniform and was sorting through the files of his son.

Bella said it wasn't right.

'That you should have *her* in the house,' she said. 'It's disgusting.'

'She has a diploma,' Tomas said.

'And how are you going to pay her? You don't have any patients.'

This discussion took place in the second floor sitting room after the children were asleep. It was the room where Bella and Abraham used to go to have their privacy.

'At first I thought maybe you didn't recognize her,' Bella started again, 'and so I said to myself, what sort of joke is this? Maybe she didn't get enough the first time, maybe she has to come back for more.'

'It was an accident,' Tomas said.

'So you forgive her?' Bella challenged. She had a strong, bell-like voice which, when she and Abraham were first married, had been a family joke, one even she would laugh at; but since his death the tone had grown rusty and sepulchral.

Tomas shrugged.

'I don't forgive her,' Bella said.

'It was an accident,' Tomas said. 'She has to work it out of her system.'

'What about me? How am I going to work it out of my system?'

At thirty, Bella was even more beautiful than when she had been married. The children had made her heavy, but grief had carved away the excess flesh. She had jet-black hair and olive skin that her children had both inherited. Now she began to cry and Tomas, as always during these nightly outbursts of tears, went to stand by the window.

'Well?' Bella insisted. 'What do you expect me to do?'

When she had asked this question before, Tomas advised her to go to sleep with the aid of a pill. But now he hesitated. For how many months, for how many years could he tell her to obliterate her evenings in sleeping pills.

'You're the saint,' Bella said. 'You never wanted anyone after Marguerita.'

'I was lucky,' Tomas said. 'I had a family.'

'I have a family.'

'I was older,' Tomas said.

'So,' Bella repeated dully, 'you never did want anyone else.'

Tomas was silent. When Abraham brought her home he had asked Tomas what he thought of her. 'She's very beautiful,' Tomas had said. Abraham had happily agreed. Now she was more beautiful but, Tomas thought, also more stupid.

'It is very hard,' Tomas said, 'for a man my age to fall in love.'

'Your wife died many years ago . . . '

Tomas shrugged. 'I always felt old,' he said, 'ever since we came to Canada.' All this time he had been standing at the window, and now he made sure his back was turned so that she wouldn't see his tears. The day Abraham had been killed he had cried with her. Since then, even at the funeral, he had refused to let her see his tears. Why? He didn't know. The sight of her, even the smell of her walking into a room, seemed to freeze his heart.

'If there was—' Bella started. She stopped. Tomas knew that he should help her, that she shouldn't have to fight Abraham's ghost *and* his father, but he couldn't bring himself to reach out. It was like watching an ant trying to struggle its way out of a pot of honey.

'If there was someone else,' Bella said. 'Even a job.'

'What can you do?' Tomas asked, but the question was rhetorical; Bella had married Abraham the year after she had finished high school. She couldn't even type.

'*I* could be your receptionist, instead of that—'

'Nurse,' Tomas interrupted. 'I need a nurse, Bella.'

'I can put a thermometer in someone's mouth,' Bella said. 'Are people going to die while you're next door in the office?'

'A doctor needs a nurse,' Tomas said. 'I didn't invent the rules.'

'There's a rule?'

'It's a custom, Bella.'

He turned from the window.

'And anyway,' Bella said, 'who's going to take care of the children?'

'That's right, the children need a mother.'

'We need Bella in the kitchen making three meals a day so at night she can cry herself to sleep—while the murderer is working off her guilt so at night she can go out and play with the boys, her conscience clean.'

'You don't know what she does at night—'

'You're such a saint,' Bella said suddenly. 'You are such a saint the whole world admires you, do you know that?'

'Bella—'

'The holy Doctor Benares. At seventy-four years of age he ends his retirement and begins work again to provide for his widowed daughter and his two orphaned grandchildren. Has the world ever seen such a man? At the *shul* they're talking about adding a sixth book to the Torah.' She looked at Tomas, and Tomas, seeing her go out of control, could only stand and watch. She was like an ant, he was thinking. Now the ant was at the lip of the pot. It might fall back into the honey, in which case it would drown; or it might escape after all.

'You're such a saint,' Bella said in her knife-edge voice, 'you're such a saint that you think poor Bella just wants to go out and get laid.'

She was teetering on the edge now, Tomas thought.

'You should see your face now,' Bella said. '*Adultery*, you're thinking. *Whore*.'

'It's perfectly normal for a healthy—'

'Oh, healthy *shit*!' Bella screamed. 'I just want to go out. Out, out, *out*!'

She was standing in the doorway, her face beet-red, panting with her fury. Tomas, staying perfectly still, could feel his own answering blush searing the backs of his ears, surrounding his neck like a hot rope.

'Even the saint goes for a walk,' Bella's voice had dropped again. 'Even the saint can spend the afternoon over at Herman Levine's apartment, playing cards and drinking beer.'

Tomas could feel his whole body burning and chafing inside his suit. *The saint*, she was calling him. And what had he done to her? Offered her and her family a home when they needed it. 'Did I make Abraham stay here?' Tomas asked. And then realized, to his shame, that he had said the words aloud.

He saw Bella in the doorway open her mouth until it looked like the muzzle of a cannon. Her lips struggled and convulsed.

The room filled with unspoken obscenities.

Tomas reached a hand to touch the veins in his neck. They were so engorged with blood he was choking. He tore at his tie, forced his collar open.

'Oh, God,' Bella moaned.

Tomas was coughing, trying to free his throat and chest. Bella was in the corner of his hazed vision, staring at him in the same detached way he had watched her only a few moments before.

The saint, Tomas was thinking, *she calls me the saint*. An old compartment of his mind suddenly opened, and he began to curse at her in Spanish. Then he turned his back and walked upstairs to his third floor bedroom.

In the small hours of the morning, Tomas Benares was lying in the centre of his marriage bed, looking up at the ceiling of the bedroom and tracing the shadows with his tired eyes. These shadows: cast by the streetlights they were as much a part of his furniture as was the big oak bed, or the matching dressers that presided on either side—still waiting, it seemed, for the miraculous return of Marguerita.

As always he was wearing pyjamas—sewing had been another of Marguerita's talents—and like the rest of his clothes they had been cleaned and ironed by the same Bella who had stood in the doorway of the second floor living room and bellowed and panted at him like an animal gone mad. The windows were open and while he argued with himself Tomas could feel the July night trying to cool his skin, soothe him. But he didn't want to be soothed, and every half hour or so he raised himself on one elbow and reached for a cigarette, flaring the light in the darkness and feeling for a second the distant twin of the young man who had lived in Madrid forty years ago, the young man who had taken lovers (all of them beautiful in retrospect), whispered romantic promises (all of them ridiculous), and then had the good fortune to fall in love and marry a woman so beautiful and devoted that even his dreams could never have imagined her. And yet it was true, as he had told Bella, that when he came to Canada his life had ended. Even lying with Marguerita in this bed he had often been unable to sleep, had often, with this very gesture, lit up a small space in the night in order to feel close to the young man who had been deserted in Spain.

Return? Yes, it had occurred to him after the war was finished. Of course, Franco was still in power then, but it was his country and there were others who had returned. And yet, what would have been the life of an exile returned? The life of a man keeping his lips perpetually sealed, his thoughts to himself; the life of a man who had sold his heart in order to have the sights and smells that were familiar.

Now, Tomas told himself wryly, he was an old man who had lost his heart for nothing at all. Somehow, over the years, it had simply disappeared; like a beam of wood being eaten from the inside, it had dropped away without him knowing it.

Tomas Benares, on his seventy-fourth birthday, had just put out a cigarette and lain back with his head on the white linen pillow to resume his study of the shadows, when he heard the footsteps on the stairs up to his attic. Then there was the creak of the door opening and Bella, in her nightgown and carrying a candle, tiptoed into the room.

Tomas closed his eyes.

The footsteps came closer, he felt the bed sag with her weight. He could hear her breathing in the night, it was soft and slow; and then, as he realized he was holding his own breath, he felt Bella's hand come to rest on his forehead.

He opened his eyes. In the light of the candle her face was like stone, etched and lined with grief.

'I'm sorry,' Tomas said.

'I'm the sorry one. And imagine, on your birthday.'

'That's all right. We've been too closed-in here, since—' Here he hesitated, because for some reason the actual event was never spoken. 'Since Abraham died.'

Bella now took her hand away, and Tomas was aware of how

cool and soft it had been. Sometimes, decades ago, Marguerita had comforted him in this same way when he couldn't sleep. Her hand on his forehead, fingers stroking his cheeks, his eyes, soothing murmurs until finally he drifted away, a log face-down in the cool water.

'There are still lives to be lived,' Bella was saying. 'The children.'

'The children,' Tomas repeated. Not since Marguerita had there been a woman in this room at night. For many years he used to lock the door when he went to bed, and even now he would still lock it on the rare times he was sick in case someone— who?—should dare to come on a mission of mercy.

'I get tired,' Bella said. Her head drooped and Tomas could see, beyond the outline of her nightdress, the curve of her breasts, the fissure between. A beautiful woman, he had thought before. . . . He was not as saintly as Bella imagined. On certain of the afternoons Bella thought he was at Herman Levine's, Tomas had been visiting a different apartment, that of a widow who was once his patient. She, too, knew what it was like to look at the shadows on the ceiling for one year after another, for one decade after another.

Now Tomas reached out for Bella's hand. Her skin was young and supple, not like the skin of the widow, or his own. There came a time in every person's life, Tomas thought, when the inner soul took a look at the body and said: Enough, you've lost what little beauty you had and now you're just an embar- rassment—I'll keep carrying you around, but I refuse to take you seriously. Tomas, aside from some stray moments of vanity, had reached that point long ago; but Bella, he knew, was still in love with her body, still wore her own bones and skin and flesh as a proud inheritance and not an aging inconvenience.

'Happy birthday,' Bella said. She lifted Tomas' hand and pressed it to her mouth. At first, what he felt was the wetness of her mouth. And then it was her tears that flowed in tiny, warm streams around his fingers.

She blew out the candle at the same time that Tomas reached for her shoulder; and then he drew her down so she was lying beside him—her on top of the covers and him beneath, her thick, jet hair folded into his neck and face, her perfume and the scent of her mourning skin wrapped around him like a garden. Chastely he cuddled her to him, her warm breath as soothing as Marguerita's had once been. He felt himself drifting into sleep, and he turned towards the perfume, the garden, turned towards Bella to hold her in his arms the way he used to hold Marguerita in that last exhausted moment of waking.

Bella shifted closer, herself breathing so slowly that Tomas thought she must be already asleep. He remembered, with relief, that his alarm was set for six o'clock; at least they would wake before the children. Then he felt his own hand, as if it had a life of its own, slide in a slow caress from Bella's shoulder to her elbow, touching, in an accidental way, her sleeping breast.

Sleep fled at once, and Tomas felt the sweat spring to his skin. Yet Bella only snuggled closer, breasts and hips flooding through the blanket like warm oceans. Tomas imagined reaching for and lighting a cigarette, the darkness parting once more. A short while ago he had been mourning his youth and now, he reflected, he was feeling as stupid as he ever had. Even with the widow there had been no hesitation. Mostly on his visits they sat in her living room and drank tea; sometimes, by a mutual consent that was arrived at without discussion, they went to her bedroom and performed sex like a warm and comfortable bath. A bath, he thought to himself, that was how he and Bella should become; chaste, warm, comforts to each other in the absence of Abraham. It wasn't right, he now decided, to have frozen his heart to this woman—his daughter-in-law, after all; surely she had a right to love, to the warmth and affection due to a member of the family. *Bella*, he was ready to proclaim, *you are the mother of my grandchildren, the chosen wife of my son. And if you couldn't help shouting, at least you were willing to comfort me.*

Tomas held Bella closer. Her lips, he became aware, were

pressed against the hollow of his throat, moving slowly, kissing the skin and now sucking gently at the hairs that curled up from his chest. Tomas let his hand find the back of her neck. There was a delicate valley that led down from her skull past the thick, black hair. He would never have guessed she was built so finely.

Now Bella's weight lifted away for a moment, though her lips stayed glued to his throat, and then suddenly she was underneath the covers, her leg across his groin, her hand sliding up his chest.

Tomas felt something inside of him break. And then, as he raised himself on top of Bella the night, too, broke open; a gigantic black and dreamless mouth, it swallowed them both. He kissed her, tore at her nightgown to suck at her breast, penetrated her so deeply that she gagged; yet though he touched and kissed her every private place; though they writhed on the bed and he felt the cool sweep of her lips as they searched out his every nerve; though he even opened his eyes to see the pleasure on her face, her black hair spread like dead butterflies over Marguerita's linen pillows, her mouth open with repeated climax, the night still swallowed them, obliterated everything as it happened, took them rushing down its hot and endless gorge until Tomas felt like Jonah in the belly of the whale; felt like Jonah trapped in endless flesh and juice. And all he had to escape with was his own sex: like an old sword he brandished it in the blackness, pierced open tunnels, flailed it against the wet walls of his prison.

'Bella, Bella, Bella.' He whispered her name silently. Every time he shaped his lips around her name, he was afraid the darkness of his inner eye would part, and Abraham's face would appear before him. But it didn't happen. Even as he scratched Bella's back, bit her neck, penetrated her from behind, he taunted himself with the idea that somewhere in this giant night Abraham must be waiting. His name was on Tomas' lips: Abraham his son. How many commandments was he breaking? Tomas wondered, pressing Bella's breasts to his parched cheeks.

Tomas felt his body, like a starved man at a banquet, go out of control. Kissing, screwing, holding, stroking: everything he did Bella wanted, did back, invented variations upon. For one brief second he thought that Marguerita had never been like this, then his mind turned on itself and he was convinced that this *was* Marguerita, back from the dead with God's blessing to make up, in a few hours, a quarter century of lost time.

But as he kissed and cried over his lost Marguerita, the night began to lift and the first light drew a grey mask on the window.

By this time he and Bella were lying on their stomachs, side by side, too exhausted to move.

The grey mask began to glow, and as it did Tomas felt the dread rising in him. Surely God Himself would appear to take His revenge, and with that thought Tomas realized he had forgotten his own name. He felt his tongue searching, fluttering between his teeth, tasting again his own sweat and Bella's fragrant juices. He must be, he thought, in Hell. He had died and God, to drive his wicked soul crazy, had given him this dream of his own daughter-in-law, his dead son's wife.

'Thank you, Tomas.'

No parting kiss, just soft steps across the carpet and then one creak as she descended the stairs. Finally, the face of his son appeared. It was an infant's face, staring uncomprehendingly at its father.

Tomas sat up. His back was sore, his kidneys felt trampled, one arm ached, his genitals burned. He stood up to go to the bathroom and was so dizzy that for a few moments he had to cling to the bedpost with his eyes closed. Then, limping and groaning, he crossed the room. When he got back to the bed there was no sign that Bella had been there—but the sheets were soaked as they sometimes were after a restless night.

He collapsed on the covers and slept dreamlessly until the alarm went off. When he opened his eyes his first thought was of Bella, and when he swung out of bed there was a sharp sting in his groin. But as he dressed he was beginning to speculate, even to hope, that the whole episode had been a dream.

A few minutes later, downstairs at breakfast, Tomas found the children sitting alone at the table. Between them was a sealed envelope addressed to 'Dr Tomas Benares, M.D.'

'Dear Tomas,' the letter read, 'I have decided that it is time for me to seek my own life in another city. Miss Rankin has already agreed to take care of the children for as long as necessary. I hope you will all understand me and remember that I love you. As always, Bella Benares.'

On his birthday, his garden always seemed to reach that explosive point that marked the height of summer. No matter what the weather, it was this garden that made up for all other deprivations, and the fact that his ninety-fourth birthday was gloriously warm and sunny made it doubly perfect for Tomas to spend the day outside.

Despite the perfect blessing of the sky, as Tomas opened his eyes from that long doze that had carried the sun straight into the afternoon, he felt a chill in his blood, the knowledge that Death, that companion he'd grown used to, almost fond of, was starting to play his tricks. Because sitting in front of him, leaning towards him as if the worlds of waking and sleeping had been forced together, was Bella herself.

'Tomas, Tomas, it's good to see you. It's Bella.'

'I know,' Tomas said. His voice sounded weak and grumpy; he coughed to clear his throat.

'Happy birthday, Tomas.'

He pushed his hand across his eyes to rid himself of this illusion.

'Tomas, you're looking so good.'

Bella: her face was fuller now, but the lines were carved deeper, bracketing her full lips and corrugating her forehead. And yet she was still young, amazing: her movements were lithe and supple; her jet-black hair was streaked, but still fell thick and wavy to her shoulders; her eyes still burned, and when she leaned forward to take his hand between her own the smell of her, dreams and remembrances, came flooding back.

'Tomas, are you glad to see me?'

'You look so young, Bella.' This in a weak voice, but Tomas' throat-clearing cough was lost in the rich burst of Bella's laughter. Tomas, seeing her head thrown back and the flash of her strong teeth, could hardly believe that he, a doddering old man, whose knees were covered by a blanket in the middle of summer, had only a few years ago actually made love to this vibrant woman. Now she was like a racehorse in voracious maturity.

'Bella, the children.'

'I know, Tomas. I telephoned Margaret; she's here. And I telephoned Joseph, too. His secretary said he was at a meeting all afternoon, but that he was coming here for dinner.'

'Bella, you're looking wonderful, truly wonderful.' Tomas had his hand hooked into hers and, suddenly aware that he was half-lying in his chair, was using her weight to try to lever himself up.

Instantly Bella was on her feet, her arm solicitously around his back, pulling him into position. She handled his weight, Tomas thought, like the weight of a baby. He felt surrounded by her, overpowered by her smell, her vitality, her cheery goodwill. *Putan*, Tomas whispered to himself. What a revenge. Twenty years ago he had been her equal; and now, suddenly—what had happened? Death was in the garden; Tomas could feel his presence, the familiar visitor turned trickster. And then Tomas felt some of his strength returning, strength in the form of contempt for Bella, who had waited twenty years to come back to this house; contempt for Death, who waited until a man was an ancient, drooling husk to test his will.

'You're the marvel, Tomas. Elizabeth says you work every day in the garden. How do you do it?'

'I spit in Death's face,' Tomas rasped. Now he was beginning to feel more himself again, and he saw that Bella was offering him a cup of coffee. All night he had slept, and then again in the daytime. What a way to spend a birthday! But coffee would heat the blood, make it run faster. He realized that he was famished.

Bella had taken out a package of cigarettes now, and offered one to Tomas. He shook his head, thinking again how he had declined in these last years. Now Joseph wouldn't let him smoke in bed, even when he couldn't sleep. He was only allowed to smoke when there was someone else in the room, or when he was outside in the garden.

'Tomas. I hope you don't mind I came back. I wanted to see you again while—while we could still talk.'

Tomas nodded. So the ant had escaped the honey pot after all, and ventured into the wide world. Now it was back, wanting to tell its adventures to the ant who had stayed home. Perhaps they hadn't spent that strange night making love after all; perhaps in his bed they had been struggling on the edge of the pot, fighting to see who would fall back and who would be set free.

'So,' Bella said. 'It's been so long.'

Tomas, watching her, refusing to speak, felt control slowly moving towards him again. He sat up straighter, brushed the blanket off his legs.

'Or maybe we should talk tomorrow,' Bella said, 'when you're feeling stronger.'

'I feel strong.' His voice surprised even himself—not the weak squawk it sometimes was now, a chicken's squeak hardly audible over the telephone, but firm and definite, booming out of his chest the way it used to. Bella: she had woken him up once, perhaps she would once more.

He could see her moving back, hurt; but then she laughed again, her rich throaty laugh that Tomas used to hear echoing through the house when his son was still alive. He looked at her left hand; Abraham's modest engagement ring was still in place, but beside it was a larger ring, a glowing bloodstone set in a fat gold band. 'Tomas,' Bella was saying, 'you really are a marvel,

I swear you're going to live to see a hundred.'

'One hundred and twenty-three,' Tomas said. 'Almost all of the Benares men live to be one hundred and twenty-three.'

For a moment, the lines deepened again in Bella's face, and Tomas wished he could someday learn to hold his tongue. A bad habit that should have long ago been entered in his diary.

'You will,' Bella finally said. Her voice had the old edge. '*Two* hundred and twenty-three, you'll dance on all our graves.'

'Bella.'

'I shouldn't have come.'

'The children—'

'They'll be glad to see me, Tomas, they always are.'

'Always?'

'Of course. Did you think I'd desert my own children?'

Tomas shook his head.

'Oh, I left, Tomas, I left. But I kept in touch. I sent them letters and they wrote me back. That woman helped me.'

'Elizabeth?'

'I should never have called her a murderer, Tomas. It was an accident.'

'They wrote you letters without telling me?'

Bella stood up. She was a powerful woman now, full-fleshed and in her prime; even Death had slunk away in the force of her presence. 'I married again, Tomas. My husband and I lived in Seattle. When Joseph went to university there, he lived in my home.'

'Joseph lived with you?'

'My husband's dead now, Tomas, but I didn't come for your pity. Or your money. I just wanted you to know that I would be in Toronto again, seeing my own children, having a regular life.'

'A regular life,' Tomas repeated. He felt dazed, dangerously weakened. Death was in the garden again, he was standing behind Bella, peeking out from behind her shoulders and making faces. He struggled to his feet. Only Bella could save him now, and yet he could see the fear on her face as he reached for her.

'Tomas, I—'

'You couldn't kill me!' Tomas roared. His lungs filled his chest like an eagle in flight. His flowering hedges, his roses, his carefully groomed patio snapped into focus. He stepped towards Bella, his balance perfect, his arm rising. He saw her mouth open, her lips begin to flutter. Beautiful but stupid, Tomas thought; some things never change. At his full height he was still tall enough to put his arm around her and lead her to the house.

'It's my birthday.' His voice boomed with the joke. 'Let me offer you a drink to celebrate your happy return.'

His hand slid from her shoulder to her arm; the skin was smooth as warm silk. Her face turned towards his: puzzled, almost happy, and he could feel the heat of her breath as she prepared to speak.

'Of course I forgive you,' Tomas said.

MAVIS GALLANT

The Chosen Husband

In 1949, a year that contained no other news of value, Mme
Carette came into a legacy of eighteen thousand dollars from a
brother-in-law who had done well in Fall River. She had suspected him of being a Freemason, as well as of other offenses,
none of them trifling, and so she did not make a show of bringing out his photograph; instead, she asked her daughters, Berthe
and Marie, to mention him in their prayers. They may have, for
a while. The girls were twenty-two and twenty, and Berthe, the
elder, hardly prayed at all.

The first thing that Mme Carette did was to acquire a better
address. Until now she had kept the Montreal habit of changing
her rented quarters every few seasons, a conversation with a
landlord serving as warranty, rent paid in cash. This time she
was summoned by appointment to a rental agency to sign a two-
year lease. She had taken the first floor of a stone house around
the corner from the church of St Louis de France. This was her
old parish (she held to the network of streets near Parc Lafontaine)
but a glorious strand of it, Rue St Hubert.

Before her inheritance Mme Carette had crept to church, eyes
lowered; had sat where she was unlikely to disturb anyone whose
life seemed more fortunate, therefore more deserving, than her
own. She had not so much prayed as petitioned. Now she ran a
glove along the pew to see if it was dusted, straightened the
unread pamphlets that called for more vocations for missionary
service in Africa, told a confessor that, like all the prosperous,

she was probably without fault. When the holy-water font looked mossy, she called the parish priest and had words with his house-keeper, even though scrubbing the church was not her job. She still prayed every day for the repose of her late husband, and the unlikelier rest of his Freemason brother, but a tone of briskness caused her own words to rattle in her head. Church was a hushed annex to home. She prayed to insist upon the refinement of some request, and instead of giving thanks simply acknowledged that matters used to be worse.

Her daughter Berthe had been quick to point out that Rue St Hubert was in decline. Otherwise, how could the Carettes afford to live here? (Berthe worked in an office and was able to pay half the rent.) A family of foreigners were installed across the road. A seamstress had placed a sign in a ground-floor window—a sure symptom of decay. True, but Mme Carette had as near neighbors a retired opera singer and the first cousins of a city councillor—calm, courteous people who had never been on relief. A few blocks north stood the mayor's private dwell-ing, with a lamppost on each side of his front door. (During the recent war the mayor had been interned, like an enemy alien. No one quite remembered why. Mme Carette believed that he had refused an invitation to Buckingham Palace, and that the English had it in for him. Berthe had been told that he had tried to annex Montreal to the State of New York and that someone had minded. Marie, who spoke to strangers on the bus, once came home with a story about Fascist views; but as she could not spell 'Fascist', and did not know if it was a kind of land-scape or something to eat, no one took her seriously. The mayor had eventually been released, was promptly reëlected, and con-tinued to add lustre to Rue St Hubert.)

Mme Carette looked out upon long façades of whitish stone, windowpanes with bevelled edges that threw rainbows. In her childhood this was how notaries and pharmacists had lived, be-fore they began to copy the English taste for freestanding houses, blank lawns, ornamental willows, leashed dogs. She recalled a moneyed aunt and uncle, a family of well-dressed, soft-spoken children, heard the echo of a French more accurately expressed than her own. She had tried to imitate the peculiarity of every syllable, sounded like a plucked string, had tried to make her little girls speak that way. But they had rebelled, refused, said it made them laughed at.

When she had nothing to request, or was tired of repeating the same reminders, she shut her eyes and imagined her funeral. She was barely forty-five, but a long widowhood strictly observed had kept her childish, not youthful. She saw the rosary twined around her hands, the vigil, the candles perfectly still, the hillock of wreaths. Until the stunning message from Fall River, death had been her small talk. She had never left the subject, once entered, without asking, 'And what will happen then to my poor little Marie?' Nobody had ever taken the question seriously except her Uncle Gildas. This was during their first Christmas dinner on Rue St Hubert. He said that Marie should pray for guidance, the sooner the better. God had no patience with last-minute appeals. (Uncle Gildas was an elderly priest with limited social opportunities, though his niece believed him to have wide and worldly connections.)

'Prayer can fail,' said Berthe, testing him.

Instead of berating her he said calmly, 'In that case, Berthe can look after her little sister.'

She considered him, old and eating slowly. His cassock exhaled some strong cleaning fluid—tetrachloride; he lived in a rest home, and nuns took care of him.

Marie was dressed in one of Berthe's castoffs—marine-blue velvet with a lace collar. Mme Carette wore a gray-white dress Berthe thought she had seen all her life. In her first year of employment Berthe had saved enough for a dyed rabbit coat. She also had an electric seal, and was on her way to sheared raccoon. 'Marie had better get married,' she said.

Mme Carette still felt cruelly the want of a husband, someone—not a daughter—to help her up the step of a streetcar,

read *La Presse* and tell her what was in it, lay down the law to
Berthe. When Berthe was in adolescence, laughing and whispering and not telling her mother the joke, Mme Carette had
asked Uncle Gildas to speak as a father. He sat in the parlor, in a
plush chair, all boots and cassock, knees apart and a hand on
each knee, and questioned Berthe about her dreams. She said
she had never in her life dreamed anything. Uncle Gildas replied that anyone with a good conscience could dream events
pleasing to God; he himself had been doing it for years. God
kept the dreams of every living person on record, like great
rolls of film. He could have them projected whenever he wanted.
Montreal girls, notoriously virtuous, had his favor, but only up
to a point. He forgave, but never forgot. He was the embodiment of endless time—though one should not take 'embodiment'
literally. Eternal remorse in a pit of flames was the same to him
as a rap on the fingers with the sharp edge of a ruler. Marie,
hearing this, had fainted dead away. That was the power of
Uncle Gildas.

Nowadays, shrunken and always hungry, he lived in retirement, had waxed linoleum on his floor, no carpet, ate tapioca
soup two or three times a week. He would have stayed in bed all
day, but the nuns who ran the place looked upon illness as fatigue, fatigue as shirking. He was not tired or lazy; he had nothing to get up for. The view from his window was a screen of
trees. When Mme Carette came to visit—a long streetcar ride,
then a bus—she had just the trees to look at: she could not stare
at her uncle the whole time. The trees put out of sight a busy
commercial garage. It might have distracted him to watch trucks
backing out, perhaps to witness a bloodless accident. In the morning he went downstairs to the chapel, ate breakfast, sat on his
bed after it was made. Or crossed the gleaming floor to a small
table, folded back the oilcloth cover, read the first sentence of a
memoir he was writing for his great-nieces: 'I was born in Montreal, on the 22nd of May, 1869, of pious Christian parents,
connected to Montreal families for whom streets and bridges

have been named.' Or shuffled out to the varnished corridor, where there was a pay phone. He liked dialling, but out of long discipline never did without a reason.

Soon after Christmas Mme Carette came to see him, wearing Berthe's velvet boots with tassels, Berthe's dyed rabbit coat, and a feather turban of her own. Instead of praying for guidance Marie had fallen in love with one of the Greeks who were starting to move into their part of Montreal. There had never been a foreigner in the family, let alone a pagan. Her uncle interrupted to remark that Greeks were usually Christians, though of the wrong kind for Marie. Mme Carette implored him to find someone, not a Greek, of the right kind: sober, established, Catholic, French-speaking, natively Canadian. 'Not Canadian from New England,' she said, showing a brief ingratitude to Fall River. She left a store of nickels, so that he could ring her whenever he liked.

Louis Driscoll, French in all but name, called on Marie for the first time on the twelfth of April, 1950. Patches of dirty snow still lay against the curb. The trees on Rue St Hubert looked dark and brittle, as though winter had killed them at last. From behind the parlor curtain, unseen from the street, the Carette women watched him coming along from the bus stop. To meet Marie he had put on a beige tweed overcoat, loosely belted, a beige scarf, a bottle-green snap-brim fedora, crêpe-soled shoes, pigskin gloves. His trousers were sharply pressed, a shade darker than the hat. Under his left arm he held close a parcel in white paper, the size and shape of a two-pound box of Laura Secord chocolates. He stopped frequently to consult the house numbers (blue-and-white, set rather high, Montreal style), which he compared with a slip of paper brought close to his eyes.

It was too bad that he had to wear glasses; the Carettes were not prepared for that, or for the fringe of ginger hair below his hat. Uncle Gildas had said he was of distinguished appearance.

He came from Moncton, New Brunswick, and was employed at the head office of a pulp-and-paper concern. His age was twenty-six. Berthe thought that he must be a failed seminarist; they were the only Catholic bachelors Uncle Gildas knew.

Peering at their front door, he walked into a puddle of slush. Mme Carette wondered if Marie's children were going to be nearsighted. 'How can we be sure he's the right man?' she said.

'Who else could he be?' Berthe replied. What did he want with Marie? Uncle Gildas could not have promised much in her name, apart from a pliant nature. There could never be a meeting in a notary's office to discuss a dowry, unless you counted some plates and furniture. The old man may have frightened Louis, reminded him that prolonged celibacy—except among the clergy—is displeasing to God. Marie is poor, he must have said, though honorably connected. She will feel grateful to you all her life.

Their front steps were painted pearl gray, to match the building stone. Louis's face, upturned, was the color of wood ash. Climbing the stair, ringing the front doorbell could change his life in a way he did not wholly desire. Probably he wanted a woman without sin or risk or coaxing or remorse; but did he want her enough to warrant setting up a household? A man with a memory as transient as his, who could read an address thirty times and still let it drift, might forget to come to the wedding. He crumpled the slip of paper, pushed it inside a tweed pocket, withdrew a large handkerchief, blew his nose.

Mme Carette swayed back from the curtain as though a stone had been flung. She concluded some private thought by addressing Marie:' . . . although I will feel better on my deathbed if I know you are in your own home.' Louis meanwhile kicked the bottom step, getting rid of snow stuck to his shoes. (Rustics kicked and stamped. Marie's Greek had wiped his feet.) Still he hesitated, sliding a last pale look in the direction of buses and streetcars. Then, as he might have turned a gun on himself, he climbed five steps and pressed his finger to the bell.

'Somebody has to let him in,' said Mme Carette.

'Marie,' said Berthe.

'It wouldn't seem right. She's never met him.'

He stood quite near, where the top step broadened to a small platform level with the window. They could have leaned out, introduced him to Marie. Marie at this moment seemed to think he would do; at least, she showed no sign of distaste, such as pushing out her lower lip or crumpling her chin. Perhaps she had been getting ready to drop her Greek: Mme Carette had warned her that she would have to be a servant to his mother, and eat peculiar food. 'He's never asked me to,' said Marie, and that was part of the trouble. He hadn't asked anything. For her twenty-first birthday he had given her a locket on a chain and a box from Maitland's, the West End confectioner, containing twenty-one chocolate mice. 'He loves me,' said Marie. She kept counting the mice and would not let anyone eat them.

In the end it was Berthe who admitted Louis, accepted the gift of chocolates on behalf of Marie, showed him where to leave his hat and coat. She approved of the clean white shirt, the jacket of a tweed similar to the coat but lighter in weight, the tie with a pattern of storm-tossed sailboats. Before shaking hands he removed his glasses, which had misted over, and wiped them dry. His eyes meeting the bright evening at the window (Marie was still there, but with her back to the street) flashed ultra-marine. Mme Carette hoped Marie's children would inherit that color.

He took Marie's yielding hand and let it drop. Freed of the introduction, she pried open the lid of the candy box and said, distinctly, 'No mice.' He seemed not to hear, or may have thought she was pleased to see he had not played a practical joke. Berthe showed him to the plush armchair, directly underneath a chandelier studded with light bulbs. From this chair Uncle Gildas had explained the whims of God; against its linen antimacassar the Greek had recently rested his head.

Around Louis's crêpe soles pools of snow water formed.

Berthe glanced at her mother, meaning that she was not to mind; but Mme Carette was trying to remember where Berthe had said that she and Marie were to sit. (On the sofa, facing Louis.) Berthe chose a gilt upright chair, from which she could rise easily to pass refreshments. These were laid out on a marble-topped console: vanilla wafers, iced sultana cake, maple fudge, marshmallow biscuits, soft drinks. Behind the sofa a large pier glass reflected Louis in the armchair and the top of Mme Carette's head. Berthe could tell from her mother's posture, head tilted, hands clasped, that she was silently asking Louis to trust her. She leaned forward and asked him if he was an only child. Berthe closed her eyes. When she opened them, nothing had changed except that Marie was eating chocolates. Louis seemed to be reflecting on his status.

He was the oldest of seven, he finally said. The others were Joseph, Raymond, Vincent, Francis, Rose, and Claire. French was their first language, in a way. But, then, so was English. A certain Louis Joseph Raymond Driscoll, Irish, veteran of Waterloo on the decent side, proscribed in England and Ireland as a result, had come out to Canada and grafted on pure French stock a number of noble traits: bright, wavy hair, a talent for public speaking, another for social aplomb. In every generation of Driscolls, there had to be a Louis, a Joseph, a Raymond. (Berthe and her mother exchanged a look. He wanted three sons.)

His French was slow and muffled, as though strained through wool. He used English words, or French words in an English way. Mme Carette lifted her shoulders and parted her clasped hands as if to say, Never mind, English is better than Greek. At least, they could be certain that the Driscolls were Catholic. In August his father and mother were making the Holy Year pilgrimage to Rome.

Rome was beyond their imagining, though all three Carettes had been to Maine and Old Orchard Beach. Louis hoped to spend a vacation in Old Orchard (in response to an ardent question from Mme Carette), but he had more feeling for Quebec City.

His father's people had entered Canada by way of Quebec.

'The French part of the family?' said Mme Carette.

'Yes, yes,' said Berthe, touching her mother's arm.

Berthe had been to Quebec City, said Mme Carette. She was brilliant, reliable, fully bilingual. Her office promoted her every January. They were always sending her away on company business. She knew Plattsburgh, Saranac Lake. In Quebec City, at lunch at the Château Frontenac, she had seen well-known politicians stuffing down oysters and fresh lobster, at taxpayers' expense.

Louis's glance tried to cross Berthe's, as he might have sought out and welcomed a second man in the room. Berthe reached past Mme Carette to take the candy box away from Marie. She nudged her mother with her elbow.

'The first time I ever saw Old Orchard,' Mme Carette resumed, smoothing the bodice of her dress, 'I was sorry I had not gone there on my honeymoon.' She paused, watching Louis accept a chocolate. 'My husband and I went to Fall River. He had a brother in the lumber business.'

At the mention of lumber, Louis took on a set, bulldog look. Berthe wondered if the pulp-and-paper firm had gone bankrupt. Her thoughts rushed to Uncle Gildas—how she would have it out with him, not leave it to her mother, if he had failed to examine Louis's prospects. But then Louis began to cough and had to cover his mouth. He was in trouble with a caramel. The Carettes looked away, so that he could strangle unobserved. 'How dark it is,' said Berthe, to let him think he could not be seen. Marie got up, with a hiss and rustle of taffeta skirt, and switched on the twin floor lamps with their cerise silk shades.

There, she seemed to be saying to Berthe. Have I done the right thing? Is this what you wanted?

Louis still coughed, but weakly. He moved his fingers, like a child made to wave goodbye. Mme Carette wondered how many contagious children's diseases he had survived; in a large family everything made the rounds. His eyes, perhaps seeking shade, moved across the brown wallpaper flecked with gold and stopped at the only familiar sight in the room—his reflection in the pier glass. He sat up straighter and quite definitely swallowed. He took a long drink of ginger ale. 'When Irish eyes are smiling,' he said, in English, as if to himself. 'When Irish eyes are smiling. There's a lot to be said for that. A lot to be said.'

Of course he was at a loss, astray in an armchair, with the Carettes watching like friendly judges. When he reached for another chocolate, they looked to see if his nails were clean. When he crossed his legs, they examined his socks. They were fixing their first impression of the stranger who might take Marie away, give her a modern kitchen, children to bring up, a muskrat coat, a charge account at Dupuis Frères department store, a holiday in Maine. Louis continued to examine his bright Driscoll hair, the small nose along which his glasses slid. Holding the glasses in place with a finger, he answered Mme Carette: His father was a dental surgeon, with a degree from Pennsylvania. It was the only degree worth mentioning. Before settling into a dentist's chair the patient should always read the writing on the wall. His mother was born Lucarne, a big name in Moncton. She could still get into her wedding dress. Everything was so conveniently arranged at home—cavernous washing machine, giant vacuum cleaner—that she seldom went out. When she did, she wore a two-strand cultured-pearl necklace and a coat and hat of Persian lamb.

The Carettes could not match this, though they were related to families for whom bridges were named. Mme Carette sat on the edge of the sofa, ankles together. Gentility was the brace that kept her upright. She had once been a young widow, hard pressed, had needed to sew for money. Berthe recalled a stricter, an unsmiling mother, straining over pleats and tucks for clients who reneged on pennies. She wore the neutral shades of half-mourning, the whitish grays of Rue St Hubert, as though everything had to be used up—even remnants of grief.

Mme Carette tried to imagine Louis's mother. She might one

day have to sell the pearls; even a dentist trained in Pennsylvania could leave behind disorder and debts. Whatever happened, she said to Louis, she would remain in this flat. Even after the girls were married. She would rather beg on the steps of the parish church than intrude upon a young marriage. When her last, dreadful illness made itself known, she would creep away to the Hôtel Dieu and die without a murmur. On the other hand, the street seemed to be filling up with foreigners. She might have to move.

Berthe and Marie were dressed alike, as if to confound Louis, force him to choose the true princess. Leaving the sight of his face in the mirror, puzzled by death and old age, he took notice of the two moiré skirts, organdie blouses, patent-leather belts. 'I can't get over those twins of yours,' he said to Mme Carette. 'I just can't get over them.'

Once, Berthe had tried Marie in her own office—easy work, taking messages when the switchboard was closed. She knew just enough English for that. After two weeks the office manager, Mr. Macfarlane, had said to Berthe, 'Your sister is an angel, but angels aren't in demand at Prestige Central Burners.'

It was the combination of fair hair and dark eyes, the enchanting misalliance, that gave Marie the look of an angel. She played with the locket the Greek had given her, twisting and unwinding the chain. What did she owe her Greek? Fidelity? An explanation? He was punctual and polite, had never laid a hand on her, in temper or eagerness, had travelled a long way by streetcar to bring back the mice. True, said Berthe, reviewing his good points, while Louis ate the last of the fudge. It was true about the mice, but he should have become more than 'Marie's Greek.' In the life of a penniless unmarried young woman, there was no room for a man merely in love. He ought to have presented himself as *something*: Marie's future.

In May true spring came, moist and hot. Berthe brought home new dress patterns and yards of flowered rayon and piqué. Louis called three evenings a week, at seven o'clock, after the supper dishes were cleared away. They played hearts in the dining room, drank Salada tea, brewed black, with plenty of sugar and cream, ate éclairs and mille-feuilles from Celentano, the bakery on Avenue Mont Royal. (Celentano had been called something else for years now, but Mme Carette did not take notice of change of that kind, and did not care to have it pointed out.) Louis, eating coffee éclairs one after the other, told stories set in Moncton that showed off his family. Marie wore a blue dress with a red collar, once Berthe's, and a red barrette in her hair. Berthe, a master player, held back to let Louis win. Mme Carette listened to Louis, kept some of his stories, discarded others, garnering information useful to Marie. Marie picked up cards at random, disrupting the game. Louis's French was not as woolly as before, but he had somewhere acquired a common Montreal accent. Mme Carette wondered who his friends were and how Marie's children would sound.

They began to invite him to meals. He arrived at half past five, straight from work, and was served at once. Mme Carette told Berthe that she hoped he washed his hands at the office, because he never did here. They used the blue-willow-pattern china that would go to Marie. One evening, when the tablecloth had been folded and put away, and the teacups and cards distributed, he mentioned marriage—not his own, or to anyone in particular, but as a way of life. Mme Carette broke in to say that she had been widowed at Louis's age. She recalled what it had been like to have a husband she could consult and admire. 'Marriage means children,' she said, looking fondly at her own. She would not be alone during her long, final illness. The girls would take her in. She would not be a burden; a couch would do for a bed.

Louis said he was tired of the game. He dropped his hand and spread the cards in an arc.

'So many hearts,' said Mme Carette, admiringly.

'Let me see.' Marie had to stand: there was a large teapot in

the way. 'Ace, queen, ten, eight, five . . . a wedding.' Before
Berthe's foot reached her ankle, she managed to ask, sincerely,
if anyone close to him was getting married this year.

Mme Carette considered Marie as good as engaged. She
bought a quantity of embroidery floss and began the ornamen-
tation of guest towels and tea towels, placemats and pillow slips.
Marie ran her finger over the pretty monogram with its intricate
frill of vine leaves. Her mind, which had sunk into hibernation
when she accepted Louis and forgot her Greek, awoke and
plagued her with a nightmare. 'I became a nun' was all she told
her mother. Mme Carette wished it were true. Actually, the dream
had stopped short of vows. Barefoot, naked under a robe of
coarse brown wool, she moved along an aisle in and out of squares
of sunlight. At the altar they were waiting to shear her hair. A
strange man—not Uncle Gildas, not Louis, not the Greek—got
up out of a pew and stood barring her way. The rough gown
turned out to be frail protection. All that kept the dream from
sliding into blasphemy and abomination was Marie's entire
unacquaintance, awake or asleep, with what could happen next.

Because Marie did not like to be alone in the dark, she and
Berthe still shared a room. Their childhood bed had been taken
away and supplanted by twin beds with quilted satin headboards.
Berthe had to sleep on three pillows, because the aluminum hair
curlers she wore ground into her scalp. First thing every morning, she clipped on her pearl earrings, sat up, and unwound the
curlers, which she handed one by one to Marie. Marie put her
own hair up and kept it that way until suppertime.

In the dark, her face turned to the heap of pillows dimly seen,
Marie told Berthe about the incident in the chapel. If dreams are
life's opposite, what did it mean? Berthe saw that there was more
to it than Marie was able to say. Speaking softly, so that their
mother would not hear, she tried to tell Marie about men—what
they were like and what they wanted. Marie suggested that she
and Berthe enter a cloistered convent together, now, while there

was still time. Berthe supposed that she had in mind the famous Martin sisters of Lisieux, in France, most of them Carmelites and one a saint. She touched her own temple, meaning that Marie had gone soft in the brain. Marie did not see; if she had, she would have thought that Berthe was easing a curler. Berthe reminded Marie that she was marked out not for sainthood in France but for marriage in Montreal. Berthe had a salary and occasional travel. Mme Carette had her Fall River bounty. Marie, if she put her mind to it, could have a lifetime of love.

'Is Louis love?' said Marie.

There were girls ready to line up in the rain for Louis, said Berthe.

'What girls?' said Marie, perplexed rather than disbelieving.

'Montreal girls,' said Berthe. 'The girls who cry with envy when you and Louis walk down the street.'

'We have never walked down a street,' said Marie.

The third of June was Louis's birthday. He arrived wearing a new seersucker suit. The Carettes offered three monogrammed hemstitched handkerchiefs—he was always polishing his glasses or mopping his face. Mme Carette had prepared a meal he particularly favored—roast pork and coconut layer cake. The sun was still high. His birthday unwound in a steady, blazing afternoon. He suddenly put his knife and fork down and said that if he ever decided to get married he would need more than his annual bonus to pay for the honeymoon. He would have to buy carpets, lamps, a refrigerator. People talked lightly of marriage without considering the cost for the groom. Priests urged the married condition on bachelors—priests, who did not know the price of eight ounces of tea.

'Some brides bring lamps and lampshades,' said Mme Carette. 'A glass-front bookcase. Even the books to put in it.' Her husband had owned a furniture shop on Rue St Denis. Household goods earmarked for Berthe and Marie had been stored with relatives for some twenty years, waxed and polished and free of dust. 'An oak table that seats fourteen,' she said, and stopped with that. Berthe had forbidden her to draw up an inventory. They were not bartering Marie.

'Some girls have money,' said Marie. Her savings—eighteen dollars—were in a drawer of her mother's old treadle sewing machine.

A spasm crossed Louis's face; he often choked on his food. Berthe knew more about men than Marie—more than her mother, who knew only how children come about. Mr Ryder, of Berthe's office, would stand in the corridor, letting elevators go by, waiting for a chance to squeeze in next to Berthe. Mr Sexton had offered her money, a regular allowance, if she would go out with him every Friday, the night of his Legion meeting. Mr Macfarlane had left a lewd poem on her desk, then a note of apology, then a poem even worse than the first. Mr Wright-Ashburton had offered to leave his wife—for, of course, they had wives, Mr Ryder, Mr Sexton, Mr Macfarlane, none of whom she had ever encouraged, and Mr Wright-Ashburton, with whom she had been to Plattsburgh and Saranac Lake, and whose private behavior she had described, kneeling, in remote parishes, where the confessor could not have known her by voice.

When Berthe accepted Mr Wright-Ashburton's raving proposal to leave his wife, saying that Irene probably knew about them anyway, would be thankful to have it in the clear, his face had wavered with fright, like a face seen underwater—rippling, uncontrolled. Berthe had to tell him she hadn't meant it. She could not marry a divorced man. On Louis's face she saw that same quivering dismay. He was afraid of Marie, of her docility, her monogrammed towels, her dependence, her glass-front bookcase. Having seen this, Berthe was not surprised when he gave no further sign of life until the twenty-fifth of June.

During his absence the guilt and darkness of rejection filled every corner of the flat. There was not a room that did not speak of humiliation—oh, not because Louis had dropped Marie but because the Carettes had honored and welcomed a clodhopper, a cheap-jack, a ginger-haired nobody. Mme Carette and Marie made many telephone calls to his office, with a variety of names and voices, to be told every time he was not at his desk. One morning Berthe, on her way to work, saw someone very like him hurrying into Windsor Station. By the time she had struggled out of her crowded streetcar, he was gone. She followed him into the great concourse and looked at the times of the different trains and saw where they were going. A trapped sparrow fluttered under the glass roof. She recalled an expression of Louis's, uneasy and roguish, when he had told Berthe that Marie did not understand the facts of life. (This in English, over the table, as if Mme Carette and Marie could not follow.) When Berthe asked what these facts might be, he had tried to cross her glance, as on that first evening, one man to another. She was not a man; she had looked away.

Mme Carette went on embroidering baskets of flowers, ivy leaves, hunched over her work, head down. Marie decided to find a job as a receptionist in a beauty salon. It would be pleasant work in clean surroundings. A girl she had talked to on the bus earned fourteen dollars a week. Marie would give her mother eight and keep six. She did not need Louis, she said, and she was sure she could never love him.

'No one expected you to love him,' said her mother, without looking up.

On the morning of the twenty-fifth of June he rang the front doorbell. Marie was eating breakfast in the kitchen, wearing Berthe's aluminum curlers under a mauve chiffon scarf, and Berthe's mauve-and-black kimono. He stood in the middle of the room, refusing offers of tea, and said that the whole world was engulfed in war. Marie looked out the kitchen window, at bare yards and storage sheds.

'Not there,' said Louis. 'In Korea.'

Marie and her mother had never heard of the place. Mme Carette took it for granted that the British had started something again. She said, 'They can't take you, Louis, because of your eyesight.' Louis replied that this time they would take everybody, bachelors first. A few married men might be allowed to make themselves useful at home. Mme Carette put her arms around him. 'You are my son now,' she said. 'I'll never let them ship you to England. You can hide in our coal shed.' Marie had not understood that the mention of war was a marriage proposal, but her mother had grasped it at once. She wanted to call Berthe and tell her to come home immediately, but Louis was in a hurry to publish the banns. Marie retired to the bedroom and changed into Berthe's white sharkskin sundress and jacket and toeless white suède shoes. She smoothed Berthe's suntan makeup on her legs, hoping that her mother would not see she was not wearing stockings. She combed out her hair, put on lipstick and earrings, and butterfly sunglasses belonging to Berthe. Then, for the first time, she and Louis together walked down the front steps to the street.

At Marie's parish church they found other couples standing about, waiting for advice. They had heard the news and decided to get married at once. Marie and Louis held hands, as though they had been engaged for a long time. She hoped no one would notice that she had no engagement ring. Unfortunately, their banns could not be posted until July, or the marriage take place until August. His parents would not be present to bless them: at the very day and hour of the ceremony they would be on their way to Rome.

The next day, Louis went to a jeweller on Rue St Denis, recommended by Mme Carette, but he was out of engagement rings. He had sold every last one that day. Louis did not look anywhere else; Mme Carette had said he was the only man she trusted. Louis's mother sent rings by registered mail. They had been taken from the hand of her dead sister, who had wanted them passed on to her son, but the son had vanished into Springfield and no longer sent Christmas cards. Mme Carette shook her own wedding dress out of tissue paper and made a few adjustments so that it would fit Marie. Since the war it had become impossible to find silk of that quality.

Waiting for August, Louis called on Marie every day. They rode the streetcar up to Avenue Mont Royal to eat barbecued chicken. (One evening Marie let her engagement ring fall into a crack of the corrugated floor of the tram, and a number of strangers told her to be careful, or she would lose her man, too.) The chicken arrived on a bed of chips, in a wicker basket. Louis showed Marie how to eat barbecue without a knife and fork. Fortunately, Mme Carette was not there to watch Marie gnawing on a bone. She was sewing the rest of the trousseau and had no time to act as chaperon.

Berthe's office sent her to Buffalo for a long weekend. She brought back match folders from Polish and German restaurants, an ashtray on which was written 'Buffalo Hofbrau', and a number of articles that were much cheaper down there, such as nylon stockings. Marie asked if they still ate with knives and forks in Buffalo, or if they had caught up to Montreal. Alone together, Mme Carette and Berthe sat in the kitchen and gossiped about Louis. The white summer curtains were up; the coal-and-wood range was covered with clean white oilcloth. Berthe had a new kimono—white, with red pagodas on the sleeves. She propped her new red mules on the oven door. She smoked now, and carried everywhere the Buffalo Hofbrau ashtray. Mme Carette made Berthe promise not to smoke in front of Uncle Gildas, or in the street, or at Marie's wedding reception, or in the front parlor, where the smell might get into the curtains. Sometimes they had just tea and toast and Celentano pastry for supper. When Berthe ate a coffee éclair, she said, 'Here's one Louis won't get.'

The bright evenings of suppers and card games slid into the past, and by August seemed long ago. Louis said to Marie, 'We knew how to have a good time. People don't enjoy themselves anymore.' He believed that the other customers in the barbecue restaurant had secret, nagging troubles. Waiting for the wicker basket of chicken, he held Marie's hand and stared at men who might be Greeks. He tried to tell her what had been on his mind between the third and twenty-fifth of June, but Marie did not care, and he gave up. They came to their first important agreement: neither of them wanted the blue-willow-pattern plates. Louis said he would ask his parents to start them off with six place settings of English Rose. She seemed still to be listening, and so he told her that the name of her parish church, St Louis de France, had always seemed to him to be a personal sign of some kind: an obscure force must have guided him to Rue St Hubert and Marie. Her soft brown eyes never wavered. They forgot about Uncle Gildas, and whatever it was Uncle Gildas had said to frighten them.

Louis and Marie were married on the third Saturday of August, with flowers from an earlier wedding banked along the altar rail, and two other wedding parties waiting at the back of the church. Berthe supposed that Marie, by accepting the ring of a dead woman and wearing the gown of another woman widowed at twenty-six, was calling down the blackest kind of misfortune. She remembered her innocent nakedness under the robe of frieze. Marie had no debts. She owed Louis nothing. She had saved him from a long journey to a foreign place, perhaps even from dying. As he placed the unlucky ring on her finger, Berthe wept. She knew that some of the people looking on—Uncle Gildas, or Joseph and Raymond Driscoll, amazing in their ginger likeness—were mistaking her for a jealous older sister, longing to be in Marie's place.

Marie, now Mme Driscoll, turned to Berthe and smiled, as she used to when they were children. Once again, the smile said, Have I done the right thing? Is this what you wanted? Yes, yes, said Berthe silently, but she went on crying. Marie had always turned to Berthe; she had started to walk because she wanted to be with Berthe. She had been standing, holding on to a kitchen chair, and she suddenly smiled and let go. Later, when Marie was three, and in the habit of taking her clothes off and showing what must never be seen, Mme Carette locked her into the storage shed behind the kitchen. Berthe knelt on her side of the door, sobbing, calling, 'Don't be afraid, Marie. Berthe is here.' Mme Carette relented and unlocked the door, and there was Marie, wearing just her undershirt, smiling for Berthe.

Leading her mother, Berthe approached the altar rail. Marie seemed contented; for Berthe, that was good enough. She kissed her sister, and kissed the chosen husband. He had not separated them but would be a long incident in their lives. Among the pictures that were taken on the church steps, there is one of Louis with an arm around each sister and the sisters trying to clasp hands behind his back.

The wedding party walked in a procession down the steps and around the corner: another impression in black-and-white. The August pavement burned under the women's thin soles. Their fine clothes were too hot. Children playing in the road broke into applause when they saw Marie. She waved her left hand, showing the ring. The children were still French-Canadian; so were the neighbors, out on their balconies to look at Marie. Three yellow leaves fell—white, in a photograph. One of the Driscoll boys raced ahead and brought the party to a stop. There is Marie, who does not yet understand that she is leaving home, and confident Louis, so soon to have knowledge of her bewildering ignorance.

Berthe saw the street as if she were bent over the box camera, trying to keep the frame straight. It was an important picture, like a precise instrument of measurement: so much duty, so much love, so much reckless safety—the distance between last April and now. She thought, It had to be done. They began to walk again. Mme Carette realized for the first time what she and Uncle Gildas and Berthe had brought about: the unredeemable loss of Marie. She said to Berthe, 'Wait until I am dead before you get married. You can marry a widower. They make good husbands.' Berthe was nearly twenty-four, just at the limit. She had turned away so many attractive prospects, with no explanation, and had frightened so many others with her skill at cards and her quick blue eyes that word had spread, and she was not solicited as before.

Berthe and Marie slipped away from the reception—moved, that is, from the parlor to the bedroom—so that Berthe could help her sister pack. It turned out that Mme Carette had done the packing. Marie had never had to fill a suitcase, and would not have known what to put in first. For a time, they sat on the edge of a bed, talking in whispers. Berthe smoked, holding the Buffalo Hofbrau ashtray. She showed Marie a black lacquer cigarette lighter she had not shown her mother. Marie had started to change her clothes; she was just in her slip. She looked at the lighter on all sides and handed it back. Louis was taking her to the Château Frontenac, in Quebec City, for three nights—the equivalent of ten days in Old Orchard, he had said. After that, they would go straight to the duplex property, quite far north on Boulevard Pie IX, that his father was helping him buy. 'I'll call you tomorrow morning,' said Marie, for whom tomorrow was still the same thing as today. If Uncle Gildas had been at Berthe's mercy, she would have held his head underwater. Then she thought, Why blame him? She and Marie were Montreal girls, not trained to accompany heroes, or to hold out for dreams, but just to be patient.

KATHERINE GOVIER

The Dragon

Pamela, they were saying, was one of those women who attracted violence. While he was simply a man who wanted to help people.

As a child, he did not understand the world. All around himself he saw people trying to escape their pain and calling it the pursuit of happiness. At seventeen he entered a seminary to train as a priest: at eighteen he met a woman and lost his calling. But she rejected him, cruelly. Having lost faith in God and woman simultaneously, he entered medical school. He studied hard and made his way to a big hospital in New York as a resident in psychiatry. He embraced certain theories and battled others, emerging despite it all with an intact belief in the possibility of human compassion.

He came home and set up office in a new, half-empty highrise in the centre of Toronto, the tracks of commerce shunting twelve stories beneath him. The walls were egg-shell, the curtains un-bleached jute. Light came from frosted tubes running in trenches around the periphery of the ceiling. The rug was the colour of damp sand. In the centre of the room was arranged an unstated circle: a chair with a chiselled heavy base, shallow swivel seat, and upright back and a matching but smaller chair opposite. Between the two was a table with an ashtray, although the psychiatrist, for that is how he had begun to see himself, as a psychiatrist, did not smoke himself. Apart from the digital clock discreetly placed, there was nothing else in the room.

The psychiatrist practised sitting in his chair and looking at the chair opposite. He swivelled around to look through his windows to the towers that were his neighbours. Beneath him were the faint rumblings of the fire-breathing city; up here there was only silence, austerity, and the moods of the sun.

Of necessity he became businesslike. He enlisted an answering service. He had bills printed on white sheets of paper, his name in light italic at the top. He began to get referrals from physicians and clinics: people began to petition him through his answering service. Please call, the messages said, urgent. The telephone answerer spelled out the names to him—Mrs. Horgan, Theodore First, Germaine Wilson—and repeated their telephone numbers. Calling, he discovered the numbers to be the city's government offices, department stores, and public schools. Need for him had sprung up just like that, full-blown, from the troubled brow of the city.

So it began. He opened his door to a patient. He took up his seat across the room from another human being less learned in the vagaries of the human psyche than himself, but no less sensitive, no less intelligent. His training let him ride his patients' aimless talk like a falcon, weightless, but with a claw of steel. He listened, mostly. He watched for clues—the twist of the mouth, the overflow of tear ducts. He did not wish to take notes while his patients poured forth their disappointments, so he grew adept at a kind of shadow filing, clearing out and aligning of information.

His patients' tales transported him. A man humiliating himself in ladies' clothing, a girl slashing her throat on her parents' bed, artists hacking their self-hate into icons, fathers crucifying their sons. And the women—he had thought he understood woman as he did man. But as he heard the virgin's terror of invasion, the matron's used emptiness, he did not want to learn what he was learning. He detached the names from the cases. He took cold showers in the mornings to forget his nightmares. At times he thought he suffered too much, but he persevered in his work. Sometimes he would come very near the heart of the other person; he could lean back in his chair and almost see the puffs of smoke separate from his body, in a kind of exorcism. Then he would deliver the standard apologia to the weeping person across the room: 'I have done what I can for you. You know I cannot go out and slay the dragon.'

So he learned to wear the hood of professionalism and live the role of the impersonal intimate. As he listened, his patients' neuroses bellied and broke. Sometimes there was healing. A few came to be free of their need for him, and more came to the door. The psychiatrist worked long hours. Sometimes at dusk when the last supplicant had departed, he would turn his chair to the window. The city smoke would fire the sunset to deep reds and burnished orange. Bewildered light would strike the curtains and lay itself on his pale walls. He'd see the tapestry of flesh and strife realized there, see a town lit by dragon breath and poised in positions of torture, the fat squashing the small, the weak scratching off the backs of the strong, as he sat cold-eyed in his swivel chair. What else there was of life for him—a renovated townhouse, dinners at good restaurants—continued somehow, tired as a vine wintering on rock.

It was in early September of his tenth year of practice that he received a request to see a new patient. While it would not be entirely true to say that his wan curiosity was quickened from the start by this man, because of what happened later the name William Kirk stood distinct when others disappeared.

A telephone message gave Mr Kirk's business number, which proved to be the head office of a large advertising agency. The psychiatrist was put through several intermediaries before being allowed to speak to Mr Kirk himself. When they were connected, the psychiatrist heard a sound like static electricity in the other man's voice, a sound of broadloom carpets and chrome bannisters. The man explained that he was plagued by certain worries and would like to speak to someone in the interest of preventing some later crisis. They arranged an appointment for Tuesday at 10:30.

Tuesday at 10:20 Mrs Horgan left, her whorled peacock tail of guilt spread behind her, his pink tissues clutched in her soft fingers. The psychiatrist sighed. He had ten minutes to regenerate. Freud had prescribed classical music for the clinician between appointments, but he found music too stirring; most often he wanted only silence. He faced the window and waited. There was a soft click at the outside door, then an almost noiseless footfall on the carpet. From a corner of his eye the psychiatrist watched nine minutes pass on the digital clock. Then he opened the door and walked into the waiting room.

A thick-boned man whose wide still hands lay flat on his knees looked up at him. His broad forehead was slanted forward, his nose pinched, his eyes scooped deep, and his chin set as if by the grip of clenched fingers. He'd have looked surly if he had not been blond as a birch.

Kirk stood. They shook hands. The patient walked into the office behind the psychiatrist, choosing the correct chair without hesitation. He leaned back slightly. He lit a cigarette without asking. The two men eyed each other.

'Well, Mr Kirk, what seems to be the difficulty?' The psychiatrist lowered his head and fastened a serene eye on Kirk's thick lids.

It was always difficult to name the problem. William Kirk, however, was more articulate than most. He had lost interest in his work and was unable to concentrate. He drank too much and couldn't seem to get a hold on himself. Oh yes, and he'd been divorced and now was involved with a woman named Pamela, who was an artist.

The psychiatrist found himself liking this man. He was more than a little relieved not to hear tales of motelroom whippings and the courting of small boys, for one thing. Kirk sounded gentle and intelligent. When the fifty minutes had elapsed, the two men shook hands again and the patient took himself to the door, opened it, and left the room. The door hissed along the carpet as it shut. The psychiatrist sat with his forefingers propped on the knob of his chin. Some of that love, that will to understand and make whole which he had once felt, stirred in him.

The second visit with Kirk was aimed at filling in the background. With a minimum of prodding, Kirk monologued in his modulated tones about an ambitious father, a pretty white house with hedges, and a mother who went to church. The psychiatrist was pleased. Kirk was a good storyteller; the professional was able to absorb the feelings almost as if it were his own small self pouring wine at the long dinner table, his own body drawn in the paternal embrace, with its smell of pipe tobacco and rough wool.

But when Kirk reached his adulthood and the woman who was to become his wife, the psychiatrist asked him to stop. He didn't want to hear that yet. Instead he asked about the drinking.

Kirk grew excited. He spoke of alcohol as a beautiful destroyer, a she-devil. It makes me see heaven, he said, and drives me to a fury because it is all a lie. The psychiatrist said that alcohol was after all only an agent. And then, rashly disclosing something he barely knew he felt, said that he too had that anger, that wish to destroy. Where did it come from? At the question Kirk fell silent. When the session was over the two men parted awkwardly, as if they might have touched.

At their next meeting the psychiatrist hid his shyness in a stern, expectant look, and Kirk had difficulty speaking. He looked for long minutes at his fingernails with the day's dust under them. Then he said he had begun to realize how much was unknown in that room. He could create any self he wished for the psychiatrist: the other's vision was confined by the rigid corners of the office and took in no authority but Kirk's own. It therefore was beginning to seem impossible to Kirk that he would learn anything he did not already know. The psychiatrist suggested that he might realize that he knew more than he now was able to acknowledge. He did not say so, but he was hurt: he felt he had a lot to give to Kirk. They decided to try to increase the momentum of the therapy by meeting twice a week. They set the second hour for Friday at 5:30, the end of a long day and week for both of them.

The therapy did pick up intensity in the foggy ease of late afternoon. The psychiatrist settled in to listen like a needy child to a bedtime story, and Kirk spoke readily of how, when he was sixteen, his father had left the family to live with his mistress. He had come home from work at five o'clock, packed a bag, called Kirk's sister into the den to tell her, and then had gone away. From his bedroom upstairs, the boy had watched him drive off. He hated the mistress, although he never met her.

The psychiatrist remained wrapped in the story over the next weeks: the formal family meetings in hotel suites, the shrill voice of the mother alone at home; all of this seemed to sink into some empty place in him. (In his training he had long since worked through his own personal history.) For the first time he exceeded his schooled empathy. Moved nearly to tears by Kirk's first wounds inflicted by a woman, he linked his patient's prolonged virginity with his own celibacy. But again, when Kirk approached the story of his marriage, the psychiatrist made him stop. Claiming fatigue, he ended the session early.

When Kirk was gone, the psychiatrist sat alone, his hands pressed on his chest like bricks. He looked out the office window. It was evening, and the light drained off the city over the skyline, leaving only the glassy baubles that were the streetlights. The psychiatrist stood up stiffly, like a man tarred. Without knowing why, he moved around to the other side of the circle and lowered himself into Kirk's chair. He felt smaller. He saw a different vista. The sun had slid behind the bank tower, bronzing the windows along its path. It made a passage that seemed to stretch away from him, whitish and paved in glare, leading to some estate where he might have been welcome. That this path out was offered to the patient but not the practitioner seemed to him brutally unfair.

Clearly, by this time the psychiatrist's interest in Kirk had surpassed that allowed in the profession. The other patients were suffering from the inequity: the man who drank but was less poetic about it became a little boring; the woman who wanted more attention from her husband became petulant. Sitting there, the psychiatrist thought about William Kirk. He loved his patients gracefully, as the rescuer loves the victim. But with Kirk he had lost his distance. In his mind their two chairs had begun to spin around the circle, to spin and to blur like buckets on a wheel. He waited until the sun had gone down and then he told himself to go home and live his own life. The psychiatrist knew all about transferring love to a patient, and it was not the love which caused the scene in the end. The psychiatrist concealed his feelings.

The following Tuesday was the first day of winter. The sky was dark, and the wind was white. William Kirk arrived late and announced that he was reluctant to carry on the meetings. The psychiatrist was alarmed. He suggested that Kirk was resisting because they were nearing the most difficult, therefore the most significant, parts of the process; this resistance was nothing more than a fear that he, the professional, could not deal with the patient's darkest secrets. He assured Kirk that this was not so: he welcomed further intimacy. Kirk dropped his chin toward his chest. Tears stood over the depths of his pale eyes. They would carry on. The psychiatrist had won.

With that, they were in dangerous territory. Kirk spoke of his wife, a strong woman who had nevertheless fallen into step behind her husband like an oriental concubine. Kirk saw her draw her hair back behind her ears and become lifeless. She grew thin, her breasts drooped, and he stopped loving her. When their daughter was born, Kirk felt disappointed and excluded. Why? interjected the psychiatrist. Kirk thought that it was because the baby daughter seemed strange, foreign. A son he would have known as another like himself. But a girl—the baby frightened him. He had no idea what little girls were like.

'What are women like?' the psychiatrist asked softly across the circle.

And Kirk said, 'I don't know. Women are mysterious.'

'Yes,' said the psychiatrist.

'The unknown,' said Kirk.

'Quite,' said the psychiatrist. He said nothing more, letting the words drain down to the carpet. He thought he had never known a woman. The young lady who had humiliated him passed through his mind. He had been seeking something unknown all these years; perhaps it dwelt where she was.

Then Kirk told how he'd left his wife, a story which shamed him, for afterwards she became so ill she was put in a convalescent home. The psychiatrist assured Kirk that the woman had found what she wanted. All that remained of the marriage was the daughter. The girl was no longer alien, but his, and Kirk felt that between himself and the girl there was perfect love. Of course, she was only eight years old. But the very existence of this love called into question his feelings for the woman Pamela: he could never love her that way.

It's not fair, said Pamela. She kept repeating that she'd never met the man. Perhaps she did something, said something to him. The violence seemed to have nothing to do with her. After it happened, she spent weeks powdering herself to cover the bruises and had to revamp her hairstyle because of the bald patches.

The psychiatrist and Kirk had suddenly arrived at the crux of the problem and almost as quickly at the solution. Kirk had never admitted before that it was the way Pamela made him feel that had brought him into therapy in the first place. She had been telling a story to her co-workers at the art gallery when Kirk had first seen her. He wanted to speak to her. Refusing to be interrupted by his awkward presence, she continued the anecdote in a delivery punctuated with trills and gutter sounds, accompanied by waving arms. But he waited, and by the time the story ended, Kirk was in love. He pursued her; she gave resistance, but in time he won and was drawn into Pamela's crazy-wheeling life.

Pamela was dark-haired, gypsyish, he said. She looked thin as sticks in her dresses, but she was soft and white, like a cloud, in his bed. The first night Kirk slept with her she'd begun to bleed before dawn; her blood had streaked their bodies.

Night after night they spent together. They were in love. The only trouble was, said Kirk, that Pamela was a bitch. She had a very sharp tongue. The more he loved her, the more they fought. They argued about sex and food and light fixtures. Anything set them off, and each fight was more passionate. Pamela's words blinded and mocked him. Her little nails tore his flesh. Kirk felt himself turning inside out. He was like a bear, wanting to maul and crush. Pamela's small body simply went supple in his grip. He was forced, he said, to actual blows. Here he knew his advantage. He did not want to hurt her, but it was a battle with himself for control. He thought sometime he might kill her, by mistake. And there in the sand-carpeted office right in front of the psychiatrist, the favorite patient put his forehead in his hands and wept.

The psychiatrist panicked. He could not bear to hear this from Kirk, although, as always, the other man's experience was validated in his own body. At this moment when it was so important that he say something, he knew only his own forbidden feelings.

He let his mind lift from the room. That day driving to work he'd seen a whirlwind, a small, dark, city whirlwind, a thing that had no substance except for what it caught in its path. Dead leaves, tin foil from cigarette packs, and balls of dry grass were lifted into it. It was cone-shaped, condensed, a world in itself. It spun on the sidewalk. He remembered that he sat at the steering wheel without moving when the thing passed in front of him. Only when it was gone did he drive on.

It seemed to the psychiatrist then that the whirlwind had come into the room. It spun up and around the circle between himself and Kirk, taking the form of a bottle, of a woman, of himself. But the psychiatrist knew a hallucination when he saw one, and this he shook from his head impatiently. It seemed then to go right into his body. His heart pounded, and he was furious at the woman, the dragon, the way his perfect love had failed. And he knew that he could go no further: the treatment was ended.

You have gained considerable insight here, said the psychiatrist, and this itself can be a control on your actions. This is as far as I can go. And as an afterthought, as usual, he added that he could not, indeed, no one could, go out and slay the dragon.

In turn, Kirk said he felt remarkably eased by his admission. The fear seemed to have passed out of him. He would control himself. Perhaps he would continue with Pamela in peace, perhaps he would not see her any more. He felt cured.

Then they stood and clasped right hands, and William Kirk walked out of the office for the last time, the eye of the psychiatrist following him, glittering like an old stone.

He kept himself in a tight rein after that. He filled the empty spot in his timetable; he said the same things again and again to patients, sometimes with failure, sometimes with success. The city rumbled on below; the sun bled into the skyline. A year went by.

One Friday evening, the psychiatrist sat in his swivel chair after his last consultation. It was already dark, for winter brought down the night so early that people had to visit their therapists by streetlight. He had been working very hard. An invitation to a Christmas cocktail party lay in his briefcase. Looking down from his window to where the lights of cars drew their lines along the streets, the psychiatrist felt moved by a whim. Light of foot for the first time in months, he took his boxy leather coat from its hanger in the waiting room, descended in the quilt-walled elevator to where his car was stowed, and became one of those he watched all day.

In the moonlight the shadows of stripped trees marbled the snow. Through the bay window he saw that the party was an elegant one. The people in their holiday armour dazzled him. His feet slipped on the swept flagstone steps. And then he was inside, standing in the draft of the doorway, not at all certain that anyone knew him. Wineglasses winked, chrome caps on the light fixtures caught the belled reflections of a hundred mouthing guests. A host appeared. He closed the door and took away the newcomer's coat. Given a glass, the psychiatrist wedged himself into the mass. Milling, as if a leader might be thrust up before them to draw them away. A gap opened ahead; he moved toward it. And then he saw William Kirk.

Their eyes met. Kirk's face, smooth and sculpted in this light, opened with a smile. When he came forward the psychiatrist had to change his drink to his left hand to shake. The grip of hands, palm to palm, knuckles protruding, was like the wild thump of a heart. Kirk said something in his ear, but it was too noisy in the room. The only word the psychiatrist heard was Pamela.

The woman with Kirk was small, agitated, and dark, her face shaded by a disarray of hair. Her dress was loosely draped from a yoke resting on her shoulders. At the base of her neck was a small purple half-moon. Her eyes were very black, and she seemed to emit a musk. The psychiatrist hated her. He felt a flash of heat under his skin, and a great peace came to him even as he leapt to attack.

Almost no-one remembered seeing it happen. Too soon, there was only the detritus, the farcical final poses. A woman's shoulder soaked in red wine. A glass, his glass, unbroken on the carpet. A livid Kirk, pacing. The psychiatrist, prone in a corner. Pamela, bloody and screaming, surrounded by women.

The psychiatrist had struck William a sound manly blow to

the lower jaw, out of a kind of respect: he must dispense with him first. Then he was at Pamela, lunging forward like a bear, arms curved above her in a mock embrace. He stumbled, then heaved his weight upright. A fist came out, retreated. Finding her body too small to strike, he closed his hands on her hair. He pulled. Masses of it came out softly, like dry moss, from her white scalp. She did not fall. She stood, thick red threads appearing around her forehead and running down her temples. She was still standing, clutching the empty wineglass whose liquid was spreading through the satin of her skirt, when they dragged him away from her. There was silence for a moment, then she started crying, and everyone began to talk. By the next day it was all over town, and some said poor woman and some said poor man.

W.P. KINSELLA

The Thrill of the Grass

1981: the summer the baseball players went on strike. The dull
weeks drag by, the summer deepens, the strike is nearly a month
old. Outside the city the corn rustles and ripens in the sun. Summer without baseball: a disruption to the psyche. An unexplain-
able aimlessness engulfs me. I stay later and later each evening
in the small office at the rear of my shop. Now, driving home
after work, the worst of the rush hour traffic over, it is the time
of evening I would normally be heading for the stadium.

I enjoy arriving an hour early, parking in a far corner of the
lot, walking slowly toward the stadium, rays of sun dropping
softly over my shoulders like tangerine ropes, my shadow gliding with me, black as an umbrella. I like to watch young families beside their campers, the mothers in shorts, grilling
hamburgers, their men drinking beer. I enjoy seeing little boys
dressed in the home team uniform, barely toddling, clutching
hotdogs in upraised hands.

I am a failed shortstop. As a young man, I saw myself diving
to my left, graceful as a toppling tree, fielding high grounders
like a cat leaping for butterflies, bracing my right foot and toss-
ing to first, the throw true as if a steel ribbon connected my
hand and the first baseman's glove. I dreamed of leading the
American League in hitting—being inducted into the Hall of
Fame. I batted .217 in my senior year of high school and aver-
aged 1.3 errors per nine innings.

I know the stadium will be deserted; nevertheless I wheel my car down off the freeway, park, and walk across the silent lot, my footsteps rasping and mournful. Strangle-grass and creeping charlie are already inching up through the gravel, surreptitious, surprised at their own ease. Faded bottle caps, rusted bits of chrome, an occasional paper clip, recede into the earth. I circle a ticket booth, sun-faded, empty, the door closed by an oversized padlock. I walk beside the tall, machinery-green, board fence. A half mile away a few cars hiss along the freeway; overhead a single-engine plane fizzes lazily. The whole place is silent as an empty classroom, like a house suddenly without children.

It is then that I spot the door-shape. I have to check twice to be sure it is there: a door cut in the deep green boards of the fence, more the promise of a door than the real thing, the kind of door, as children, we cut in the sides of cardboard boxes with our mothers' paring knives. As I move closer, a golden circle of lock, like an acrimonious eye, establishes its certainty.

I stand, my nose so close to the door I can smell the faint odour of paint, the golden eye of a lock inches from my own eyes. My desire to be inside the ballpark is so great that for the first time in my life I commit a criminal act. I have been a locksmith for over forty years. I take the small tools from the pocket of my jacket, and in less time than it would take a speedy runner to circle the bases I am inside the stadium. Though the ballpark is open-air, it smells of abandonment; the walkways and seating areas are cold as basements. I breathe the odours of rancid popcorn and wilted cardboard.

The maintenance staff were laid off when the strike began. Synthetic grass does not need to be cut or watered. I stare down at the ball diamond, where just to the right of the pitcher's mound, a single weed, perhaps two inches high, stands defiant in the rain-pocked dirt.

The field sits breathless in the orangy glow of the evening sun. I stare at the potato-coloured earth of the infield, that wide, dun arc, surrounded by plastic grass. As I contemplate the prickly turf, which scorches the thighs and buttocks of a sliding player as if he were being seared by hot steel, it stares back in its uniform ugliness. The seams that send routinely hit ground balls veering at tortuous angles, are vivid, grey as scars.

I remember the ballfields of my childhood, the outfields full of soft hummocks and brown-eyed gopher holes.

I stride down from the stands and walk out to the middle of the field. I touch the stubble that is called grass, take off my shoes, but find it is like walking on a row of toothbrushes. It was an evil day when they stripped the sod from this ballpark, cut it into yard-wide swathes, rolled it, memories and all, into great green-and-black cinnamonroll shapes, trucked it away Nature temporarily defeated. But Nature is patient.

Over the next few days an idea forms within me, ripening, swelling, pushing everything else into a corner. It is like knowing a new, wonderful joke and not being able to share. I need an accomplice.

I go to see a man I don't know personally, though I have seen his face peering at me from the financial pages of the local newspaper, and the *Wall Street Journal*, and I have been watching his profile at the baseball stadium, two boxes to the right of me, for several years. He is a fan. Really a fan. When the weather is intemperate, or the game not close, the people around us disappear like flowers closing at sunset, but we are always there until the last pitch. I know he is a man who attends because of the beauty and mystery of the game, a man who can sit during the last of the ninth with the game decided innings ago, and draw joy from watching the first baseman adjust the angle of his glove as the pitcher goes into his windup.

He, like me, is a first-base-side fan. I've always watched baseball from behind first base. The positions fans choose at sporting events are like politics, religion, or philosophy: a view of the world, a way of seeing the universe. They make no sense to anyone, have no basis in anything but stubbornness.

I brought up my daughters to watch baseball from the first-base side. One lives in Japan and sends me box scores from Japanese newspapers, and Japanese baseball magazines with pictures of superstars politely bowing to one another. She has a season ticket in Yokohama; on the first-base side.

'Tell him a baseball fan is here to see him,' is all I will say to his secretary. His office is in a skyscraper, from which he can look out over the city to where the prairie rolls green as mountain water to the limits of the eye. I wait all afternoon in the artificially cool, glassy reception area with its yellow and mauve chairs, chrome and glass coffee tables. Finally, in the late afternoon, my message is passed along.

'I've seen you at the baseball stadium,' I say, not introducing myself.

'Yes,' he says. 'I recognize you. Three rows back, about eight seats to my left. You have a red scorebook and you often bring your daughter . . . '

'Granddaughter. Yes, she goes to sleep in my lap in the late innings, but she knows how to calculate an ERA and she's only in Grade 2.'

'One of my greatest regrets,' says this tall man, whose moustache and carefully styled hair are polar-bear white, 'is that my grandchildren all live over a thousand miles away. You're very lucky. Now, what can I do for you?'

'I have an idea,' I say. 'One that's been creeping toward me like a first baseman when the bunt sign is on. What do you think about artificial turf?'

'Hmmmf,' he snorts, 'that's what the strike should be about. Baseball is meant to be played on summer evenings and Sunday afternoons, on grass just cut by a horse-drawn mower,' and we smile as our eyes meet.

'I've discovered the ballpark is open, to me anyway,' I go on. 'There's no one there while the strike is on. The wind blows through the high top of the grandstand, whining until the pigeons in the rafters flutter. It's lonely as a ghost town.'

'And what is it you do there, alone with the pigeons?'

'I dream.'

'And where do I come in?'

'You've always struck me as a man who dreams. I think we have things in common. I think you might like to come with me. I could show you what I dream, paint you pictures, suggest what might happen . . . '

He studies me carefully for a moment, like a pitcher trying to decide if he can trust the sign his catcher has just given him.

'Tonight?' he says. 'Would tonight be too soon?'

'Park in the northwest corner of the lot about 1:00 a.m. There is a door about fifty yards to the right of the main gate. I'll open it when I hear you.'

He nods.

I turn and leave.

The night is clear and cotton warm when he arrives. 'Oh, my,' he says, staring at the stadium turned chrome-blue by a full moon. 'Oh, my,' he says again, breathing in the faint odours of base-ball, the reminder of fans and players not long gone.

'Let's go down to the field,' I say. I am carrying a cardboard pizza box, holding it on the upturned palms of my hands, like an offering.

When we reach the field, he first stands on the mound, makes an awkward attempt at a windup, then does a little sprint from first to about half-way to second. 'I think I know what you've brought,' he says, gesturing toward the box, 'but let me see anyway.'

I open the box in which rests a square foot of sod, the grass smooth and pure, cool as a swatch of satin, fragile as baby's hair.

'Ohhh,' the man says, reaching out a finger to test the moist-ness of it. 'Oh, I see.'

We walk across the field, the harsh, prickly turf making the bottoms of my feet tingle, to the left-field corner where, in the angle formed by the foul line and the warning track, I lay down the square foot of sod. 'That's beautiful,' my friend says, kneeling beside me, placing his hand, fingers spread wide, on the verdant square, leaving a print faint as a veronica.

I take from my belt a sickle-shaped blade, the kind used for cutting carpet. I measure along the edge of the sod, dig the point in and pull carefully toward me. There is a ripping sound, like tearing an old bed sheet. I hold up the square of artificial turf like something freshly killed, while all the time digging the sharp point into the packed earth I have exposed. I replace the sod lovingly, covering the newly bared surface.

'A protest,' I say.

'But it could be more,' the man replies.

'I hoped you'd say that. It could be. If you'd like to come back . . . '

'Tomorrow night?'

'Tomorrow night would be fine. But there will be an admission charge . . . '

'A square of sod?'

'A square of sod two inches thick . . . '

'Of the same grass?'

'Of the same grass. But there's more.'

'I suspected as much.'

'You must have a friend . . . '

'Who would join us?'

'Yes.'

'I have two. Would that be all right?'

'I trust your judgement.'

'My father. He's over eighty,' my friend says. 'You might have seen him with me once or twice. He lives over fifty miles from here, but if I call him he'll come. And my friend . . . '

'If they pay their admission they'll be welcome . . . '

'And *they* may have friends . . . '

'Indeed they may. But what will we do with this?' I say, holding up the sticky-backed square of turf, which smells of glue and fabric.

'We could mail them anonymously to baseball executives, politicians, clergymen.'

'Gentle reminders not to tamper with Nature.'

We dance toward the exit, rampant with excitement.

'You will come back? You'll bring others?'

'Count on it,' says my friend.

They do come, those trusted friends, and friends of friends, each making a live, green deposit. At first, a tiny row of sod squares begins to inch along toward left-centre field. The next night even more people arrive, the following night more again, and the night after there is positively a crowd. Those who come once seem always to return accompanied by friends, occasionally a son or young brother, but mostly men my age or older, for we are the ones who remember the grass.

Night after night the pilgrimage continues. The first night I stand inside the deep green door, listening. I hear a vehicle stop; hear a car door close with a snug thud. I open the door when the sound of soft soled shoes on gravel tells me it is time. The door swings silent as a snake. We nod curt greetings to each other. Two men pass me, each carrying a grasshopper-legged sprinkler. Later, each sprinkler will sizzle like frying onions as it wheels, a silver sparkler in the moonlight.

During the nights that follow, I stand sentinel-like at the top of the grandstand, watching as my cohorts arrive. Old men walking across a parking lot in a row, in the dark, carrying coiled hoses, looking like the many wheels of a locomotive, old men who have slipped away from their homes, skulked down their sturdy sidewalks, breathing the cool, grassy, after-midnight air. They have left behind their sleeping, grey-haired women, their immaculate bungalows, their manicured lawns. They continue to walk across the parking lot, while occasionally a soft wheeze, a nibbling, breathy sound like an old horse might make, divulges their humanity. They move methodically toward the baseball stadium which hulks against the moon-blue sky like a small mountain. Beneath the tint of starlight, the tall light standards which rise above the fences and grandstand glow purple, necks bent forward, like sunflowers heavy with seed.

My other daughter lives in this city, is married to a fan, but one who watches baseball from behind third base. And like marrying outside the faith, she has been converted to the third-base side. They have their own season tickets, twelve rows up just to the outfield side of third base. I love her, but I don't trust her enough to let her in on my secret.

I could trust my granddaughter, but she is too young. At her age she shouldn't have to face such responsibility. I remember my own daughter, the one who lives in Japan, remember her at nine, all knees, elbows and missing teeth—remember peering in her room, seeing her asleep, a shower of well-thumbed baseball cards scattered over her chest and pillow.

I haven't been able to tell my wife—it is like my compatriots and I are involved in a ritual for true believers only. Maggie, who knew me when I still dreamed of playing professionally myself—Maggie, after over half a lifetime together, comes and sits in my lap in the comfortable easy chair which has adjusted through the years to my thickening shape, just as she has. I love to hold the lightness of her, her tongue exploring my mouth, gently as a baby's finger.

'Where do you go?' she asks sleepily when I crawl into bed at dawn.

I mumble a reply. I know she doesn't sleep well when I'm gone. I can feel her body rhythms change as I slip out of bed after midnight.

'Aren't you too old to be having a change of life,' she says, placing her toast-warm hand on my cold thigh.

I am not the only one with this problem.

'I'm developing a reputation,' whispers an affable man at the ballpark. 'I imagine any number of private investigators following any number of cars across the city. I imagine them creeping about the parking lot, shining pen-lights on licence plates, trying to guess what we're up to. Think of the reports they must prepare. I wonder if our wives are disappointed that we're not out discoing with frizzy-haired teenagers?'

Night after night, virtually no words are spoken. Each man seems to know his assignment. Not all bring sod. Some carry rakes, some hoes, some hoses, which, when joined together, snake across the infield and outfield, dispensing the blessing of water. Others, cradle in their arms bags of earth for building up the infield to meet the thick, living sod.

I often remain high in the stadium, looking down on the men moving over the earth, dark as ants, each sodding, cutting, watering, shaping. Occasionally the moon finds a knife blade as it trims the sod or slices away a chunk of artificial turf, and tosses the reflection skyward like a bright ball. My body tingles. There should be symphony music playing. Everyone should be humming 'America the Beautiful'.

Toward dawn, I watch the men walking away in groups, like small patrols of soldiers, carrying instead of arms, the tools and utensils which breathe life back into the arid ballfield.

Row by row, night by night, we lay the little squares of sod, moist as chocolate cake with green icing. Where did all the sod come from? I picture many men, in many parts of the city, surreptitiously cutting chunks out of their own lawns in the leafy midnight darkness, listening to the uncomprehending protests of their wives the next day—pretending to know nothing of it— pretending to have called the police to investigate.

When the strike is over I know we will all be here to watch the workouts, to hear the recalcitrant joints crackling like twigs after the forced inactivity. We will sit in our regular seats, scattered like popcorn throughout the stadium, and we'll nod as we pass on the way to the exits, exchange secret smiles, proud as new fathers.

For me, the best part of all will be the surprise. I feel like a magician who has gestured hypnotically and produced an elephant from thin air. I know I am not alone in my wonder. I know that rockets shoot off in half-a-hundred chests, the excitement of birthday mornings, Christmas eves, and home-town doubleheaders, boils within each of my conspirators. Our secret rites have been performed with love, like delivering a valentine to a sweetheart's door in that blue-steel span of morning just before dawn.

Players and management are meeting round the clock. A settlement is imminent. I have watched the stadium covered square foot by square foot until it looks like green graph paper. I have stood and felt the cool odours of the grass rise up and touch my face. I have studied the lines between each small square, watched those lines fade until they were visible to my eyes alone, then not even to them.

What will the players think, as they straggle into the stadium and find the miracle we have created? The old-timers will raise their heads like ponies, as far away as the parking lot, when the thrill of the grass reaches their nostrils. And, as they dress, they'll recall sprawling in the lush outfields of childhood, the grass as cool as a mother's hand on a forehead.

'Goodbye, goodbye,' we say at the gate, the smell of water, of sod, of sweat, small perfumes in the air. Our secrets are safe with each other. We go our separate ways.

Alone in the stadium in the last chill darkness before dawn, I drop to my hands and knees in the centre of the outfield. My palms are sodden. Water touches the skin between my spread fingers. I lower my face to the silvered grass, which, wonder of wonders, already has the ephemeral odours of baseball about it.

NORMAN LEVINE

Django, Karfunkelstein, & Roses

In late October, on the morning of my fiftieth birthday, we had breakfast early—my wife and three daughters. On the plain wooden table: a black comb, a half-bottle of brandy, a red box of matches from Belgium, a felt pen, a couple of Dutch cigars, a card of Pissarro's *Lower Norwood Under Snow*, and a record. They wished me happy birthday. And we kissed.

After breakfast the children went to school. We continued to talk, without having to finish sentences, over another cup of coffee. Then my wife went to make the beds, water the plants, do the washing. And I went to the front room, lit the coal fire, smoked a Dutch cigar, drank some of the brandy, put the record on, listened to Django Reinhardt and Stephane Grappelli—The Hot Club of France. And looked out for the postman.

The mimosa tree was still in bloom in the small front garden as were some roses. To the left, a road of terraced houses curved as it sloped down to the church steeple and the small shops. And at the end of the road—above houses, steeple, shops—was the white-blue water of the bay.

Directly opposite, past the garden and across the road, was Wesley Street. A short narrow street of stone cottages. I watched the milkman leave bottles on the granite by the front doors. Mr Veal—a tall man with glasses, a retired carpenter, a Plymouth brethren ('I have my place up there when I die' he told me pointing to the sky)—came out of his cottage holding a white tablecloth. He shook the tablecloth in the street. From the slate roofs, the red chimney pots, came jackdaws, sparrows, and a few gulls. They were waiting for him. Mr Veal swirled the tablecloth—as if it was a cape—and over his shoulder it folded neatly on his back. He stood in the centre of the street with the white table-cloth on his back, the birds near his feet ('I need to get wax out of my ears,' he said when we were walking. 'I don't hear people—but I hear the birds'). Then he went inside.

The postman appeared and walked past the house. This morning it didn't matter. My wife hung the washing in the courtyard and pulled up the line. Then left the house to buy the food for the day. The sun came through the coloured glass of the inside front door and onto the floor in shafts of soft yellow, blue, and red. I went upstairs to the large attic room. And got on with the new story . . .

Within a few years this life changed. And for my wife it ended. The children left home. I would get up early—the gulls woke me—wondering what to do (I wasn't writing anything). Living by oneself like this, I thought, how long the day is. How slow it goes by. I went from one empty room to another . . . looked outside . . . such a nice-looking place . . . and wondered how to go on. And there were times when I wondered why go on?

Then a letter came from Zurich. It came from the people who worked in a literary agency. They told me that my literary agent was going to be 70. They were planning a surprise party. Could I come?

At the airport a young man with curly brown hair and glasses, just over medium height, was holding a sheet of paper with my name on it. He was shy (No, he hadn't been waiting long). He smiled easily. He said he did the accounts.

'You have not met Ruth?'

'No,' I said.

'How long is she your agent?'

'14 years.'

Zurich was busy. In sunny end-of-May weather he drove to the heights above . . . to a *cul-de-sac* of large houses. They had signs, *Achtung Hund* . . . except in front of the large house where he stopped.

As he opened the door there were red roses, in the hallway, lots of them. And more red roses at the bottom of the wide stairs. The wall opposite the front door was mostly books. But in a space, waist high, a small sink with the head of a brass lion. Water came out of its mouth. There were more roses, as well as books, in the large carpeted rooms that he led me through. Then outside, down a few steps, to a grass lawn. People were standing in clusters talking and eating. A tall attractive woman with straight blonde hair was cooking over a barbecue. She talked loudly in Italian. A man in his 30s—regular clean cut face, black curly hair—was moving around slowly with a handheld camera, stopping, then moving again.

The person at the airport came towards me with a lively short woman. She looked very alert, intelligent, and with a sense of fun.

'What a surprise,' she said. We embraced quickly and kissed. Then we moved apart and looked at one another.

'This is very moving,' she said quietly.

I could hear the whirr of the film camera.

'You must be hungry.'

She linked arms, led me to the barbecue, and introduced me to Giuli—the tall blonde Italian who was her housekeeper (She would die, unexpectedly, in two years). There were frankfurters, hamburgers, salad, grapes. I had a couple of frankfurters and walked to the lawn's edge and to an immediate drop. The churches, the buildings, the houses of Zurich spread out below and in front. Across some water I could see wooded hills. And further away, hardly visible against the skyline, mountains.

More people kept arriving. I could now hear French and German. It was pleasantly warm. Sparrows flitted around us. Giuli, and others, threw them bits of bread.

That night cars brought the guests into Zurich. The birthday party was in a Guildhall near the centre. A narrow river was outside. The water looked black. I could see several white swans on it. The guests came from different parts of Western Europe. They were mostly publishers. But I did meet Alfred Andersch. A gentle man with a pleasant face, a nice smile ('Why write novels if you can write short stories'). He would die within a year. And Elias Canetti. A short stocky man with a large face, high forehead, thick black hair brushed back (He would be awarded the Nobel Prize).

There were speeches, toasts, in English. Then the guests went in line to another room where—on a long table with white tablecloths—there were lit candles and all sorts of food. Platters of shrimp . . . asparagus . . . a large cooked salmon . . . roast beef . . . the salads were colourful. I looked ahead to the far end where the cakes were. And saw, on the table, what I thought was one of the white swans from the river. As I came closer I realized it was made of butter.

Later that night, in the house, seven of us who were staying as guests sat with Ruth in the kitchen. We talked and drank. I was the only male. The women's ages spread from the late 30s into the 70s. The youngest was the girl from upstairs who rented a room and worked in Zurich. She was waiting for her gentleman friend to phone to let her know when he would be in Zurich. After she spoke to him she came down and joined us and she started to sing, *It's All Right With Me*. She had a fine voice. We joined in. There were more Cole Porter songs. And Jerome Kern. Then the older ladies sang, very enthusiastically. European socialist songs. And went on to folk songs, mostly German (Ruth was born in Hamburg). The one that made an impression was a slow sad tune about the black death.

Giuli, sitting beside me, said in broken English how her husband, a pilot in the Italian air force, was killed while flying. And how lucky she was to find Ruth. Then, with more wine, she began to talk Italian to everyone and stood up wanting us all to dance. We formed a chorus line, Ruth in the middle. We kicked our legs up and sang as we moved around the kitchen. Then tired we sat down. This time Ruth was beside me, a little out of breath. While our glasses were being filled again I asked her— what was she thinking when she saw those large bunches of roses all over the house?

And she said, that during the last war she worked as a courier for the resistance. They sent her to Holland. The Nazis tracked her down. 'Things became difficult. I was on a wanted list. I had to stay inside my small room. I couldn't go out.

'In the next room there was a man called Karfunkelstein. He told me he was going to commit suicide. I asked him why.

' "One can't live with a name like Karfunkelstein in these times."

'I managed to talk him out of it.

' "Wait," he said. And left me.

'When he came back he had his arms full of roses and other flowers.

' "For you," he said.

'And gave them to me.

'My small room was full of flowers. And I couldn't go out to sell a rose for food.'

Four and a half years later, early this December, I saw Ruth again. I had been invited to Strasbourg to give a lecture at the university. After the lecture I took a train to Zurich. Outside the station I went into a waiting taxi. I gave the driver the name of the street.

He replied with the number I wanted.

'How did you know?'

'Many people go there.'

This time no guests or flowers. But the same warm welcome. The young man who met me at the airport was still doing the accounts, still looked shy, and smiled easily. His hair was grey. I met the new housekeeper, Juliette. She came from France. About the same age as Ruth.

It was cold and foggy. At dusk I could see the lights of Zurich below. Juliette brought in some coffee and for over an hour Ruth and I talked business. She phoned up the Canadian embassy in Bonn and spoke to the cultural attaché about an East German translation. She phoned a radio station in Cologne about a short story that had been broadcast. We went over a contract line by line. Then Ruth said.

'I must go and lie down for 20 minutes.'

She went upstairs. I went into the kitchen. And talked to Juliette while she was preparing the food. Juliette told me she used to be a photographer in Paris before the war. Then worked in London. She had a studio in Knightsbridge. And talked nostalgically of the time she lived there. A small radio was on. Someone was playing a guitar. I said I liked Django Reinhardt.

'I knew him,' Juliette said. 'My husband Andre was his best friend for some years.'

Ruth appeared looking less tired.

'You didn't stay 20 minutes,' Juliette said in mock anger.

Ruth and I finished the rest of our business over a drink. Then it was time for supper. The three of us sat around a small table in the kitchen, in a corner, by the stove. We had red wine. We clinked glasses and drank to our next meeting.

Juliette passed the salad bowl.

I asked her about Django Reinhardt.

'He couldn't read or write. He was a gypsy,' she said. 'Very black hair but good white teeth. You know how he got those two fingers? His wife was in a caravan making artificial flowers when there was a fire. Django ran in and saved her. His hand was burned . . . Oh, he was a bad driver. He had so many accidents . . . the car looked a wreck. One time he came to see us with a new shirt, a tie, and a new suit. He asked my husband what was the proper way to wear it? Andre showed him. Django stood in front of the mirror wearing the new clothes, looking at himself, very pleased at the way he looked.' (Juliette acted this out with little movements of her face and hands as she spoke). 'We listened to him play . . . he would play for hours . . . if I could have recorded it . . . He only began to make records so he could give them to his friends. But he could be difficult. To get him to the recording studio on time my husband would say 'Django, you are late . . . the machinery is all set up . . . there are people waiting . . . they have their jobs.' And Django would not go. Andre tried again. And Django got angry.

' "I need my freedom. If I can't have my freedom . . . it's not my life."

'Later he bought a Chateau near Paris. That life didn't suit him. He was ruined . . . by money . . . by women . . . fame. He couldn't handle it.'

Juliette stood up and from the stove brought a small casserole and served the meat and the vegetables.

'What happened to Karfunkelstein?' I asked Ruth.

'He probably committed suicide,' she said in a flat voice. 'In those days people like him did . . .

'On May 10th 1940,' she went on, 'The Germans came into Holland. Next day there was an epidemic of suicides. There weren't enough coffins. They put them in sacks.

'I knew this young family. They had two small boys. The man was a teacher. His wife was in love with him. She would go along with whatever he wanted. And he wanted to commit suicide. He kept saying: "Life as it is going to be . . . will not be worth living."

'I knew someone in the American Embassy. I arranged for them to see him next morning so they could get out of Holland. But I wanted to make sure they would be there.

'I went to their house. The man was still saying that life without freedom to live the way he had lived would be impossible . . . when the youngest boy swallowed a small bulb from a flashlight. (At least his mother said that he did). She was very worried. She asked me: What should she do? How could she get a doctor? After a while the child got better. Because I saw how worried she had been I thought it was all right to leave them for the night. I said I would be back in the morning.

'When I arrived. The two boys were dead. The man and the wife had sealed all the doors and windows. Turned on the gas. And they had cut their wrists.'

When we had finished, Juliette began to clear and wash up while Ruth went into the other room to dictate letters into a machine for the secretary next morning. I went up to the room where I would sleep the night—a large bare room in the attic with a low double bed, books all over, and a wide window with a view of Zurich. I looked at the lights and thought of the people who had come to Zurich, from other countries, for different reasons. And how few of them stayed.

Juliette came to the door and said, 'There is a Canadian film on television. Have you heard of it? It is called *Mon Oncle Antoine.*'

'It's the best Canadian film I have seen,' I said.

'Then we shall all see it,' she said.

I went down with her.

Juliette drew the curtains. Ruth put in a hearing aid. 'I only do this for television,' she said.

I looked forward to seeing the film again. I had seen it, about 20 years ago, in St Ives on television and remembered how moved I had been by it.

'There is a marvellous shot,' I said while the news was on. 'It is winter. On the extreme left of the picture there is a horse and a sleigh with a young boy and his uncle. The horse has stopped. And on the extreme right of the picture is a coffin that has fallen off the sleigh. Inbetween there is this empty field of snow. It is night. The wind is blowing . . . no words spoken. But that image I have remembered all these years.'

Mon Oncle Antoine came on. The first surprise—it was in colour. I remembered it in black and white. Then I realized . . . it was because in St Ives we had then a black and white TV set. There were other disappointments. It might have been because of the German subtitles, or my memory.

I told them the scene was about to come on.

When it did—it wasn't memorable at all.

Was it because it was in colour? Or had it been cut? I remembered it as lasting much longer. And it was the length of the shot, in black and white, that made it so poignant.

When the film was over I could see they were disappointed.

'I remember it differently,' I said. And told them how I had seen it on a black-and-white TV set.

'It would have been better in black and white,' Ruth said.

'There may have been cuts.'

'It seemed very jumpy,' Juliette said. 'You could see it had the possibility of a good movie.'

That night in the attic, in bed, I heard midnight by the different clocks in Zurich. I didn't count how many. But there were several. Each one starting a few seconds after another . . . and thought about *Mon Oncle Antoine*. How it differed from what I remembered. I saw how I had changed that shot. Just as I had switched the candles from around the man in the coffin at the start. And had them around the boy in the coffin at the end. I had, over the years, changed these things in order to remember them. Is this what time does? Perhaps it was a good film because it could suggest these things.

And was this what Juliette had done when she told about Django Reinhardt. And Ruth with Karfunkelstein?

But some things don't change.

I remembered my wife having to go into Penzance hospital to drain off some fluid. It was in the last two weeks of her life. She hadn't been outside for over a year but in that front room where I brought down a bed. And from there she looked at the granite of Wesley Street and Mr Veal feeding the birds. Two men carried her out on a canvas and put her in the back of the ambulance.

When she returned she said, 'It's so beautiful. The sky . . . the clouds . . . the trees . . . the fields . . . the hedges. I was lying on my back and I could see through the windows . . . '

Early next morning Ruth drove me to the railway station. The
streets were quite empty. The sun was not high above the horizon. And here it was snowing. The sun caught the glass of the
buildings, the houses, and lit them up. And now the snow was
falling . . . thick flakes.

'My aunt in Israel is 90,' Ruth said. 'And drives her car. Isn't
that marvellous.'

We were going down a turning road, down a slope, then it
straightened out. I asked her.

'Will you go on living in Zurich?'

'I don't know. The only other country would be Holland. I
like Holland.'

After she left I went inside the station and gave all the Swiss
change I had to a plump young girl who was selling things from
a portable kiosk. In return I had a bar of chocolate, a large green
apple, and a yellow pack of five small cigars.

JOYCE MARSHALL

My Refugee

This should be, in part at least, an apology to Kurt. Though he wouldn't find much of it new; I was fairly apparent in those days. I should also, while I'm at it, thank him for his patience which, granted the circumstances of his life and mine, was far greater than I deserved or had any right to demand. For I did demand it. In excuse, if it is an excuse, I can only say that I was quite desperately unhappy—and bitterly ashamed of myself, my unhappiness, my life, all of which seemed, like the world itself at that time, to be completely out of control. I felt that I could see what was happening, to the world and to myself, that I even knew why it was happening. But I couldn't stop it and no-one else would.

We met during the last winter of so-called peace, at a party given for refugees by the mother of one of my friends. (Hitler was screaming again. There'd be another march quite soon, we knew—this time into Czechoslovakia—another loss.) He was from Vienna, he told me, and had been a lawyer there—a big man of much rather wobbly flesh, a pale clownish face, and a narrow pulpy mouth whose movements were at once too small and too elaborate to make proper English sounds. He'd come to the party, as he claimed he went most places, to meet girls though not, he assured me then and later, to meet a girl who was in any way like me. I wasn't his type. Kurt's type possessed a vague European attribute called temperament, which had something to do, I gathered, with not always trying (ploddingly) to tell the truth or showing their emotions on their faces. I hadn't come to meet men, or not specifically, for there was always the hope, small but persistent, that some day, perhaps when I least expected it, someone would turn up and do for me what I seemed unable to do for myself, sweep me away, save me. And a tragic victim of history would have done so nicely. I was expected, of course, to pass around sandwiches and tea, as the other young women were doing. I'd come, however, to listen and learn. Though I didn't go so far as to think it was good to be a refugee, I did think it was better to know. I believed in Experience, and History was shaping out of my sight, permitting us to have so little. We listened to Hitler scream over the radio, we sang the song about the peat-bog soldiers, raised money for Spain, demonstrated for China, without jobs most of us, while History decided what it would do with us. We knew all too well, had known for years, that war was what it would do, made bleak little jokes: 'And then there'll be jobs for us all.' Meanwhile our days, which seem so swift in their downward-rushing now but at the time dragged leadenly, were cruelly the same. And that isn't what one wants when one is young.

'Tell me what it was like,' I longed to say to the people milling about the room that snowy Sunday in their European clothes so different from ours—the men's suit-coats waisted, which, with a certain stiffness of movement, gave them the appearance of being in uniform, the women in drab confused colours, their garments flounced or trailing, or both flounced and trailing. I'd thought they might talk about their Experience, or make statements about Democracy, without prompting. No-one did and I was too shy to ask.

So I did what I could to show my goodwill, smiled at various people, asked how they liked Toronto. All said they liked it. People were kind. They were delighted with this party. If everyone was truly so kind, why were they so delighted, I wondered, to be standing around this rather ordinary Toronto living-room with cups of tea. I didn't realize that they were being grateful because they knew they had to be, that they were people who'd never expected such gratitude to be required of them—people of substance, professionals in many cases.

Kurt saw what I was up to, of course. I was aware several times of a big bulky man with a pale, often expressionless face who was studying me. A distracted woman had just rushed up to me with a flutter of muddy-coloured garments and asked whether I knew anyone who wanted German lessons. She spoke a pure high German, she was assuring me, not a trace of dialect, repeating this several times, not a trace, when Kurt was suddenly at my side, addressing me in almost incomprehensible English and getting rid of the fluttery lady. (I've often wondered what he said to her.) It took a great deal of talking from him, a great many 'I'm sorry, I can't quite' from me, for us to exchange names and basic facts. By that time he'd decided, he informed me, that I spoke the clearest English of anyone he'd met and that he wanted me to be his English coach. My lack of teaching experience was of no importance. He'd bought an English book, which we'd read paragraph by paragraph in turn. Then followed another five minutes' mouthing and apology while he struggled to tell me the name of his book. I said, finally, embarrassed by his sweating and my inability to stop staring at his mouth, that I'd never heard of the book. Everyone had heard of it, he said. And indeed everyone had. It was John O'Hara's *Appointment in Samarra*, as I discovered a week or so later when I went round to his ground-floor room in the Annex for our first lesson.

It was a large room with an off-centre bay window, the former drawing-room of one of those great clumsy turreted houses that still stand here and there on dwindling streets. There were probably interesting architectural features—panelling, stained glass—but I was interested only in the furniture, whether it was better (and steadier) than mine. I moved often and had become in a very few years quite a connoisseur of such things. My current quarters held, besides the standard lumpy studio-couch

(Kurt's was green, mine a dirty orange), an assortment of garden rejects—two wicker chairs with ravelling crocheted backs,
a pedestal table that shook and tottered when I typed on it, a
lamp with a charred shade. Kurt's rejects were Victorian—
awkwardly shaped chairs like the ones at my grandparents',
upholstered in a similarly abrasive goldy-brown plush, and a
number of those wrought-iron stands that are supposed to hold
plants. (Such furnishings would be considered trendy now, with a
little paint and jacking up. We who lived with them in our young
poor days are not enamoured of such things.) Kurt's was a 'light-
housekeeping' room so there was a hot-plate behind a flowery
curtain in one corner. Another held a big scuffed desk, for he
carried on his business—selling real estate, he told me—from
this room.

We settled ourselves on two of the square-seated chairs and
commenced our lesson. Kurt read a few sentences. I read the
same sentences. He then reread the sentences. He tried to imitate me. I tried to correct him. Kurt's efforts to move his lips as
I moved mine, scarcely at all, his rubbery face pinched into a
comically girlish expression—he seemed incapable of copying
my mouth without copying my entire face—produced strangled
squeaks that reduced us both to helpless laughter. I'd been watching him as closely as he watched me—not only closely, with
fascination—and by the time he decided we'd done enough work
and should now have coffee, I'd begun to purse my mouth as he
did his and to thicken my own sounds. Kurt caught this at once.
His ear was always much more accurate than his tongue. 'The
teacher should not learn from the pupil, she should teach the
pupil,' he said indignantly and I promised to try to do better.

We continued these 'lessons' at intervals of a week or two,
though we soon gave up reading-in-turn as dull as well as non-
productive and simply met to talk. Kurt's English sounds did
become a little less smudged, though whether my correcting
and patient demonstration had anything to do with this I cannot
say. I still often stared at his mouth and then he'd exaggerate its

movements, and his own difficulties, in absurdly comical ways. I knew little about him at this time except his age—37—and that he'd left Vienna on skis the day the Nazis arrived. (I always held a tiny picture in my mind—the Germans goose-stepping in at one end of the city while Kurt puffed up a mountain at the other end. Slithered and scrambled up—I assumed that he was physically awkward in every respect—then coasted down into Switzerland.) He didn't seem anxious to tell his story, not nearly as eager as I had been to tell mine. The details of my unhappy entanglement spilled out of me at our second or third meeting, which was surprising since I was almost pathologically reticent in those days. I suppose I badly needed to talk and found Kurt as an outsider less threatening. The emotion itself is gone from me now. It simply sits there, in my life, as it will sit in the middle of these incidents, not nearly as unusual or as tragic as I thought it was but encompassing, the source of bitter self-dislike. Kurt's response, then and later, was wry, not quite amused enough to offend me, rather chiding. 'Still tied up with that guy?' he'd ask me from time to time, and I'd say that I loved 'that guy', I just couldn't help it. If I was particularly unhappy, he'd suggest that I stay the night—not, he always hastened to add, that I was in any way his type; he was goodhearted and willing to sacrifice time that might more profitably be spent with sensible women to prove to me that there were other men in the world. (Kurt was attractive to women and usually, at the time I knew him, involved with at least two. They were often the sort who called late at night; I would listen to their excited rushing voices and Kurt's soothing replies. So few Canadian women had tempera-ment, he said sadly.) These invitations, whether they were seri-ously meant or not, and I've never known which, gave me the opportunity to decline, careful not to hurt his feelings. Not that his feelings were in danger of being hurt, he assured me often; I was the loser, not he.

Perhaps he didn't tell his story sooner because he couldn't trust my discretion. (He wasn't aware that I talked to my friends about ''my'' refugee. Or was he? At least suspicious?) Perhaps he saw how anxious I was to make him into a tragic victim and didn't want, by indulging me, to weaken himself. He was gay always and as witty as his graceless English would let him be—a buffoon the rest of the time. I was too full of myself to realize that this gaiety might have to be made afresh each day—each minute even. He gave me bits of his story when it suited him, often when I was feeling particularly sad and fearful; not, I believe, to cap my experience with his own but as an offering, a distraction. The fact that he was in Canada illegally came out the night I almost agreed to stay with him, had risen wildly and removed my blouse. He gave a queer little sound, half snort and told me to put it on again. Since I insisted upon acting like a schoolgirl, he, who preferred women of the world, women with temperament, would rather just have coffee and talk. So we did and when I was feeling a little steadier (and rather foolish), he mentioned his status—or rather lack of status. Casually, as a joke on himself. He'd entered Canada on false pretenses (a complicated story he'd tell me some other time) and might in theory be deported at any moment.

This country has a poor record for admitting refugees during the thirties. 'About 1100 Jews from all countries' is the figure given; there is no indication whether all of these were refugees. Still I'd like to register a small cheer for some bureaucrat (or bureaucrats) in the Immigration Department who, faced with this one flagrantly illegal immigrant, did not send him back. They didn't tell him he could stay, simply delayed the final formality. There was never even a crisis. I hoped, at least half hoped, that there would be, that I'd be able for once to *do something*, strike a personal blow against Hitler, and kept reminding Kurt that he must leave some signal for me if he were picked up (though I could never think of any satisfactory or even sensible way—breadcrumbs, chalk on the door?—that this could be done) and that he should call me at once if he as much as felt himself in danger. I'd hide him somehow, farm him out among my friends, claim him as a brother to deceive my Baptist landlady—a deaf-mute brother presumably if I could find some way to keep him silent. He wasn't any more ironic than usual as I hatched my schemes, didn't even remind me that there were others who'd be more useful in such emergency than me. Perhaps that was the secret of Kurt's remarkable patience. I was as much a distraction to him as he was to me.

He didn't give me the full story till the war had started, seven or eight months after our meeting. I'd told myself I must remember the last hours and minutes of peace, that I'd need this memory later in the darkness. But there'd been too many crises; I couldn't force myself to make or note down gestures. Nothing much happened, in any event. No-one came across a lawn, waving a newspaper and shouting 'We are at war!' I must have switched on my radio first thing and listened to the bleating voice of Chamberlain, later to the King; I can't remember. The war became real to me a fortnight later as I was walking over to see Kurt in the early evening. Young men, my fellows, not yet provided with uniforms, were drilling stripped to the waist on the university campus. I looked at the hollow chests, the bones breaking the bad skin, all the other signs of malnutrition, and told myself, with the first sense of drama the war had brought me, that this was one thing I must remember, I must remember it very clearly.

Kurt said, 'So they realize finally that Nazism isn't just an internal matter.' There was a bite in his voice. He'd organized a meeting of Toronto refugees, he told me, and they'd sent Mackenzie King a telegram, promising full support of our war effort. There'd be no question now of deportation. He'd have to register with the other 'enemy' aliens and that, we knew, would be that. The man Kurt always called 'that guy' had been talking of enlisting. I believe I mentioned this to Kurt, tried at some length to untangle my feelings—I was beginning to suspect that the neurosis wasn't all on my side, 'that guy' was every bit as bound to me as I was to him, and if he should leave me now, leave me to go into danger, I wouldn't be free, I'd be more firmly attached than ever—and that Kurt listened in his astringent, not-quite-mocking way. (I needn't have worried, as it happened. The enlistment talk was only talk. He spent a profitable and quite interesting war making gunsights. It was the first real work he'd had.) Our conversation that evening kept dribbling into silence—no-one could make pronouncements in those days (though we wanted to) or plan or even think of planning—and at some point Kurt decided to make tea. His story came out in brief quiet sentences while the kettle boiled. He'd met an American woman tourist in July of 1934. That bloody month of that damn bloody year. Did I remember? Dolfuss, the chancellor, shot by the Nazis and left to die very slowly in his own blood—no great loss perhaps but still. . . . In the midst of all the horror and blood he'd had an affair with this woman and she'd offered the help of herself and her husband if he should decide to emigrate. That's how he put it—he had, she offered—in the tone of an adult addressing a child, his usual tone with me, so that I couldn't judge how much was connivance, how much happenstance. He thought about it. Kept putting it off. Various reasons. His widowed mother, for one. He was her only child. Finally, when it was almost too late, he decided to take up the offer and the husband, a manufacturer of kitchen gadgets, obtained a visa for Kurt to visit them in New York. It came through just in time to be in his knapsack the day he skied out of the city. (Again I saw that neat small scene—the Nazis goose-stepping in at one side while Kurt huffed and puffed up that mountain on the other side.) But the visa was only for six months and couldn't be extended. Kurt would have to leave the country and re-apply. Canada was handy but to apply from here he must first get in. It was decided that he should pretend to be investigating opportunities to set up a plant here and, armed with a sample of his sponsor's goods—a cap for a teapot spout that was supposed to catch drips—Kurt boarded a train for Toronto. He dug out the gadget, which was still attached to its card. We decided to try it out at once; interestingly enough, it wouldn't

fit on Kurt's teapot—or on mine when I took it home. But with
its help Kurt talked his way into Canada. These things were to
be manufactured by the millions, providing thousands of jobs.
He didn't dare stop, he told me, lest he be asked for more proof
than this one sample and a two-paragraph letter from his sponsor. For some reason, perhaps he was dazed by the barrage of
half-intelligible words, the immigration inspector let Kurt in.
He'd been provided with money and settled down to wait for a
permanent visa. Then the sponsor made a false move. Or was it
a false move? I can't say, not knowing the true facts of the Vienna
affair, the invitation to come to New York. He declared himself
willing to provide Kurt with support—and to give him a job
This effectively foxed the application; the US needed all available jobs for its own people.

Kurt was stuck, in a country that might send him back to
Austria at any moment. He'd begun, by the time I met him, to
support himself by selling real estate in what wasn't yet called the
ethnic community. There wasn't much trade in property at that
time but Kurt lived by it—a store here, a row house there—
even after a time employed an acquaintance he'd helped bring
to Toronto. I happened to be with him the evening this man and
his family arrived. Kurt had obtained a room for them above his
own—a large pleasant room with cots in an alcove for the two
children. They were all tired after the train-journey from New
York and went at once to the room. In no time the man was back
downstairs. His wife couldn't sleep in that room, he said, speaking part of the time in English out of courtesy to me, because
the bedspreads were not white. It was no use Kurt's assuring
him, as he did in English first, then in German, that he'd find
something suitable the next day. The woman was upstairs crying,
not on one of the print-covered beds but sitting upright in a chair.
There was no resident landlady so Kurt began to root about in
cupboards. I helped him and eventually we found clean sheets
to cover the beds. He wasn't furious, as I'd have expected and
as I was on his account; just ironic and a touch exasperated as

156 | Joyce Marshall

he so often was with me. I understand now what I imagine Kurt realized at the time. Only so much strangeness can be accepted. This woman had been wrenched from everything safe and known in her life. She was proving herself a human being with tastes and a past. Bedspreads were white in her world.

Other refugees sometimes turned up during our lessons. Kurt could find a room, a bed, even at times a job, and always advice for everyone. There must have been a number like him in the refugee community—men and women with energy, with patience, with the ability to force or charm or, as in Kurt's case I've always felt, talk their way through. The people who came to Kurt's room in the early evening weren't quite the band of brothers and sisters I'd expected them to be. Some would have been neurotics and simple whiners anywhere, I imagine; others were learning, with pain, the loss of self, the little deaths, that come from being in a place one didn't choose, perhaps never would have chosen, and cannot seem to fit.

All this time, despite his own lack of status, Kurt had been trying to get his mother out of Austria, raise money, obtain influence. (I'm glad to say that although we often discussed it I refrained from offering hare-brained schemes.) Till the US entered the war, he was able to correspond with her through the American Red Cross. Then even letters stopped.

He was already sending parcels to two cousins, at least one ex-girlfriend and several other people of his acquaintance who'd managed to reach London. He even found stockings for me when I couldn't find any for myself—tubes of thick woody rayon whose toes had to be cobbled together again each day. I wore them for an entire winter. But that was after the war had dragged on for two or three years. Before that he had a visitor of another sort and I saw another Kurt, another side of his life.

It was early June, the close of one of the flawless days of that flawless season when news came to us in a code we learned to read. ('German dead piled high' meant approaching disaster. 'Withdrawal to previously prepared position' was a rout.) I'd

been ill and had struggled out of anaesthetic after minor surgery
to hear that Paris had been declared an open city. France had
fallen now, Hitler would soon strut down the Champs Elysées
(which I hadn't seen, was convinced now I'd never see) and we
were hamming it up, laughing, I think, at Kurt's efforts to move
his lips like mine, his face pinched together and girlish, when
there was a knock and in came a man I recall only as tall and
rather seedy-looking. (We all went into the war shabby and came
out shabbier.) I'd never seen anyone so quick-moving; he seemed
to leap into the room. 'I'm from the city police,' he said, pulling out some sort of badge or card and, whether we'd recognized it or not, putting it back again. He proceeded to question
Kurt about his citizenship, status in the country, date of entry,
point of entry. Kurt, always so swift with not always compre-
hensible words, collapsed, quivered, could not remember places,
circumstances. I listened for as long as I could, then decided to
answer a question myself. It was about the bridge by which he'd
entered Canada. 'The Erie Bridge,' I said firmly though I had
no idea whether this was so. 'And who are you, young lady?'
the policeman asked. I replied with my full name and the
announcement that I was a citizen of this country and as such did
not like to see my innocent friend intimidated in this way, intended
furthermore to make sure that he was treated correctly by the
police who after all were responsible ultimately to me. The cop
assured me of his lack of any desire to intimidate. Someone had
reported the presence of an enemy alien in the house and he was
simply investigating the truth of this as he was bound to do.
He completed his note-taking, examined the proof of registration
Kurt, after much fumbling, found for him and left us amiably
enough. I learned then the reason for Kurt's collapse. He'd heard
the cop's introductory words as 'I'm from the secret police,'
had felt that he'd climbed that imaginary mountain of mine and
crossed the ocean for nothing, they were here too.

It would make a better story if there'd been some real brutal-
ity, a show, even a hint, of racism. (There were such incidents,

I know. The policeman who accused me three or four years later of making notes about military insignia, which I was in fact doing for future literary reference, wasn't nearly so agreeable.) But Kurt's cop was on the whole quite friendly and called him 'son' at the last. This was my one experience of the world of the knock in the night.

The war went on. They killed us as we'd known they would—at Hong Kong, by the sea-wall at Dieppe, on the Normandy beaches, at Arnhem, haphazardly here and there, in ditches, beside barns. Those of us who were able to stay behind had jobs, heard bad news over the radio in the early morning. It was just as we'd known it would be, as if our own imaginations were opening again and again, showing us what we'd always known would come. Then when war, like the bad peace that preceded it, seemed to have been with us forever, it ended. Though I hate to say this in the same breath, my own personal unhappiness ended at about this time, as if the two things had really been bound up together, and the exhaustion of one brought the exhaustion of the other.

Kurt received the worst possible news about his mother. Rather promptly, for though we were daily learning more about the camps, it could still seem possible that news of an elderly Jewish widow might be good, and when he said 'Yes, I've heard,' his clown-face blank, in response to a question from me, I was gazing at his mouth, its baby-movements making baby-sounds, so ready to laugh and say 'Oh I'm glad' that I almost did.

Kurt became a Canadian citizen, settled down, prospered. There were no more English lessons. We met less and less frequently till finally, without intention on either side, I believe, he slipped into being one of those people one still considers a friend but never sees. For years he used to call me from time to time and announce, without troubling to introduce himself—and of course this wasn't necessary, no-one of my acquaintance ever made such a mess of English sounds—some fact or bit of news. One day it was 'The policeman loves you.' He'd been to a police station on a routine errand, had encountered our cop, now promoted to a desk. The cop had recognized Kurt and they'd reminisced about the occasion of the knock in the night.

'How's that hot-tempered girlfriend of yours?' the cop had inquired. I was a real fighter, he'd said; any sensible man would prefer to have me on his side and not against. More too, which Kurt wouldn't tell me because, as he put it, they were the sort of things men say to each other when there are no ladies to hear them.

It was nice to be appreciated, even by a policeman on a distasteful errand. I'd rather liked him too. He was shabby like the rest of us and he called Kurt 'son'. My intervention on that occasion was my one chance to do a big thing for Kurt, strike a personal blow against Hitler. I'm glad it was seen as such.

ALICE MUNRO

Miles City, Montana

My father came across the field, carrying the body of the boy who had been drowned. There were several men together, returning from the search, but he was the one carrying the body. The men were muddy and exhausted, and walked with their heads down, as if they were ashamed. Even the dogs were dispirited, dripping from the cold river. When they all set out, hours before, the dogs were nervy and yelping, the men tense and determined, and there was a constrained, unspeakable excitement about the whole scene. It was understood that they might find something horrible.

The boy's name was Steve Gauley. He was eight years old. His hair and clothes were mud-colored now and carried some bits of dead leaves, twigs, and grass. He was like a heap of refuse that had been left all winter. His face was turned in to my father's chest, but I could see a nostril, an ear, plugged up with greenish mud.

I don't think I really saw all this. Perhaps I saw my father carrying him, and the other men coming with him, and the dogs, but I would not have been allowed to get close enough to see something like mud in his nostril. I must have heard someone talking about that and imagined that I saw it. I see his face unaltered except for the mud—Steve Gauley's familiar, sharp-honed, sneaky-looking face—and it wouldn't have been like that; it would have been bloated and changed and perhaps muddied all over after so many hours in the water.

To have to bring back such news, such evidence, to a waiting family, particularly a mother, would have made searchers move heavily, but what was happening here was worse. It seemed a worse shame (to hear people talk) that there was no mother, no woman at all—no grandmother or aunt, or even a sister—to receive Steve Gauley and give him his due of grief. His father was a hired man, a drinker but not a drunk, an erratic man without being entertaining, not friendly but not exactly a troublemaker. His fatherhood seemed accidental, and the fact that the child had been left with him when the mother went away, and that they continued living together, seemed accidental. They lived in a steep-roofed, gray-shingled hillbilly sort of house that was just a bit better than a shack—the father fixed the roof and put supports under the porch, just enough and just in time—and their life was held together in a similar manner; that is, just well enough to keep the Children's Aid at bay. They didn't eat meals together or cook for each other, but there was food. Sometimes the father would give Steve money to buy food at the store, and Steve was seen to buy quite sensible things, such as pancake mix and macaroni dinner.

I had known Steve Gauley fairly well. I had not liked him more often than I had liked him. He was two years older than I was. He would hang around our place on Saturdays, scornful of whatever I was doing but unable to leave me alone. I couldn't be on the swing without him wanting to try it, and if I wouldn't give it up he came and pushed me so that I went crooked. He teased the dog. He got me into trouble—deliberately and maliciously, it seemed to me afterward—by daring me to do things I wouldn't have thought of on my own: digging up the potatoes to see how big they were, when they were still only the size of marbles, and pushing over the stacked firewood to make a pile we could jump off. At school we never spoke to each other. He was solitary, though not tormented. But on Saturday mornings when I saw his thin, self-possessed figure sliding through the cedar hedge I knew I was in for something, and he would decide what. Sometimes it was all right. We pretended we were cow-boys who had to tame wild horses. We played in the pasture by the river, not far from the place where Steve drowned. We were horses and riders both, screaming and neighing and bucking and waving whips of tree branches beside a little nameless river that flows into the Saugeen, in southern Ontario.

The funeral was held in our house. There was not enough room at Steve's father's place for the large crowd that was expected, because of the circumstances. I have a memory of the crowded room but no picture of Steve in his coffin, or of the minister, or of wreaths of flowers. I remember that I was hold-ing one flower, a white narcissus, which must have come from a pot somebody forced indoors, because it was too early for even the forsythia bush or the trilliums and marsh marigolds in the woods. I stood in a row of children, each of us holding a narcis-sus. We sang a children's hymn, which somebody played on our piano: 'When He Cometh, When He Cometh, to Make Up His Jewels.' I was wearing white ribbed stockings, which were disgustingly itchy and which wrinkled at the knees and ankles. The feeling of these stockings on my legs is mixed up with another feeling in my memory. It is hard to describe. It had to do with my parents. Adults in general but my parents in particu-lar. My father, who had carried Steve's body from the river, and my mother, who must have done most of the arranging of this funeral. My father in his dark-blue suit and my mother in her brown velvet dress with the creamy satin collar. They stood side by side opening and closing their mouths for the hymn, and I stood removed from them, in the row of children, watching. I felt a furious, and sickening, disgust. Children sometimes have an access of disgust concerning adults. The size, the lumpy shapes, the bloated power. The breath, the coarseness, the hairi-ness, the horrid secretions. But this was more. And the accom-panying anger had nothing sharp and self-respecting about it. There was no release, as when I would finally bend and pick up a stone and throw it at Steve Gauley. It could not be understood or expressed, though it died down after a while into a heaviness, then just a taste, an occasional taste—a thin, familiar misgiving.

Twenty years or so later, in 1961, my husband, Andrew, and I got a brand-new car, our first—that is, our first brand-new. It was a Morris Oxford, oyster-colored (the dealer had some fancier name for the color)—a big small car, with plenty of room for us and our two children. Cynthia was six and Meg three and a half.

Andrew took a picture of me standing beside the car. I was wearing white pants, a black turtleneck, and sunglasses. I lounged against the car door, canting my hips to make myself look slim.

'Wonderful,' Andrew said. 'Great. You look like Jackie Kennedy.' All over this continent probably, dark-haired, reasonably slender young women were told, when they were stylishly dressed or getting their pictures taken, that they looked like Jackie Kennedy.

Andrew took a lot of pictures of me, and of the children, our house, our garden, our excursions and possessions. He got copies made, labelled them carefully, and sent them back to his mother and his aunt and uncle, in Ontario. He got copies for me to send to my father, who also lived in Ontario, and I did so, but less regularly than he sent his. When he saw pictures he thought I had already sent lying around the house, Andrew was perplexed and annoyed. He liked to have this record go forth.

That summer we were presenting ourselves, not pictures. We were driving back from Vancouver, where we lived, to Ontario, which we still called 'home', in our new car. Five days to get there, ten days there, five days back. For the first time, Andrew had three weeks' holiday. He worked in the legal department at B.C. Hydro.

On a Saturday morning we loaded suitcases, two thermos bottles—one filled with coffee and one with lemonade—some fruit and sandwiches, picture books and coloring books, crayons, drawing pads, insect repellent, sweaters (in case it got cold in the mountains), and our two children into the car. Andrew locked the house and Cynthia said ceremoniously, 'Goodbye, house.'

Meg said, 'Goodbye, house.' Then she said, 'Where will we live now?'

'It's not goodbye forever,' said Cynthia. 'We're coming back. Mother! Meg thought we weren't ever coming back!'

'I did not,' said Meg, kicking the back of my seat.

Andrew and I put on our sunglasses and we drove away, over the Lions Gate Bridge and through the main part of Vancouver. We shed our house, the neighborhood, the city, and—at the crossing point between Blaine, Washington, and British Columbia— our country. We were driving east across the United States, taking the most northerly route, and would cross into Canada again at Sarnia, Ontario. I don't know if we chose this route because the Trans-Canada Highway was not completely finished at the time or if we just wanted the feeling of driving through a foreign, a very slightly foreign, country—that extra bit of interest and adventure.

We were both in high spirits. Andrew congratulated the car several times. He said he felt so much better driving it than our old car, a 1951 Austin that slowed down dismally on the hills and had a fussy-old-lady image. So Andrew said now.

'What kind of image does this one have?' said Cynthia. She listened to us carefully and liked to try out new words such as 'image'. Usually she got them right.

'Lively,' I said. 'Slightly sporty. It's not showoff.'

'It's sensible, but it has class,' Andrew said. 'Like my image.'

Cynthia thought that over and said with a cautious pride, 'That means like you think you want to be, Daddy?'

As for me, I was happy because of the shedding. I loved taking off. In my own house, I seemed to be often looking for a place to hide—sometimes from the children but more often from the jobs to be done and the phone ringing and the sociability of the neighborhood. I wanted to hide so that I could get busy at my real work, which was a sort of wooing of distant parts of myself. I lived in a state of siege, always losing just what I wanted to hold on to. But on trips there was no difficulty. I could be talking to Andrew, talking to the children and looking at whatever they wanted me to look at—a pig on a sign, a pony in a field, a Volkswagen on a revolving stand—and pouring lemonade into plastic cups, and all the time those bits and pieces would be flying together inside me. The essential composition would be achieved. This made me hopeful and lighthearted. It was being a watcher that did it. A watcher, not a keeper.

We turned east at Everett and climbed into the Cascades. I showed Cynthia our route on the map. First I showed her the map of the whole United States, which showed also the bottom part of Canada. Then I turned to the separate maps of each of the states we were going to pass through. Washington, Idaho, Montana, North Dakota, Minnesota, Wisconsin. I showed her the dotted line across Lake Michigan, which was the route of the ferry we would take. Then we would drive across Michigan to the bridge that linked the United States and Canada, at Sarnia. Ontario. Home.

Meg wanted to see, too.

'You won't understand,' said Cynthia. But she took the road atlas into the back seat.

'Sit back,' she said to Meg. 'Sit still. I'll show you.'

I could hear her tracing the route for Meg, very accurately, just as I had done it for her. She looked up all the states' maps, knowing how to find them in alphabetical order.

'You know what that line is?' she said. 'It's the road. That line is the road we're driving on. We're going right along this line.'

Meg did not say anything.

'Mother, show me where we are right this minute,' said Cynthia.

I took the atlas and pointed out the road through the mountains, and she took it back and showed it to Meg. 'See where the road is all wiggly?' she said. 'It's wiggly because there are so many turns in it. The wiggles are the turns.' She flipped some pages and waited a moment. 'Now,' she said, 'show me where we are.' Then she called to me, 'Mother, she understands! She pointed to it! Meg understands maps!'

It seems to me now that we invented characters for our children. We had them firmly set to play their parts. Cynthia was bright and diligent, sensitive, courteous, watchful. Sometimes we teased her for being too conscientious, too eager to be what we in fact depended on her to be. Any reproach or failure, any rebuff, went terribly deep with her. She was fair-haired, fair-skinned, easily showing the effects of the sun, raw winds, pride, or humiliation. Meg was more solidly built, more reticent—not rebellious but stubborn sometimes, mysterious. Her silences seemed to us to show her strength of character, and her negatives were taken as signs of an imperturbable independence. Her hair was brown, and we cut it in straight bangs. Her eyes were a light hazel, clear and dazzling.

We were entirely pleased with these characters, enjoying the contradictions as well as the confirmations of them. We disliked the heavy, the uninventive, approach to being parents. I had a dread of turning into a certain kind of mother—the kind whose body sagged and ripened, who moved in a woolly-smelling, milky-smelling fog, solemn with trivial burdens. I believed that all the attention these mothers paid, their need to be burdened, was the cause of colic, bed-wetting, asthma. I favored another approach—the mock desperation, the inflated irony of the professional mothers who wrote for magazines. In those magazine pieces the children were splendidly self-willed, hard-edged, perverse, indomitable. So were the mothers, through their wit, indomitable. The other mothers I warmed to were the sort who would phone up and say, 'Is my embryo Hitler by any chance over at your house?' They cackled clear above the milky fog.

We saw a dead deer strapped across the front of a pickup truck.

'Somebody shot it,' Cynthia said. 'Hunters shoot the deer.'

'It's not hunting season yet,' Andrew said. 'They may have hit it on the road. See the sign for deer crossing?'

'I would cry if we hit one,' Cynthia said sternly.

I had made peanut-butter-and-marmalade sandwiches for the children and salmon-and-mayonnaise for us. But I had not put any lettuce in, and Andrew was disappointed.

'I didn't have any,' I said.

'Couldn't you have got some?'

'I'd have had to buy a whole head of lettuce just to get enough for sandwiches, and I decided it wasn't worth it.'

This was a lie. I had forgotten.

'They're a lot better with lettuce.'

'I didn't think it made that much difference.' After a silence I said, 'Don't be mad.'

'I'm not mad. I like lettuce on sandwiches.'

'I just didn't think it mattered that much.'

'How would it be if I didn't bother to fill up the gas tank?'

'That's not the same thing.'

'Sing a song,' said Cynthia. She started to sing:

> *Five little ducks went out one day,*
> *Over the hills and far away.*
> *One little duck went*
> *'Quack-quack-quack.'*
> *Four little ducks came swimming back.*

Andrew squeezed my hand and said, 'Let's not fight.'

'You're right. I should have got lettuce.'

'It doesn't matter that much.'

I wished that I could get my feelings about Andrew to come together into serviceable and dependable feeling. I had even tried writing two lists, one of things I liked about him, one of things I disliked—in the cauldron of intimate life, things I loved and things I hated—as if I hoped by this to prove something, to come to a conclusion one way or the other. But I gave it up when I saw that all it proved was what I already knew—that I had violent contradictions. Sometimes the very sound of his footsteps seemed to me tyrannical, the set of his mouth smug and mean, his hard, straight body a barrier interposed—quite consciously, even dutifully, and with a nasty pleasure in its masculine authority— between me and whatever joy or lightness I could get in life. Then, with not much warning, he became my good friend and most essential companion. I felt the sweetness of his light bones and serious ideas, the vulnerability of his love, which I imagined to be much purer and more straight-forward than my own. I could be greatly moved by an inflexibility, a harsh propriety, that at other times I scorned. I would think how humble he was, really, taking on such a ready-made role of husband, father, breadwinner, and how I myself in comparison was really a secret monster of egotism. Not so secret, either—not from him.

At the bottom of our fights we served up what we thought were the ugliest truths. ''I know there is something basically self-ish and basically untrustworthy about you,'' Andrew once said. 'I've always known it. I also know that that is why I fell in love with you.'

'Yes,' I said, feeling sorrowful but complacent.

'I know that I'd be better off without you.'

'Yes. You would.'

'You'd be happier without me.'

'Yes.'

And finally—finally—racked and purged, we clasped hands and laughed, laughed at those two benighted people, ourselves. Their grudges, their grievances, their self-justification. We leap-frogged over them. We declared them liars. We would have wine for dinner, or decide to give a party.

I haven't seen Andrew for years, don't know if he is still thin, has gone completely gray, insists on lettuce, tells the truth, or is hearty and disappointed.

We stayed the night in Wenatchee, Washington, where it hadn't rained for weeks. We ate dinner in a restaurant built about a tree—not a sapling in a tub but a tall, sturdy cottonwood. In the early-morning light we climbed out of the irrigated valley, up dry, rocky, very steep hillsides that would seem to lead to more hills, and there on the top was a wide plateau, cut by the great Spokane and Columbia Rivers. Grainland and grassland, mile after mile. There were straight roads here, and little farming towns with grain elevators. In fact, there was a sign announcing that this county we were going through, Douglas County, had one of the highest wheat yields of any county in the United States. The towns had planted shade trees. At least, I thought they had been planted, because there were no such big trees in the countryside.

All this was marvellously welcome to me. 'Why do I love it so much?' I said to Andrew. 'Is it because it isn't scenery?'

'It reminds you of home,' said Andrew. 'A bout of severe nostalgia.' But he said this kindly.

When we said 'home' and meant Ontario, we had very different places in mind. My home was a turkey farm, where my father lived as a widower, and though it was the same house my mother had lived in, had papered, painted, cleaned, furnished, it showed the effects now of neglect and of some wild sociability. A life went on in it that my mother could not have predicted or condoned. There were parties for the turkey crew, the gutters and pluckers, and sometimes one or two of the young men would be living there temporarily, inviting their own friends and having their own impromptu parties. This life, I thought, was better for my father than being lonely, and I did not disapprove, had certainly no right to disapprove. Andrew did not like to go there, naturally enough, because he was not the sort who could sit around the kitchen table with the turkey crew, telling jokes. They were intimidated by him and contemptuous of him, and it seemed to me that my father, when they were around, had to be on their side. And it wasn't only Andrew who had trouble. I could manage those jokes, but it was an effort.

I wished for the days when I was little, before we had the

turkeys. We had cows, and sold the milk to the cheese factory. A turkey farm is nothing like as pretty as a dairy farm or a sheep farm. You can see that the turkeys are on a straight path to becoming frozen carcasses and table meat. They don't have the pretense of a life of their own, a browsing idyll, that cattle have, or pigs in the dappled orchard. Turkeys barns are long, efficient buildings—tin sheds. No beams or hay or warm stables. Even the smell of guano seems thinner and more offensive than the usual smell of stable manure. No hints of hay coils and rail fences and songbirds and the flowering hawthorn. The turkeys were all let out into one long field, which they picked clean. They didn't look like great birds there but like fluttering laundry.

Once, shortly after my mother died and I was married—in fact, I was packing to join Andrew in Vancouver—I was at home alone for a couple of days with my father. There was a freakishly heavy rain all night. In the early light we saw that the turkey field was flooded. At least, the low-lying parts of it were flooded—it was like a lake with many islands. The turkeys were huddled on these islands. Turkeys are very stupid. (My father would say, 'You know a chicken? You know how stupid a chicken is? Well, a chicken is an Einstein compared with a turkey.') But they had managed to crowd to higher ground and avoid drowning. Now they might push each other off, suffocate each other, get cold and die. We couldn't wait for the water to go down. We went out in an old rowboat we had. I rowed and my father pulled the heavy, wet turkeys into the boat and we took them to the barn. It was still raining a little. The job was difficult and absurd and very uncomfortable. We were laughing. I was happy to be working with my father. I felt close to all hard, repetitive, appalling work, in which the body is finally worn out, the mind sunk (though sometimes the spirit can stay marvellously light), and I was homesick in advance for this life and this place. I thought that if Andrew could see me there in the rain, red-handed, muddy, trying to hold on to turkey legs and row the boat at the same time, he would only want to get me out of there and make me forget about it. This raw life angered him. My attachment to it angered him. I thought that I shouldn't have married him. But who else? One of the turkey crew?

And I didn't want to stay there. I might feel bad about leaving, but I would feel worse if somebody made me stay.

Andrew's mother lived in Toronto, in an apartment building looking out on Muir Park. When Andrew and his sister were both at home, his mother slept in the living room. Her husband, a doctor, had died when the children were still too young to go to school. She took a secretarial course and sold her house at Depression prices, moved to this apartment, managed to raise her children, with some help from relatives—her sister Caroline, her brother-in-law Roger. Andrew and his sister went to private schools and to camp in the summer.

'I suppose that was courtesy of the Fresh Air Fund?' I said once, scornful of his claim that he had been poor. To my mind, Andrew's urban life had been sheltered and fussy. His mother came home with a headache from working all day in the noise, the harsh light of a department-store office, but it did not occur to me that hers was a hard or admirable life. I don't think she herself believed that she was admirable—only unlucky. She worried about her work in the office, her clothes, her cooking, her children. She worried most of all about what Roger and Caroline would think.

Caroline and Roger lived on the east side of the park, in a handsome stone house. Roger was a tall man with a bald, freckled head, a fat, firm stomach. Some operation on his throat had deprived him of his voice—he spoke in a rough whisper. But everybody paid attention. At dinner once in the stone house—where all the dining-room furniture was enormous, darkly glowing, palatial—I asked him a question. I think it had to do with Whittaker Chambers, whose story was then appearing in *The Saturday Evening Post*. The question was mild in tone, but he guessed its subversive intent and took to calling me Mrs. Gromyko, referring to what he alleged to be my "sympathies." Perhaps he really craved an adversary, and could not find one. At that dinner I saw Andrew's hand tremble as he lit his mother's cigarette. His Uncle Roger had paid for Andrew's education, and was on the board of directors of several companies.

'He is just an opinionated old man,' Andrew said to me later. 'What is the point of arguing with him?'

Before we left Vancouver, Andrew's mother had written, "Roger seems quite intrigued by the idea of your buying a small car!" Her exclamation mark showed apprehension. At that time, particularly in Ontario, the choice of a small, European car over a large, American car could be seen as some sort of declaration—a declaration of tendencies Roger had been sniffing after all along.

'It isn't that small a car,' said Andrew huffily.

'That's not the point,' I said. 'The point is, it isn't any of his business!'

'He's bored.'

We spent the second night in Missoula. We had been told in Spokane, at a gas station, that there was a lot of repair work going on along Highway 2, and that we were in for a very hot, dusty drive, with long waits, so we turned onto the interstate, and drove through Coeur d'Alene and Kellogg into Montana. After Missoula we turned south, toward Butte, but detoured to see Helena, the state capital. In the car we played Who Am I?

Cynthia was somebody dead, and an American, and a girl. Possibly a lady. She was not in a story. She had not been seen on television. Cynthia had not read about her in a book. She was not anybody who had come to the kindergarten, or a relative of any of Cynthia's friends.

'Is she human?' said Andrew, with a sudden shrewdness.

'No! That's what you forgot to ask!'

'An animal,' I said reflectively.

'Is that a question? Sixteen questions!'

'No, it is not a question. I'm thinking. A dead animal.'

'It's the deer,' said Meg, who hadn't been playing.

'That's not fair!' said Cynthia. 'She's not playing!'

'What deer?' said Andrew.

I said, 'Yesterday.'

'The day before,' said Cynthia. 'Meg wasn't playing. Nobody got it.'

'The deer on the truck,' said Andrew.

'It was a lady deer, because it didn't have antlers, and it was an American and it was dead,' Cynthia said.

Andrew said, 'I think it's kind of morbid, being a dead deer.'

'I got it,' said Meg.

Cynthia said, 'I think I know what morbid is. It's depressing.'

Helena, an old silver-mining town, looked forlorn to us even in the morning sunlight. Then Bozeman and Billings, not forlorn in the slightest—energetic, strung-out towns, with miles of blinding tinsel fluttering over used-car lots. We got too tired and hot even to play Who Am I? These busy, prosaic cities reminded me of similar places in Ontario, and I thought about what was really waiting there—the great tombstone furniture of Roger and Caroline's dining room, the dinners for which I must iron the children's dresses and warn them about forks, and then the other table a hundred miles away, the jokes of my father's crew. The pleasures I had been thinking of—looking at the countryside or drinking a Coke in an old-fashioned drugstore with fans and a high, pressed-tin ceiling—would have to be snatched in between.

'Meg's asleep,' Cynthia said. 'She's so hot. She makes me hot in the same seat with her.'

'I hope she isn't feverish,' I said, not turning around.

What are we doing this for, I thought, and the answer came—to show off. To give Andrew's mother and my father the pleasure of seeing their grandchildren. That was our duty. But beyond that we wanted to show them something. What strenuous children we were, Andrew and I, what relentless seekers of approbation. It was as if at some point we had received an unforgettable, indigestible message—that we were far from satisfactory, and that the most common-place success in life was probably beyond us. Roger dealt out such messages, of course—that was his style—but Andrew's mother, my own mother and father couldn't have meant to do so. All they meant to tell us was 'Watch out. Get along.' When I was in high school my father teased me that I was getting to think I was so smart I would never find a boyfriend. He would have forgotten that in a week. I never forgot it. Andrew and I didn't forget things. We took umbrage.

'I wish there was a beach,' said Cynthia.

'There probably is one,' Andrew said. 'Right around the next curve.'

'There isn't any curve,' she said, sounding insulted.

'That's what I mean.'

'I wish there was some more lemonade.'

'I will just wave my magic wand and produce some,' I said. 'O.K., Cynthia? Would you rather have grape juice? Will I do a beach while I'm at it?'

She was silent, and soon I felt repentant. 'Maybe in the next town there might be a pool,' I said. I looked at the map. 'In Miles City. Anyway, there'll be something cool to drink.'

'How far is it?' Andrew said.

'Not so far,' I said. 'Thirty miles, about.'

'In Miles City,' said Cynthia, in the tones of an incantation, 'there is a beautiful blue swimming pool for children, and a park with lovely trees.'

Andrew said to me, 'You could have started something.'

But there was a pool. There was a park, too, though not quite the oasis of Cynthia's fantasy. Prairie trees—cottonwoods and poplars—worn grass, and a high wire fence around the pool. Within this fence, a wall, not yet completed, of cement blocks. Nobody was around. There were no shouts or splashes. Over the entrance I saw a sign that said the pool was closed every day from noon until two o'clock. It was then twenty-five after twelve.

Nevertheless I called out, 'Is anybody there?' I thought some-body must be around, because there was a small truck parked near the entrance. On the side of the truck were these words: 'We have Brains, to fix your Drains. (We have Roto-Rooter too.)'

A girl came out, wearing a red lifeguard's shirt over her bath-ing suit. 'Sorry, we're closed.'

'We were just driving through,' I said.

'We close every day from twelve until two. It's on the sign.' She was eating a sandwich.

'I saw the sign,' I said. 'But this is the first water we've seen for so long, and the children are awfully hot, and I wondered if they could just dip in and out—just five minutes. We'd watch them.'

A boy came into sight behind her. He was wearing jeans and a T-shirt with the words 'Roto-Rooter' on it.

I was going to say that we were driving from British Colum-bia to Ontario, but I remembered that Canadian place names usually meant nothing to Americans. 'We're driving right across the country,' I said. 'We haven't time to wait for the pool to open. We were just hoping the children could get cooled off.'

Cynthia came running up barefoot behind me. 'Mother. Mother, where is my bathing suit?' Then she stopped, sensing the serious adult negotiations. Meg was climbing out of the car—just wakened, with her top pulled up and her shorts pulled down, showing her pink stomach.

'Is it just those two?' the girl said.

'Just the two. We'll watch them.'

'I can't let any adults in. If it's just the two, I guess I could watch them. I'm having my lunch.' She said to Cynthia, 'Do you want to come in the pool?'

'Yes, please,' said Cynthia firmly.

Meg looked at the ground.

'Just a short time, because the pool is really closed,' I said. 'We appreciate this very much,' I said to the girl.

'Well, I can eat my lunch out there, if it's just the two of them.' She looked toward the car as if she thought I might try to spring some more children on her.

When I found Cynthia's bathing suit, she took it into the changing room. She would not permit anybody, even Meg, to see her naked. I changed Meg, who stood on the front seat of the car. She had a pink cotton bathing suit with straps that crossed and buttoned. There were ruffles across the seat.

'She *is* hot,' I said. 'But I don't think she's feverish.'

I loved helping Meg to dress or undress, because her body still had the solid unself-consciousness, the sweet indifference, something of the milky smell, of a baby's body. Cynthia's body had long ago been pared down, shaped and altered, into Cynthia. We all liked to hug Meg, press and nuzzle her. Sometimes she would scowl and beat us off, and this forthright independence, this ferocious bashfulness, simply made her more appealing, more apt to be teased and tickled in the way of family love.

Andrew and I sat in the car with the windows open. I could hear a radio playing, and thought it must belong to the girl or her boyfriend. I was thirsty, and got out of the car to look for a concession stand, or perhaps a soft-drink machine, somewhere in the park. I was wearing shorts, and the backs of my legs were slick with sweat. I saw a drinking fountain at the other side of the park and was walking toward it in a roundabout way, keeping to the shade of the trees. No place became real till you got out of the car. Dazed with the heat, with the sun on the blistered houses, the pavement, the burned grass, I walked slowly. I paid attention to a poor thin leaf, ground a Popsicle stick under the heel of my sandal, squinted at a trash can strapped to a tree that I would never see again.

Where are the children?

I turned around and moved quickly, not quite running, to a part of the fence beyond which the cement wall was not completed. I could see some of the pool. I saw Cynthia, standing about waist-deep in the water, fluttering her hands on the surface and discreetly watching something at the end of the pool, which I could not see. I thought by her pose, her discretion, the look on her face that she must be watching some byplay between the lifeguard and her boyfriend. I couldn't see Meg, but I thought she must be playing in the shallower water—both the shallow and the deep ends of the pool were out of my sight.

'Cynthia!' I had to call twice before she knew where my voice was coming from. 'Cynthia! Where's Meg?'

It always seems to me, when I recall this scene, that Cynthia turns very gracefully toward me, then turns all around in the water—making me think of a ballerina on point—then spreads her arms in a gesture of the stage 'Dis-ap-peared!'

Cynthia was naturally graceful, and she did take dancing lessons, so these movements may have been as I have described. She did say 'Disappeared,' after looking all around the pool, but the strangely artificial style of speech and gesture, the lack of urgency, is more likely my invention. The fear I felt instantly when I couldn't see Meg—even while I was telling myself she must be in the shallower water—must have made Cynthia's movements seem unbearably slow and inappropriate to me, and the tone in which she could say 'Disappeared' before the implications struck her (or was she covering, at once, some ever-ready guilt?) was heard by me as quite exquisitely, monstrously self-possessed.

I cried out for Andrew, and the lifeguard came into view. She was pointing toward the deep end of the pool, saying, 'What's that?'

There, just within my view, a cluster of pink ruffles appeared, a bouquet, beneath the surface of the water. Why would a lifeguard stop and point, why would she ask what that was, why didn't she just dive into the water and swim to it? She didn't swim, she ran all the way around the edge of the pool. But by this time Andrew was over the fence. So many things seemed not quite plausible—Cynthia's behavior, then the lifeguard's—and now I had the impression that Andrew jumped with one bound over this fence, which seemed about seven feet high. He must have climbed it very quickly, getting a grip on the wire.

I could not jump or climb it, so I ran to the entrance, where there was a sort of latticed gate, locked. It was not very high, and I did pull myself over it. I ran through the cement corridors, through the disinfectant pool for your feet, and came out on the edge of the pool.

The drama was over.

Andrew had got to Meg first, and had pulled her out of the water. He just had to reach over and grab her, because she was swimming somehow, with her head underwater—she was moving toward the edge of the pool. He was carrying her now, and the lifeguard was trotting along behind. Cynthia had climbed out of the water and was running to meet them. The only person aloof from the situation was the boyfriend, who had stayed on the bench at the shallow end, drinking a milkshake. He smiled at me, and I thought that unfeeling of him, even though the danger was past. He may have meant it kindly. I noticed that he had not turned the radio off, just down.

Meg had not swallowed any water. She hadn't even scared herself. Her hair was plastered to her head and her eyes were wide open, golden with amazement.

'I was getting the comb,' she said. 'I didn't know it was deep.'

Andrew said, 'She was swimming! She was swimming by herself. I saw her bathing suit in the water and then I saw her swimming.'

'She nearly drowned,' Cynthia said. 'Didn't she? Meg nearly drowned.'

'I don't know how it could have happened,' said the lifeguard. 'One moment she was there, and the next she wasn't.'

What had happened was that Meg had climbed out of the water at the shallow end and run along the edge of the pool toward the deep end. She saw a comb that somebody had dropped lying on the bottom. She crouched down and reached in to pick it up, quite deceived as to the depth of the water. She went over the edge and slipped into the pool, making such a light splash that nobody heard—not the lifeguard, who was kissing her boyfriend, nor Cynthia, who was watching them. That must have been the moment under the trees when I thought, Where are the children? It must have been the same moment. At that moment Meg was slipping, surprised, into the treacherously clear blue water.

'It's O.K.,' I said to the lifeguard, who was nearly crying. 'She can move pretty fast.' (Though that wasn't what we usually said about Meg at all. We said she thought everything over and took her time.)

'You swam, Meg,' said Cynthia, in a congratulatory way. (She told us about the kissing later.)

'I didn't know it was deep,' Meg said. 'I didn't drown.'

We had lunch at a takeout place, eating hamburgers and fries at a picnic table not far from the highway. In my excitement I forgot to get Meg a plain hamburger, and had to scrape off the relish and mustard with plastic spoons, then wipe the meat with a paper napkin, before she would eat it. I took advantage of the trash can there to clean out the car. Then we resumed driving east, with the car windows open in front. Cynthia and Meg fell asleep in the back seat.

Andrew and I now talked quietly about what had happened. Suppose I hadn't had the impulse just at that moment to check on the children? Suppose we had gone uptown to get drinks, as we had thought of doing? How had Andrew got over the fence? Did he jump or climb? (He couldn't remember.) How had he reached Meg so quickly? And think of the lifeguard not watching. And Cynthia, taken up with the kissing. Not seeing anything else. Not seeing Meg drop over the edge.

Disappeared.

But she swam. She held her breath and came up swimming.

What a chain of lucky links.

That was all we spoke about—luck. But I was compelled to picture the opposite. At this moment we could have been filling out forms. Meg removed from us, Meg's body being prepared for shipment. To Vancouver—where we had never noticed such a thing as a graveyard—or to Ontario? The scribbled drawings she had made this morning would be still in the back seat of the car. How could this be borne all at once, how did people bear it? The plump, sweet shoulders and hands and feet, the fine brown hair, the rather satisfied, secretive expression—all exactly the same as when she had been alive. The most ordinary tragedy. A child drowned in a swimming pool at noon on a sunny day. Things tidied up quickly. The pool open as usual at two o'clock. The lifeguard is a bit shaken up and gets the afternoon off. She drives away with her boyfriend in the Roto-Rooter truck. The body sealed away in some kind of shipping coffin. Sedatives, phone calls, arrangements. Such a sudden vacancy, a blind sinking and shifting. Waking up groggy from the pills, thinking for a moment it wasn't true. Thinking if only we hadn't taken this route, if only they hadn't let us use the pool. Probably no one would ever have known about the comb.

There's something trashy about this kind of imagining, isn't there? Something shameful. Laying your finger on the wire to get the safe shock, feeling a bit of what it's like, then pulling back. I believed that Andrew was more scrupulous than I about such things, and that at this moment he was really trying to think about something else.

When I stood apart from my parents at Steve Gauley's funeral and watched them, and had this new, unpleasant feeling about them, I thought that I was understanding something about them for the first time. It was a deadly-serious thing. I was understanding that they were implicated. Their big, stiff, dressed-up bodies did not stand between me and sudden death, or any kind of death. They gave consent. So it seemed. They gave consent to the death of children and to my death not by anything they said or thought but by the very fact that they had made children—they had made me. They had made me, and for that reason my death—however grieved they were, however they carried on—would seem to them anything but impossible or unnatural. This was a fact, and even then I knew they were not to blame.

But I did blame them. I charged them with effrontery, hypocrisy. And not just on my own behalf. On Steve Gauley's behalf, and on behalf of all children, who knew that by rights they should have sprung up free, to live a new, superior kind of life, not to be caught in the snares of grownups, with their sex and funerals.

Steve Gauley drowned, people said, because he was next thing to an orphan and was let run free. If he had been warned enough and given chores to do and kept in check, he wouldn't have fallen from an untrustworthy tree branch into a spring pond, a full gravel pit near the river—he wouldn't have drowned. He was neglected, he was free, so he drowned. And his father took it as an accident, such as might happen to a dog. He didn't have a good suit for the funeral, and he didn't bow his head for the prayers. But he was the only grownup that I let off the hook. He was the only one I didn't see giving consent. He couldn't prevent anything, but he wasn't implicated in anything, either—not like the others, saying the Lord's Prayer in their unnaturally weighted voices, oozing religion and dishonor.

At Glendive, not far from the North Dakota border, we had a choice—either to continue on the interstate or head northeast, toward Williston, taking Route 16, then some secondary roads that would get us back to Highway 2.

We agreed that the interstate would be faster, and that it was important for us not to spend too much time—that is, money—on the road. Nevertheless, we decided to cut back to Highway 2.

'I just like the idea of it better,' I said.

Andrew said, 'That's because it's what we planned to do in the beginning.'

'We missed seeing Kalispell and Havre. And Wolf Point. I like the names.'

'We'll see them on the way back.'

Andrew's saying 'on the way back' in such an easy tone was a surprising pleasure to me. Of course, I had believed that we would be coming back, with our car and our lives and our family intact, having covered all that distance, having dealt somehow with those loyalties and problems, held ourselves up for inspection in such a foolhardy way. But it was a relief to hear him say it.

'What I can't get over,' said Andrew, 'is how you got the signal. It's got to be some kind of extra sense that mothers have.'

Partly I wanted to believe that, to bask in my extra sense. Partly I wanted to warn him—to warn everybody—never to count on it.

'What I can't understand,' I said, 'is how you got over that fence.'

'Neither can I.'

So we went on, with the two in the back seat trusting us, because of no choice, and we ourselves trusting to be forgiven in time what first had to be seen and condemned by those children: whatever was flippant, arbitrary, careless, callous—all our natural, and particular, mistakes.

LEON ROOKE

A Bolt of White Cloth

A man came by our road carrying an enormous bolt of white cloth on his back. Said he was from the East. Said whoever partook of this cloth would come to know true happiness. Innocence without heartbreak, he said, if that person proved worthy. My wife fingered his cloth, having in mind something for new curtains. It was good quality, she said. Beautifully woven, of a fine, light texture, and you certainly couldn't argue with the color.

'How much is it?' she asked.

'Before I tell you that,' the man said, 'you must tell me truthfully if you've ever suffered.'

'Oh, I've suffered,' she said. 'I've known suffering of some description every day of my natural life.'

I was standing over by the toolshed, with a big smile. My wife is a real joker, who likes nothing better than pulling a person's leg. She's known hardships, this and that upheaval, but nothing I would call down-and-out suffering. Mind you, I don't speak for her. I wouldn't pretend to speak for another person.

This man with the bolt of cloth, however, he clearly had no sense of my wife's brand of humor. She didn't get an itch of a smile out of him. He kept the cloth neatly balanced on his shoulder, wincing a little from the weight and from however far he'd had to carry it, staring hard and straight at my wife the whole time she fooled with him, as if he hoped to peer clear through to her soul. His eyes were dark and brooding and hollowed out some. He was like no person either my wife or me had ever seen before.

'Yes,' he said, 'but suffering of what kind?'

'Worse than I hope forever to carry, I'll tell you that,' my wife said. 'But why are you asking me these questions? I like your cloth and if the price is right I mean to buy it.'

'You can only buy my cloth with love,' he said.

We began right then to understand that he was some kind of oddity. He was not like anybody we'd ever seen and he didn't come from around here. He'd come from a place we'd never heard of, and if that was the East, or wherever, then he was welcome to it.

'Love?' she said. 'Love? There's *love* and there's *love*, mister. What kind are you talking about?' She hitched a head my way, rolling her eyes, as if to indicate that if it was *passionate* love he was talking about then he'd first have to do something with me. He'd have to get me off my simmer and onto full boil. That's what she was telling him, with this mischief in her eyes.

I put down my pitchfork about here, and strolled nearer. I liked seeing my wife dealing with difficult situations. I didn't want to miss anything. My life with that woman has been packed with the unusual. Unusual circumstances, she calls them. Any time she's ever gone out anywhere without me, whether for a day or an hour or for five minutes, she's come back with whopping good stories about what she's seen and heard and what's happened to her. She's come back with reports on these unusual circumstances, these little adventures in which so many people have done so many extraordinary things or behaved in such fabulous or foolish ways. So what was rare this time, I thought, was that it had come visiting. She hadn't had to go out and find it.

'Hold these,' my wife told me. And she put this washtub of clothes in my hands, and went back to hanging wet pieces on the line, which is what she'd been doing when this man with the bolt of cloth ventured up into our yard.

'Love,' she told him. 'You tell me what kind I need, if I'm to buy that cloth. I got good ears and I'm listening.'

The man watched her stick clothespins in her mouth, slap out a good wide sheet, and string it up. He watched her hang two of these, plus a mess of towels, and get her mouth full again before he spoke. He looked about the unhappiest I've ever seen any man look. He didn't have any joy in him. I wondered why he didn't put down that heavy bolt of cloth, and why he didn't step around into a spot of shade. The sun was lick-killing bright in that yard. I was worried he'd faint.

'The ordinary kind,' he said. 'Your ordinary kind of love will buy this cloth.'

My wife flapped her wash and laughed. He was really tickling her. She was having herself a wonderful time.

'What's ordinary?' she said. 'I've never known no *ordinary* love.'

He jumped right in. He got excited just for a second.

'The kind such as might exist between the closest friends,' he said. 'The kind such as might exist between a man and his wife or between parents and children or for that matter the love a boy might have for his dog. That kind of love.'

'I've got that,' she said. 'I've had all three. Last year this time I had me a fourth, but it got run over. Up on the road there, by the tall trees, by a man in a car who didn't even stop.'

'That would have been your cat,' he said. 'I don't know much about cats.'

I put down the washtub. My wife let her arms drop. We looked at him, wondering how he knew about that cat. Then I laughed, for I figured someone down the road must have told him of my wife's mourning over that cat. She'd dug it a grave under the grapevine and said sweet words over it. She sorely missed that cat.

'What's wrong with loving cats?' she asked him. 'Or beasts of the fields? I'm surprised at you.'

The man shifted his burden and worked one shoe into the

ground. He stared off at the horizon. He looked like he knew he'd said something he shouldn't.

She pushed me out of the way. She wanted to get nearer to him. She had something more to say.

'Now listen to me,' she said. 'I've loved lots of things in my life. Lots and lots. *Him!*' she said (pointing at me), '*it*' (pointing to our house), '*them!*' (pointing to the flower beds), '*that*' (pointing to the sky), '*those*' (pointing to the woods), '*this*' (pointing to the ground)—'practically *everything*! There isn't any of it I've hated, and not much I've been indifferent to. Including cats. So put that in your pipe and smoke it.'

Then swooping up her arms and laughing hard, making it plain she bore no grudge but wasn't just fooling.

Funny thing was, hearing her say it, I felt the same way. *It, them, that, those*—they were all beautiful. I couldn't deny it was love I was feeling.

The man with the cloth had turned each way she'd pointed. He'd staggered a time or two but he'd kept up. In fact, it struck me that he'd got a little ahead of her. That he knew where her arm was next going. Some trickle of pleasure was showing in his face. And something else was happening, something I'd never seen. He had his face lifted up to this burning sun. It was big and orange, that sun, and scorching-hot, but he was staring smack into it. He wasn't blinking or squinting. His eyes were wide open.

Madness or miracle, I couldn't tell which.

He strode over to a parcel of good grass.

'I believe you mean it,' he said. 'How much could you use?'

He placed the bolt of white cloth down on the grass and pulled out shiny scissors from his back pocket.

'I bet he's blind,' I whispered to my wife. 'I bet he's got false eyes.'

My wife shushed me. She wasn't listening. She had her excitement hat on; her *unusual circumstances* look. He was offering free cloth for love, ordinary love, and she figured she'd go along with the gag.

How much?

'Oh,' she said, 'maybe eight yards. Maybe ten. It depends on how many windows I end up doing, plus what hang I want, plus the pleating I'm after.'

'You mean to make these curtains yourself?' he asked. He was already down on his knees, smoothing the bolt. Getting set to roll it out.

'Why, sure,' she said. 'I don't know who else would do it for me. I don't know who else I would ask.'

He nodded soberly, not thinking about it. 'That's so,' he said casually. 'Mend your own fences first.' He was perspiring in the sun, and dishevelled, as though he'd been on the road a long time. His shoes had big holes in them and you could see the blistered soles of his feet, but he had an air of exhilaration now. His hair fell down over his eyes and he shoved the dark locks back. I got the impression that some days he went a long time between customers; that he didn't find cause to give away this cloth every day.

He got a fair bit unrolled. It certainly did look like prime goods, once you saw it spread out on the grass in that long expanse.

'It's so pretty!' My wife said. 'Heaven help me, but I think it is *prettier* than grass!'

'It's pretty, all right,' he said. 'It's a wing-dinger. Just tell me when to stop,' he said. 'Just shout yoo-hoo.'

'Hold up a minute,' she said. 'I don't want to get greedy. I don't want you rolling off more than we can afford.'

'You can afford it,' he said.

He kept unrolling. He was up past the well house by now, whipping it off fast, though the bolt didn't appear to be getting any smaller. My wife had both hands up over her mouth. Half of her wanted to run into the house and get her purse so she could pay; the other half wanted to stay and watch this man unfurl his beautiful cloth. She whipped around to me, all agitated.

'I believe he means it,' she said. 'He means us to have this cloth. What do I do?'

I shook my head. This was her territory. It was the kind of adventure constant to her nature and necessary to her well-being.

'Honey,' I said, 'you deal with it.'

The sun was bright over everything. It was whipping-hot. There wasn't much wind but I could hear the clothes flapping on the line. A woodpecker had himself a pole somewhere and I could hear him pecking. The sky was wavy blue. The trees seemed to be swaying.

He was up by the front porch now, still unrolling. It surprised us both that he could move so fast.

'Yoo-hoo,' my wife said. It was no more than a peep, the sound you might make if a butterfly lands on your hand.

'Wait,' he said. 'One thing. One question I meant to ask. All this talk of love, your *it*, your *those* and *them*, it slipped my mind.'

'Let's hear it,' my wife said. 'Ask away.' It seemed to me that she spoke out of a trance. That she was as dazzled as I was.

'You two got no children,' he said. 'Why is that? You're out here on this nice farm, and no children to your name. Why is that?'

We hadn't expected this query from him. It did something to the light in the yard and how we saw it. It was as if some giant dark bird had fluttered between us and the sun. Without knowing it, we sidled closer to each other. We fumbled for the other's hand. We stared off every which way. No one on our road had asked that question in a long, long time; they hadn't asked it in some years.

'We're not able,' we said. Both of us spoke at the same time. It seemed to me that it was my wife's voice which carried; mine was some place down in my chest, and dropping, as if it meant to crawl on the ground.

'We're not able,' we said. That time it came out pure, without any grief to bind it. It came out the way we long ago learned how to say it.

'Oh,' he said. 'I see.' He mumbled something else. He kicked the ground and took a little walk back and forth. He seemed angry, though not at us. 'Wouldn't you know it?' he said. 'Wouldn't you know it?'

He swore a time or two. He kicked the ground. He surely didn't like it.'

'We're over that now,' my wife said. 'We're past that caring.'

'I bet you are,' he said. 'You're past that little misfortune.'

He took to unrolling his bolt again, working with his back to the sun. Down on his knees, scrambling, smoothing the material. Sweating and huffing. He was past the front porch now, and still going, getting on toward that edge where the high weeds grew.

'About here, do you think?' he asked.

He'd rolled off about fifty yards.

My wife and I slowly shook our heads, not knowing what to think.

'Say the word,' he told us. 'I can give you more if more is what you want.'

'I'd say you were giving us too much,' my wife said. 'I'd say we don't need nearly that much.'

'Never mind that,' he said. 'I'm feeling generous today.'

He nudged the cloth with his fingers and rolled off a few yards more. He would have gone on unwinding his cloth had the weeds not stopped him. He stood and looked back over the great length he had unwound.

'Looks like a long white road, don't it?' he said. 'You could walk that road and your feet never get dirty.'

My wife clenched my hand; it was what we'd both been thinking.

SnipSnipSnip. He began snipping. His scissors raced over the material. *SnipSnipSnip*. The cloth was sheared clear and clean of his bolt, yet it seemed to me the size of that bolt hadn't lessened any. My wife saw it too.

'He's got cloth for all eternity,' she said. 'He could unroll that cloth till doomsday.'

The man laughed. We were whispering this, but way up by the weeds he heard us. 'There's doom and there's doom,' he said. '*Which* doomsday?'

I had the notion he'd gone through more than one. That he knew the picture from both sides.

'It *is* smart as grass,' he said. 'Smarter. It never needs watering.' He chuckled at that, spinning both arms. Dancing a little. 'You could make *nighties* out of this,' he said. 'New bedsheets. Transform your whole bedroom.'

My wife made a face. She wasn't too pleased, talking *nighties* with another man.

Innocence without heartbreak, I thought. That's what we're coming to.

He nicely rolled up the cloth he'd sheared off and presented it to my wife. 'I hope you like it,' he said. 'No complaints yet. Maybe you can make yourself a nice dress as well. Maybe two or three. Make him some shirts. I think you'll find there's plenty here.'

'Goodness, it's light,' she said.

'Not if you've been carrying it long as I have,' he said. He pulled a blue bandanna from his pocket and wiped his face and neck. He ran his hand through his hair and slicked it back. He looked up at the sky. His dark eyes seemed to have cleared up some. They looked less broody now. 'Gets hot,' he said, 'working in this sun. But a nice day. I'm glad I found you folks home.'

'Oh, we're most always home,' my wife said.

I had to laugh at that. My wife almost never *is* home. She's forever gallivanting over the countryside, checking up on this person and that, taking them her soups and jams and breads.

'We're homebodies, us two.'

She kept fingering the cloth and sighing over it. She held it up against her cheek and with her eyes closed rested herself on it. The man hoisted his own bolt back on his shoulder; he seemed ready to be going. I looked at my wife's closed lids, at the soft look she had.

I got trembly, fearful of what might happen if that cloth didn't work out.

'Now look,' I said to him, 'what's wrong with this cloth? Is it going to rot inside a week? Tomorrow is some *other* stranger going to knock on our door saying we owe him a hundred or five hundred dollars for this cloth? Mister, I don't understand you,' I said.

He hadn't bothered with me before; now he looked me dead in the eye. 'I can't help being a stranger,' he said. 'If you never set eyes on me before, I guess that's what I would have to be. Don't you like strangers? Don't you trust them?'

My wife jumped in. Her face was fiery, like she thought I had wounded him. 'We like strangers just fine,' she said. 'We've helped out many a-one. No, I can't say our door has ever been closed to whoever it is comes by. Strangers can sit in our kitchen just the same as our friends.'

He smiled at her but kept his stern look for me. 'As to your questions,' he said, 'You're worried about the golden goose, I can see that. Fair enough. No, your cloth will not rot. It will not shred, fade, or tear. Nor will it ever need cleaning, either. This cloth requires no upkeep whatsoever. Though a sound heart helps. A sweet disposition, too. Innocence without heartbreak, as I told you. And your wife, if it's her making the curtains or making herself a dress, she will find it to be an amazingly easy cloth to work with. It will practically do the job itself. No, I don't believe you will ever find you have any reason to complain of the quality of that cloth.'

My wife had it up to her face again. She had her face sunk in it.

'Goodness,' she said, 'it's *soft*! It smells so fresh. It's like someone singing a song to me.'

The man laughed. 'It *is* soft,' he said. 'But it can't sing a note, or has never been known to.'

It was my wife singing. She had this little hum under the breath.

'This is the most wonderful cloth in the world,' she said.

He nodded. 'I can't argue with you on that score,' he said. Then he turned again to me. 'I believe your wife is satisfied,' he said. 'But if you have any doubts, if you're worried someone is going to knock on your door tomorrow asking you for a hundred or five hundred dollars, I suppose I could write you up a guarantee. I could give you a PAID IN FULL.'

He was making me feel ashamed of myself. They both were. 'No, no,' I said, 'if she's satisfied then I am. And I can see she's tickled pink. No, I beg your pardon. I meant no offense.'

'No offense taken,' he said.

But his eyes clouded a token. He gazed off at our road and up along the stand of trees and his eyes kept roaming until they snagged the sun. He kept his eyes there, unblinking, open, staring at the sun. I could see the red orbs reflected in his eyes.

'There is one thing,' he said.

I caught my breath and felt my wife catch hers. The hitch? A hitch, after all? Coming so late?

We waited.

He shuffled his feet. He brought out his bandanna and wiped his face again. He stared at the ground.

'Should you ever stop loving,' he said, 'you shall lose this cloth and all else. You shall wake up one morning and it and all else will no longer be where you left it. It will all be gone and you will not know where you are. You will not know what to do with yourself. You will wish you'd never been born.'

My wife's eyes went saucer-size.

He had us in some kind of spell.

Hocus-pocus, I thought. He is telling us some kind of hocus-pocus. Yet I felt my skin shudder; I felt the goose bumps rise.

'That's it?' my wife said. 'That's the only catch?'

He shrugged. 'That's it,' he said. 'Not much, is it? Not a whisper of menace for a pair such as yourselves.'

My wife's eyes were gauzed over; there was a wetness in them.

'Hold on,' she said. 'Don't you be leaving yet. Hold this, honey.'

She put the cloth in my arms. Then she hastened over to the well, pitched the bucket down, and drew it up running over with fresh water.

'Here,' she said, coming back with a good dipperful. 'Here's a nice drink of cool water. You need it on a day like this.'

The man drank. He held the dipper in both hands, with the tips of his fingers, and drained the dipper dry, then wiped his chin with the back of a hand.

'I did indeed,' he said. 'That's very tasty water. I thank you.'

'That's good water,' she said. 'That well has been here to a hundred years. You could stay on for supper,' she said. 'It's getting on toward that time and I have a fine stew on the stove, with plenty to spare.'

'That's kind of you,' he said back, 'and I'm grateful. But I'd best pass on up your road while there's still daylight left, and see who else might have need of this cloth.'

My wife is not normally a demonstrative woman, not in public. Certainly not with strangers. You could have knocked me over with a feather when she up and kissed him full on the mouth, with a nice hug to boot.

'There's payment,' she said, 'if our money's no good.'

He blushed, trying to hide his pleasure. It seemed to me she had him wrapped around her little finger . . . or the other way around.

'You kiss like a woman,' he said. 'Like one who knows what kissing is for, and can't hardly stop herself.'

It was my wife's turn to blush.

I took hold of her hand and held her down to grass, because it seemed to me another kiss or two and she'd fly right away with him.

He walked across the yard and up by the well house, leaving by the same route he had come. Heading for the road. At the turn, he spun around and waved.

'You could try the Hopkins place!' my wife called. 'There's a fat woman down that road got a sea of troubles. She could surely use some of that cloth.'

He smiled and again waved. Then we saw his head and his bolt of white cloth bobbing along the weeds as he took the dips and rises in the road. Then he went on out of sight.

'There's that man with some horses down that road!' my wife called. 'You be careful of him!'

It seemed we heard some sound come back, but whether it was his we couldn't say.

My wife and I stood a long time in the yard, me holding the dipper and watching her, while she held her own bolt of cloth in her arms, staring off to where he'd last been.

Then she sighed dreamily and went inside.

I went on down to the barn and looked after the animals. Getting my feeding done. I talked a spell to them. Talking to animals is soothing to me, and they like it too. They pretend to stare at the walls or the floor as they're munching their feed down, but I know they listen to me. We had us an *unusual circumstances* chat. 'That man with the cloth,' I said. 'Maybe you can tell me what you make of him.'

Thirty minutes later I heard my wife excitedly calling me. She was standing out on the back doorstep, with this incredulous look.

'I've finished,' she said. 'I've finished the windows. *Nine* windows. It beats me how.'

I started up to the house. Her voice was all shaky. Her face flushed, flinging her arms about. Then she got this new look on.

'Wait!' she said. 'Stay there! Give me ten minutes!'

And she flung herself back inside, banging the door. I laughed. It always gave me a kick how she ordered me around.

I got the milk pail down under the cow. Before I'd touched and drained all four teats she was calling again.

'Come look, come look, oh come look!'

She was standing in the open doorway, with the kitchen to her back. Behind her, through the windows, I could see the streak of a red sunset and how it lit up the swing of trees. But I wasn't looking there. I was looking at her. Looking and swallowing hard and trying to remember how a body produced human speech. I had never thought of white as a color she could wear. White, it pales her some. It leaves her undefined and washes out what parts I like best. But she looked beautiful now. In her new dress she struck me down to my bootstraps. She made my chest break.

'Do you like it?' she said.

I went running up to her. I was up against her, hugging her and lifting her before she'd even had a chance to get set. I'd never held on so tightly or been so tightly held back.

Truth is, it was the strangest thing. Like we were both so innocent we hadn't yet shot up out of new ground.

'Come see the curtains,' she whispered. 'Come see the new sheets. Come see what else I've made. You'll see it all. You'll see how our home has been transformed.'

I crept inside. There was something holy about it. About it and about us and about those rooms and the whole wide world. Something radiant. Like you had to put your foot down easy and hold it down or you'd float on up.

'That's it,' she said. 'That's how I feel too.'

That night in bed, trying to figure it out, we wondered how Ella Mae down the road had done. How the people all along our road had made out.

'No worry,' my wife said. 'He'll have found a bonanza around

here. There's heaps of decent people in this neck of the woods.'
   'Wonder where he is now?' we said.
   'Wonder where he goes next?'
   'Where he gets that cloth?'
   'Who he *is*?'

We couldn't get to sleep, wondering about that.

CAROL SHIELDS

Mrs Turner
Cutting the Grass

Oh, Mrs Turner is a sight cutting the grass on a hot afternoon in
June! She climbs into an ancient pair of shorts and ties on her
halter top and wedges her feet into crepe-soled sandals and covers her red-gray frizz with Gord's old golf cap—Gord is dead
now, ten years ago, a seizure on a Saturday night while winding
the mantel clock.

The grass flies up around Mrs Turner's knees. Why doesn't
she use a catcher, the Saschers next door wonder. Everyone
knows that leaving the clippings like that is bad for the lawn.
Each fallen blade of grass throws a minute shadow which im-
pedes growth and repair. The Saschers themselves use their clippings to make compost which they hope one day will be ripe as
the good manure that Sally Sascher's father used to spread on
his fields down near Emerson Township.

Mrs Turner's carelessness over the clippings plucks away at
Sally, but her husband Roy is far more concerned about the Killex
that Mrs Turner dumps on her dandelions. It's true that in Winnipeg the dandelion roots go right to the middle of the earth, but
Roy is patient and persistent in pulling them out, knowing exactly how to grasp the coarse leaves in his hand and how much
pressure to apply. Mostly they come up like corks with their
roots intact. And he and Sally are experimenting with new ways
to cook dandelion greens, believing as they do that the compo-

nents of nature are arranged for a specific purpose—if only that
purpose can be divined.

In the early summer Mrs Turner is out every morning by ten
with her sprinkling can of chemical killer, and Roy, watching
from his front porch, imagines how this poison will enter the
ecosystem and move by quick capillary surges into his fenced
vegetable plot, newly seeded now with green beans and lettuce.
His children, his two little girls aged two and four—that they
should be touched by such poison makes him morose and angry. But he and Sally so far have said nothing to Mrs Turner
about her abuse of the planet because they're hoping she'll go
into an old-folks home soon or maybe die, and then all will proceed as it should.

High-school girls on their way home in the afternoon see Mrs
Turner cutting her grass and are mildly, momentarily repelled
by the lapped, striated flesh on her upper thighs. At her age.
Doesn't she realize? Every last one of them is intimate with the
vocabulary of skin care and knows that what has claimed Mrs
Turner's thighs is the enemy called cellulite, but they can't understand why she doesn't take the trouble to hide it. It makes
them queasy; it makes them fear for the future.

The things Mrs Turner doesn't know would fill the Saschers'
new compost pit, would sink a ship, would set off a tidal wave,
would make her want to kill herself. Back and forth, back and
forth she goes with the electric lawn mower, the grass flying out
sideways like whiskers. Oh, the things she doesn't know! She
has never heard, for example, of the folk-rock recording star
Neil Young, though the high school just around the corner from
her house happens to be the very school Neil Young attended as
a lad. His initials can actually be seen carved on one of the desks,
and a few of the teachers say they remember him, a quiet fellow
of neat appearance and always very polite in class. The desk
with the initials N.Y. is kept in a corner of Mr Pring's home-
room, and it's considered lucky—despite the fact that the re-
nowned singer wasn't a great scholar—to touch the incised letters

just before an exam. Since it's exam time now, the second week of June, the girls walking past Mrs Turner's front yard (and shuddering over her display of cellulite) are carrying on their fingertips the spiritual scent, the essence, the fragrance, the aura of Neil Young, but Mrs Turner is as ignorant of that fact as the girls are that she, Mrs Turner, possesses a first name—which is Geraldine.

Not that she's ever been called Geraldine. Where she grew up in Boissevain, Manitoba, she was known always—the Lord knows why—as Girlie Fergus, the youngest of the three Fergus girls and the one who got herself in hot water. Her sister Em went to normal school and her sister Muriel went to Brandon to work at Eatons, but Girlie got caught one night—she was nineteen—in a Boissevain hotel room with a local farmer, married, named Gus MacGregor. It was her father who got wind of where she might be and came banging on the door, shouting and weeping. 'Girlie, Girlie, what have you done to me?'

Girlie had been working in the Boissevain Dairy since she'd left school at sixteen and had a bit of money saved up, and so, a week after the humiliation in the local hotel, she wrote a farewell note to the family, crept out of the house at midnight and caught the bus to Winnipeg. From there she got another bus down to Minneapolis, then to Chicago and finally New York City. The journey was endless and wretched, and on the way across Indiana and Ohio and Pennsylvania she saw hundreds and hundreds of towns whose unpaved streets and narrow blinded houses made her fear some conspiratorial, punishing power had carried her back to Boissevain. Her father's soppy-stern voice sang and sang in her ears as the wooden bus rattled its way eastward. It was summer, 1930.

New York was immense and wonderful, dirty, perilous and puzzling. She found herself longing for a sight of real earth which she assumed must lie somewhere beneath the tough pavement. On the other hand, the brown flat-roofed factories with their little windows tilted skyward pumped her full of happiness, as did the dusty trees, when she finally discovered them, lining the long avenues. Every last person in the world seemed to be outside, walking around, filling the streets, and every corner breezed with noise and sunlight. She had to pinch herself to believe this was the same sunlight that filtered its way into the rooms of the house back in Boissevain, fading the curtains but nourishing her mother's ferns. She sent postcards to Em and Muriel that said, 'Don't worry about me. I've got a job in the theater business.'

It was true. For eight and a half months she was an usherette in the Lamar Movie Palace in Brooklyn. She loved her perky maroon uniform, the way it fit on her shoulders, the way the strips of crinkly gold braid outlined her figure. With a little flashlight in hand she was able to send streams of light across the furry darkness of the theater and onto the plum-colored aisle carpet. The voices from the screen talked on and on. She felt after a time that their resonant declarations and tender replies belonged to her.

She met a man named Kiki her first month in New York and moved in with him. His skin was as black as ebony. *As black as ebony*—that was the phrase that hung like a ribbon on the end of his name, and it's also the phrase she uses, infrequently, when she wants to call up his memory, though she's more than a little doubtful about what *ebony* is. It may be a kind of stone, she thinks, something round and polished that comes out of a deep mine.

Kiki was a good-hearted man, though she didn't like the beer he drank, and he stayed with her, willingly, for several months after she had to stop working because of the baby. It was the baby itself that frightened him off, the way it cried probably. Leaving fifty dollars on the table, he slipped out one July afternoon when Girlie was shopping, and went back to Troy, New York, where he'd been raised.

Her first thought was to take the baby and get on a bus and go find him, but there wasn't enough money, and the thought of the baby crying all the way on the hot bus made her feel tired. She was worried about the rent and about the little red sores in the baby's ears—it was a boy, rather sweetly formed, with wonderful smooth feet and hands. On a murderously hot night, a night when the humidity was especially bad, she wrapped him in a clean piece of sheeting and carried him all the way to Brooklyn Heights where the houses were large and solid and surrounded by grass. There was a house on a corner she particularly liked because it had a wide front porch (like those in Boissevain) with a curved railing—and parked on the porch, its brake on, was a beautiful wicker baby carriage. It was here she placed her baby, giving one last look to his sleeping face, as round and calm as the moon. She walked home, taking her time, swinging her legs. If she had known the word *foundling*—which she didn't—she would have bounded along on its rhythmic back, so airy and wide did the world seem that night.

Most of these secrets she keeps locked away inside her mottled thighs or in the curled pinkness of her genital flesh. She has no idea what happened to Kiki, whether he ever went off to Alaska as he wanted to or whether he fell down a flight of stone steps in the silverware factory in Troy, New York, and died of head injuries before his 30th birthday. Or what happened to her son—whether he was bitten that night in the baby carriage by a rabid neighborhood cat or whether he was discovered the next morning and adopted by the large, loving family who lived in the house. As a rule, Girlie tries not to think about the things she can't even guess at. All she thinks is that she did the best she could under the circumstances.

In a year she saved enough money to take the train home to Boissevain. She took with her all her belongings, and also gifts for Em and Muriel, boxes of hose, bottles of apple-blossom cologne, phonograph records. For her mother she took an embroidered apron and for her father a pipe made of curious gnarled wood. 'Girlie, my Girlie,' her father said, embracing her at the Boissevain station. Then he said, 'Don't ever leave us again,' in a way that frightened her and made her resolve to leave as quickly as possible.

But she didn't go so far the second time around. She and Gordon Turner—he was, for all his life, a tongue-tied man, though he did manage a proper proposal—settled down in Winnipeg, first in St Boniface where the rents were cheap and then Fort Rouge and finally the little house in River Heights just around the corner from the high school. It was her husband, Gord, who planted the grass that Mrs Turner now shaves in the summertime. It was Gord who trimmed and shaped the caragana hedge and Gord who painted the little shutters with the cut-out hearts. He was a man who loved every inch of his house, the wide wooden steps, the oak door with its glass inset, the radiators and the baseboards and the snug sash windows. And he loved every inch of his wife, Girlie, too, saying to her once and only once that he knew about her past (meaning Gus MacGregor and the incident in the Boissevain Hotel), and that as far as he was concerned the slate had been wiped clean. Once he came home with a little package in his pocket; inside was a diamond ring, delicate and glittering. Once he took Girlie on a picnic all the way up to Steep Rock, and in the woods he took off her dress and underthings and kissed every part of her body.

After he died, Girlie began to travel. She was far from rich, as she liked to say, but with care she could manage one trip every spring.

She has never known such ease. She and Em and Muriel have been to Disneyland as well as Disneyworld. They've been to Europe, taking a sixteen-day trip through seven countries. The three of them have visited the south and seen the famous antebellum houses of Georgia, Alabama and Mississippi, after which they spent a week in the city of New Orleans. They went to Mexico one year and took pictures of Mayan ruins and queer shadowy gods cut squarely from stone. And three years ago they did what they swore they'd never have the nerve to do: they got on an airplane and went to Japan.

The package tour started in Tokyo where Mrs Turner ate, on her first night there, a chrysanthemum fried in hot oil. She saw a village where everyone earned a living by making dolls and another village where everyone made pottery. Members of the tour group, each holding up a green flag so their tour leader could keep track of them, climbed on a little train, zoomed off to Osaka where they visited an electronics factory, and then went to a restaurant to eat uncooked fish. They visited more temples and shrines than Mrs Turner could keep track of. Once they stayed the night in a Japanese hotel where she and Em and Muriel bedded down on floor mats and little pillows stuffed with cracked wheat, and woke up, laughing, with backaches and shooting pains in their legs.

That was the same day they visited the Golden Pavilion in Kyoto. The three-storied temple was made of wood and had a roof like a set of wings and was painted a soft old flaky gold. Everybody in the group took pictures—Em took a whole roll—and bought postcards; everybody, that is, except a single tour member, the one they all referred to as the Professor.

The Professor traveled without a camera, but jotted notes almost continuously into a little pocket scribbler. He was bald, had a trim body and wore Bermuda shorts, sandals and black nylon socks. Those who asked him learned that he really was a professor, a teacher of English poetry in a small college in Massachusetts. He was also a poet who, at the time of the Japanese trip, had published two small chapbooks based mainly on the breakdown of his marriage. The poems, sadly, had not caused much stir.

It grieved him to think of that paltry, guarded nut-like thing that was his artistic reputation. His domestic life had been too cluttered; there had been too many professional demands; the political situation in America had drained him of energy—these were the thoughts that buzzed in his skull as he scribbled and scribbled, like a man with a fever, in the back seat of a tour bus traveling through Japan.

Here in this crowded, confused country he discovered sim-
plicity and order and something spiritual, too, which he recognized as being authentic. He felt as though a flower, something
like a lily, only smaller and tougher, had unfurled in his hand
and was nudging along his fountain pen. He wrote and wrote,
shaken by catharsis, but lulled into a new sense of his powers.

Not surprisingly, a solid little book of poems came out of his
experience. It was published soon afterwards by a well-thought-of
Boston publisher who, as soon as possible, sent him around the
United States to give poetry readings.

Mostly the Professor read his poems in universities and col-
leges where his book was already listed on the Contemporary
Poetry course. He read in faculty clubs, student centers, class-
rooms, gymnasiums and auditoriums, and usually, part way
through a reading, someone or other would call from the back
of the room, 'Give us your Golden Pavilion poem.'

He would have preferred to read his Fuji meditation or the
tone poem on the Inner Sea, but he was happy to oblige his au-
diences, though he felt 'A Day At The Golden Pavilion' was a
somewhat light piece, even what is sometimes known on the
circuit as a 'crowd pleaser'. People (admittedly they were mostly
undergraduates) laughed out loud when they heard it; he read it
well, too, in a moist, avuncular amateur actor's voice, reminding himself to pause frequently, to look upward and raise an
ironic eyebrow.

The poem was not really about the Golden Pavilion at all, but
about three midwestern lady tourists who, while viewing the
temple and madly snapping photos, had talked incessantly and
in loud, flat-bottomed voices about knitting patterns, indigestion, sore feet, breast lumps, the cost of plastic raincoats and a
previous trip they'd made together to Mexico. They had wondered, these three—noisily, repeatedly—who back home in Manitoba should receive a postcard, what they'd give for an honest
cup of tea, if there was an easy way to remove stains from an

electric coffee maker, and where they would go the following year—Hawaii? They were the three furies, the three witches, who for vulgarity and tastelessness formed a shattering counterpoint to the Professor's own state of transcendence. He had been affronted, angered, half-crazed.

One of the sisters, a little pug of a woman, particularly stirred his contempt, she of the pink pantsuit, the red toenails, the grapefruity buttocks, the overly bright souvenirs, the garish Mexican straw bag containing Dentyne chewing gum, aspirin, breath mints, sun goggles, envelopes of saccharine, and photos of her dead husband standing in front of a squat, ugly house in Winnipeg. This defilement she had spread before the ancient and exquisitely proportioned Golden Pavilion of Kyoto, proving — and here the Professor's tone became grave—proving that sublime beauty can be brought to the very doorway of human eyes, ears and lips and remain unperceived.

When he comes to the end of 'A Day At The Golden Pavilion' there is generally a thoughtful half second of silence, then laughter and applause. Students turn in their seats and exchange looks with their fellows. They have seen such unspeakable tourists themselves. There was old Auntie Marigold or Auntie Flossie. There was that tacky Mrs Shannon with her rouge and her jewelry. They know—despite their youth they know—the irreconcilable distance between taste and banality. Or perhaps that's too harsh; perhaps it's only the difference between those who know about the world and those who don't.

It's true Mrs Turner remembers little about her travels. She's never had much of a head for history or dates; she never did learn, for instance, the difference between a Buddhist temple and a Shinto shrine. She gets on a tour bus and goes and goes, and that's all there is to it. She doesn't know if she's going north or south or east or west. What does it matter? She's having a grand time. And she's reassured, always, by the sameness of the world. She's never heard the word *commonality*, but is nevertheless fused with its sense. In Japan she was made as happy to see carrots and lettuce growing in the fields as she was to see sunlight, years earlier, pouring into the streets of New York City. Everywhere she's been she's seen people eating and sleeping and working and making things with their hands and urging things to grow. There have been cats and dogs, fences and bicycles and telephone poles, and objects to buy and take care of; it is amazing, she thinks, that she can understand so much of the world and that it comes to her as easily as bars of music floating out of a radio.

Her sisters have long forgotten about her wild days. Now the three of them love to sit on tour buses and chatter away about old friends and family members, their stern father and their mother who never once took their part against him. Muriel carries on about her children (a son in California and a daughter in Toronto) and she brings along snaps of her grandchildren to pass round. Em has retired from school teaching and is a volunteer in the Boissevain Local History Museum, to which she has donated several family mementos: her father's old carved pipe and her mother's wedding veil and, in a separate case, for all the world to see, a white cotton garment labeled 'Girlie Fergus' Underdrawers, handmade, trimmed with lace, circa 1918'. If Mrs Turner knew the word *irony* she would relish this. Even without knowing the word irony, she relishes it.

The professor from Massachusetts has won an important international award for his book of poems; translation rights have been sold to a number of foreign publishers; and recently his picture appeared in the *New York Times*, along with a lengthy quotation from 'A Day At The Golden Pavilion'. How providential, some will think, that Mrs Turner doesn't read the *New York Times* or attend poetry readings, for it might injure her deeply to know how she appears in certain people's eyes, but then there are so many things she doesn't know.

In the summer as she cuts the grass, to and fro, to and fro, she waves to everyone she sees. She waves to the high-school girls who timidly wave back. She hollers hello to Sally and Roy Sascher and asks them how their garden is coming on. She cannot imagine that anyone would wish her harm. All she's done is live her life. The green grass flies up in the air, a buoyant cloud swirling about her head. Oh, what a sight is Mrs Turner cutting her grass and how, like an ornament, she shines.

ELIZABETH SPENCER

Madonna

When alone there, coming there alone, I sometimes stop and
rub my hand across the wood on the outside banister. I lean and
smell the wood, hoping no-one to think I'm crazy is passing in
the little street, though down in that area any watcher is likely
to be crazy, too. The banister is painted grey, weather-worn,
uneven. The smell has something like damp and old paint shreds
in it, but underneath those there is the sound odour of heart-
wood, called up by the sun. Sun and wood together warm me,
make me know the back of my neck, the touch of my own hand,
the set of my ankle: all that perennially is. The bushes are
growing up taller near the door and are hanging over onto the
steps, also lifting up against the windows. Their green is June-
fresh, the leaf is large, I do not know the name.

I look, debate going in. The present tenants have kept the
off-white bleached-denim draperies I selected six years back—I
can see beyond the fold of one to the empty fireplace. If I mount
two steps more I will be pressing my face to the pane as I have
many times since the Eckleses left, seeing into the narrow hall
past the stairwell, seeing ghost images in motion. There am I as I
was five years ago, not much different; Bob Eckles is following, height overtopping me, moving in neat sand-coloured chino
trousers, and I, swaying now and then out of line with his more
direct advance, revealed to be in dark cotton, the piping of the
sleeveless shoulder cutting into deeply tanned flesh. His two steps
make an easy three of mine. Young America follows at my san-

dal heel. Young America is here on a Montreal street because of principles about the Vietnam War. High principles. Oh, very high.

He pulls the blinds. His wife is still in the hospital with the baby, coming home in a day or so, the third time they've both been sick since that hard birth back in the dark, snow-streaked winter. He knows I like her, would do anything for them, have done all I can since the moment of their appearance. 'But this is a thing apart from all that . . . different, altogether different,' he's said to me, more than once. My clothes are dropping onto a chair. His fingers touch my arm, press into my bare back. As their warmth spreads out, my nerve-ends leap to life, wild and strong. 'I don't like to do this here,' I murmur. 'Why not?' 'You know why not.' 'Anywhere's the same.' 'After a point, I guess.' 'You guess? You know.' We're kissing, and the words float out toward nothing.

At the memory, my spine shudders, I spin off as if from a physical blow, lean against the warm wood, face down.

I have to ring the bell now. Somebody will notice I'm just standing there like a woman in a dream, or drunk, or fainting from the sun. The street is a narrow old one where some people stay on for years and some of those, secluded penny-counters, see life from windows only, a patch of pavement, two façades, a changing tree. I mount to the landing, ring. The face that appears in the left of two oblong window panes that flank the door is not that of Bob or Mary Eckles. It is a woman, gaunt and ugly, with an Indian's large bone structure at the eye sockets. Mary Eckles was gentle with long light-coloured hair; at a time when good little American madonna faces might be found with a joint stuck between their lips, she never smoked, sipped milk, was coaxed to eat enough. She had a musical voice, pleasant and low. The large woman back of the door recognizes me; her landlady, after all. She yanks the door open, lets out a squawk like an old phonograph record.

'Oah! It's yew.'

'Excuse me, Mrs Welford,' I go into my lie. 'I had a call from a tenant on my Ansaphone—I couldn't make the name out. I had to come down this way, so I thought I'd ask. Was it you?'

'No, we ain't called I know of. You remember about them storm windows, eh?'

'Oh, that's being taken care of. You'll get them back before fall.'

'No, it wasn't us.'

'Sorry to bother you.'

'Why don't your husband never come?'

'I told you before. He's tied up downtown and in Westmount. These below St. Catherine are my job.'

Shall I say: I never dreamed of managing any rental property, low-rent or high-rent, before the Eckleses came. Then I begged. 'I can take some of them off your hands. You think I enjoy life? Lunching with other women, shopping for clothes, giving dinner parties? I've had enough of it. Fire me if I'm not good.' Even after the Eckleses left, I held on; to keep those houses tended gave life to my memories, but what are you, Mrs Welford, doing in this very house, making a discord of the past? My fault, of course, for having rented to you at all. But Mary Eckles herself had made the first of the discords, as she'd had a perfect right to do. I can hear her still in that living-room I glimpsed just now through the window, and again, from the hall, through the open door:

'Benefactress! Lady bountiful! Thanks a lot! If there was any way to take it all and wad it up and throw it at you, I'd do it! It was bad enough already, a draft-evader's wife, walked away from at parties, cut dead on the street, as soon as anybody finds out about you, out you go. Oh, everybody's against that war, all right. Oh, yes! Against it till they meet somebody who's done the honest thing and refused to fight it. And you our only friend. It was you who "understood". Oh, yes, you were just wonderful to us! You were *great*!'

I wish I could get angry in return, but I can't. I hate seeing her smooth features distort and change, hate the tears that smear off into her long hair.

'Aren't you a little angry with Bob, too?' I ask, and almost smile, for there's a wry humour in it all. Bob and I ironically had landed in a thicket of desire without meaning to, from having to sit together so often and worry over her precarious pregnancy. It was close to the truth that I was their only friend. Had she rather Bob and I had sat about lusting? Plucking out the thorns of desire? Watching the salt blood flow? Avoiding eyes and touch? I *had* helped them: got him work, found them a reasonable place to stay, even located people uncritical or detectors, who would invite them out for company and talk. 'I thought you knew all along,' I told her, quietly honest.

'How long did it go on?' She's getting calmer, looking fretfully aside. As a child she must have exploded into short, intense tantrums, wanting to burst with rage, found there wasn't any way to, then calmed down into plain humanity again, having changed nothing.

'I can't remember.' This is true. Reality like that is not boarded up with time; does she think that? 'Not so long.' In my turn, I am outraged too. 'Oh, you could be fairer than this!' Their marriage was never at stake with me. A man so much younger could only be temporary, even as a lover. A man so much younger could, at a certain point, be exactly what a woman needs. 'It's Bob you ought to talk to; not me.' I ought to tell her what I used to ask myself: Question: What's sadder than two waifs together? Answer: Two waifs apart. Q: What must I do? A: You must let go.

She's crying softly now, the soft rain after the hard, exploding cloudburst. 'I've so little . . . so little to go on. Only just him . . . and Kathy. I can't go back home, the family's against me. Oh, they're crazy. My mother is crazy. She was that way for a long time before I met Bob. She would turn on me. I told you, long ago, all about that. The little life I had, I trusted you to come into it. And you've damaged it. It won't, ever, be the same. It's all messed up.'

So it's me you're telling about it, I think. I think: these Americans! I sit in the living-room with her most of that September day. She had telephoned me in the morning, having to see me. The baby's asleep, the room is chilling down toward evening. She needs me. Hates me, resents me, has to see me. Has found some passionate note from me, stuck away in a drawer where he'd saved it. The street outside, its leaves turning, its narrow modest French-Canadian look, is no part of her. Grey stone façades, green leaves in summer, grey stone with green leaves, leaves turning orange, grey stone in the snow—that's Canada. And dormer windows above in the mansard's drop, painted to match the doorways—white or yellow, or blue, or red—and always the steep steps in shining grey paint: that's Montreal, French Montréal, and no part of her. Nor am I. Shall I say: everything I have and am, have had, have been, will have and be, always gets 'messed up', as you put it, one way or another. It happens to everybody. It is nothing but acceptance to recognize that.

Suddenly, out of thinking these things, I discover something. Americans want somewhere, somehow, a purity, an inviolability. But why then did Bob Eckles, strong in his marriage, young husband, young father, 'mess up' this enviable estate by an affair with me? Because—I saw now—his act against the war was purity enough already. I saw that it might have been enough for her too if she'd ever been entirely involved in his act, close to his thinking. Then some affair of his would have cost her no more tears than a gnat in her eye. But peasant intellectual, striding shoulder to shoulder with her mate, Mary Eckles was not. She had let me do things for her too acceptingly. She was an American college girl, spoiled by parents. The smooth Madonna face was a neutrality, a perfect balance maintained over the tensions she daily survived, never presumed to take in hand. How far back this must go. To that 'craziness' she had talked about, more than once. Young people often talk of crazy parents, but suppose this talk of hers was true? Then my sympathy could reach that, the source of her weakness.

'I loved him,' I told her. I thought she ought, at least, to know that.

What had she answered on that September afternoon? I can't remember. The voice, slight and distant, whirls away in time.

Now in this summer weather, empty of the Eckleses, the sun beats constantly on the tin roof, but in the back bedroom where the baby slept, the rez de chaussée, across from the kitchen, it is cool, sheltered by the shrubs grown up at the windows, darkened by the dusty Venetian blinds he always drew closed for us (they tilt unevenly). His heels are always sounding behind me in that hallway, two steps to my three, repeated four times—five times?—over. Did I love him? I called it that. He aroused me, I desired him, his touch fled out to every nerve, sought inward to the dark core. He fitted, suited, all I physically am. And more. When we discussed something, we spoke equally; when we laughed, we laughed together. ('You know about that war?' I said. 'You know what I think about it . . . you want to know? I don't think anything, nothing at all. It's funny, isn't it?' 'I'm dying laughing it's so funny.' 'Don't you think I should?' 'It's not your country. Why care?') At times it seemed that Mary and the baby both were our children. That was the heart of what we reached to. That's fine, if apolitical. ('I go alone,' he said once. 'Alone, and I don't mind.')

'Let me go on managing those old houses,' I said to my husband, after the Eckleses left. 'You know I'm good at it. Who could you find half as good?'

My consenting husband, 'charming host', 'effective man in the English-speaking business community', he takes it for granted that steps have followed me down any number of hallways, that the blinds drawn for me are numerous. He overestimates. Seeking is easy, finding is hard. If Mary Eckles could but know it, when she and her husband appeared, I wasn't even looking.

I had first seen their faces before me one day when shopping downtown. I had stopped by my husband's office and, finding him and his secretary both gone to lunch, had sat down at the front desk. So they, entering for the first time, took me for the secretary, able to answer something about an apartment. 'Have you got anything for us?' He was tall and bearded, with rust-coloured hair to the shoulders; she young and fair and pregnant, and the snow outside had melted away. I had noticed a haze of green on a willow near a parking-lot, buds on trees red and swollen, the sky a melting blue. They stood hand in hand. Out of the talk between them as they'd entered I had caught her name: 'Mary'. Her skin was pale but luminous, her grey-blue eyes steadily serious, her mouth unaware of makeup. 'A room at the inn, perhaps?' I almost said, the first I'd thought of convent days in many a year. I could recall the rustle of nuns' skirts along polished corridors, see the flat arrangement of furniture, the harsh colours of cheap religious pictures: I had hated it, I thought, but a secret meaning hidden beneath its surfaces was broken open for me now, and in this living presence I found tears rising to my eyes. Such summoning power is angelic: I was theirs from that moment. . . .

'Sorry to have to trouble you, Mrs Welford.'

Did I say that before? The memory has done all it can; it has taken me back to the beginning of itself, to that day at the secretary's desk, to a vision's fleetingness and its power to remain.

I leave the little house in the poor street, and going think of one other thing. To re-enter the country he came from, Bob Eckles had to get, through channels tricky to deal with, a false identity, faked documents and, further, to alter his fingerprints by scarring them with acid. Necessary or not—I don't know. He had thought it was. There had been directions to find, or learn somehow, and equipment to obtain. He himself, alone, had bent to this punishing task. Politics is powerful, reaching in to change the imprint of a lover's touch.

Mary Eckles, were you hurt by that?

Mary Eckles, if I see you again, will I get to say: did it hurt you as much as it hurt me, to think of his fingers burnt and changed?

AUDREY THOMAS

Crossing the Rubicon

Today is the ides of February, February 13th. I was actually looking up 'idiot' in my Concise Oxford (*n*. Person so deficient in mind as to be permanently incapable of rational conduct; utter fool. f. Gk. *idiōtēs* private person, [*idios*, own, private]) when I noticed 'ides' at the top of the page. I knew what it meant, of course, or thought I did; but as it is virtually impossible for me to stop with one word when consulting a dictionary, I read the definition anyway: '*n.pl.* (Rom. Ant.) Eighth day after nones (15th day of March, May, July, October; 13th of other months)'. That surprised me. I had always assumed, because of Caesar, that the ides invariably fell on the 15th. And yet here it is today, by one of those strange coincidences, the ides of the month I am in. Another piece of trivia, I thought, to cram into my ragbag of a mind, where reside such useless bits of information as the Harvard telephone number of my first real boyfriend (Kirkland 7-1044), a man whom I have not seen or heard of in twenty-five years; or the day of the week on which my sister, then aged eleven, had her appendix out. And yet, yesterday, I couldn't remember where I put the car keys.

I am trying to write a story which I do not particularly want to write. But it nags at me, whines, rubs against the side of my leg, begs for attention. I won't be able to go on to anything else until I deal with it. In this context, the fact that it is the ides of February seems ominous—'Beware, beware'—and I wonder if I might be better off doing something, anything, else.

Tomorrow is Valentine's Day and my daughter has announced that, when she comes home from school, she and her girlfriend, who has been invited to stay the night, are going to make Valentine cupcakes for all the boys in their class. This is really not much of a task: we live on an island and the total population of the school, boys and girls, is fifty-one. If they make cupcakes for all the boys in the top three classes, it will come to little more than a dozen.

'What are you going to make for the *girls*?' I call sarcastically. I am standing on the porch in my flannel nightdress and she is running down the path to catch the yellow school bus.

'Paper Valentines. Handmade. We can do that while the cakes are cooking.'

I do not make any political comment; she is already out of earshot and what would be the use? Nothing ever really changes. The boys will accept the cupcakes as their due; the other girls will understand. That is the way it is in elementary school, even in the Enlightened Year of Our Lord 1980. In grade seven, my sister and her girlfriend, Shirley, held their first boy-girl party on Valentine's Day and they worked for hours on the food. This was partly to impress the other girls (it always is), but mostly to impress the boys. I remember that they borrowed a heart cutter from Shirley's mother's bridge-sandwich set and made two or three dozen heart-shaped egg salad or tuna fish sandwiches. My mother and I sat upstairs while the party was going on, eating all the 'surrounds', as it were, and playing gin rummy. One of the naughtier boys fused the lights by putting a penny in the light socket and then screwing the light back in, and my mother got really mad when she found out what had happened. My father was out, so she had to go down the steep steps to the cellar, carrying a candle, and she was afraid of the dark. Later on, she gave my sister and Shirley a lecture on 'promiscuity'. (She had heard the squeals and giggles in the dark, oh yes.) I had never heard that word before, but listening outside my sister's bedroom door, I soon caught the drift of the conversation. My mother wanted to have a word with the boy's mother. My sister vowed that she would never go to school again, never ever, if my mother said even one word. Later on, I could hear the two girls giggling and re-living the party when they were supposed to be asleep.

I was in town the other day and bought a half-pound of candy hearts—the flat pastel ones with mottoes—and I expect that some of these, carefully chosen, will go on top of the cupcakes. They are just like the ones we used to buy when we were kids, although they don't seem to taste as nice. These leave a bitter taste, like candy-coated pills, if you suck on them too long. But the taste isn't the important thing, it's the mottoes. What surprised me was that most of the mottoes are the same as they were when I was a kid growing up in the forties. Because I don't want to begin my story, I have taken some of the hearts out of the glass jar, where we've been keeping them, and have shaken them onto the kitchen table (which is also my desk). I've turned them right side up. 'TO EACH HIS OWN', 'WHY NOT SAY YES', 'BE GOOD TO ME', 'LET'S GET TOGETHER', 'KISS ME', 'BE MY SUGAR DADDY'. I pick up a pink 'LOVE ME' and pop it in my mouth. It seems rather touching that these things are still sold in a big city like Vancouver, where the number one hit song recently was, 'Good Girls Don't—But I Do'. Good girls certainly didn't when I was growing up, only bad girls, girls from the East Side who hung around the lockers in the basement of the high school where the vocational boys hung out. They had loud, defiant laughs, these girls, and red lips, and their sweaters were too tight. (Or so it seemed to me, seeing them through my mother's eyes.) Everybody knew about them, of course, but nobody wrote songs about what was going on. And if a good girl got into trouble, she went to Arizona for a few months—for her asthma.

'YOU'RE A SLICK CHICK', says this one. Good heavens, where are these made? In some small town, by-passed by the Trans-Canada; in some equally obscure factory, where the women still wear snoods and current jargon never filters in? 'SLICK CHICK', indeed! I must try to find out where these hearts come from. Do the workers in the candy factory still jitterbug in the staff canteen and listen to a skinny Frankie singing, 'That Old Black Magic's Got Me in Its Spell'?

My story is set in Montréal and it will begin with a woman on a Number 24 bus, heading East along Sherbrooke Street. She is on her way to meet a man who used to be her lover. The bus passes a clock, and seeing that at this rate she will be early, she decides to get off at Peel and walk the rest of the way. They have arranged over the telephone to meet at Place Ville Marie at noon and go somewhere nice for lunch. She is staying with an old friend and when she wakes up, there is a note shoved under her door. 'Ma belle, back soon. Will drive you anywhere.' But she has decided that she does not want to talk this morning, even to her dear, dear friend, so she has dressed carefully, had a quick cup of coffee in the empty kitchen, and gone for a walk, until it is time to catch the bus. She likes being in Montréal again, likes the bilingual chatter, likes the business of the place, likes the little shopgirls and secretaries in their smart clothes. Vancouver, where she lives, is a veritable frontier town as far as *couture* is concerned. And she likes old things and old places— the patina that they have. Old people too. One of her very best friends is eighty-five. She has noticed, while still on the bus, a Hundertwasser exhibition at the art gallery. If things get too tense, she will tell him that she planned to go to that. The conference for which she is here does not officially begin until this evening.

'The boys are getting paper Valentines as well,' my daughter calls from across the road, 'the cupcakes will be extra.' When I was at the candy counter in the Bay, I bought her a bag of solid chocolate hearts, which she does not know about, and upstairs, in Fabrics, enough heart-embroidered braid to make hairbands for her and her two best friends. Later, in a drugstore, I saw a button which said: 'Cinderella married for money.' I knew that she would find that funny, so I bought that too. Some of the buttons were very crude and I couldn't imagine who would wear them. Bad girls, I suppose. But maybe not. In Delhi, India, last year, a friend of mine saw an otherwise perfectly respectable-looking American girl walking along the Raj Path in a T-shirt depicting a drunken kitten holding a martini glass in its paw. Underneath was written in pink letters: 'Happiness is a tight pussy'. How could even a bad girl wear a thing like that? How could she pick it out of the pile and hand it to the cashier? How could she wear it in India, let alone back home? Sometimes, I feel like old Miniver Cheevy in our high school literature books. 'Born too late'. How we laughed at *him* in grade nine!

He had fallen in love with her, and one afternoon, they had slept together. Then, he went home and told his wife. They called her up and asked her to come and see them, to talk, to try and untangle this thing. She couldn't go right then, she said, because she was alone in the house and her children were sleeping. She did not suggest that they, being childless and more mobile, should come and see her. She imagined tears and shouting, and coward-like, she did not want her children to be a witness to all that. The next day, his wife came to see her. 'If it had been a girl off the streets,' she said, 'I could have dealt with it better. But *you*. I can't compete against you.'

She wanted to say, 'Oh, my dear, it's not a competition,' but it was. It always, to some degree, is.

'It won't happen again,' she said. 'I think that he's just feeling restless and unsure.'

'I feel as though I've been walking around in a bubble for the last six years,' his wife said, 'and now, it's burst.'

So, the woman in my story will get off at Peel, one fine October morning, and walk down to and along St Catherines. The last time she has seen him was at Dorval Airport, six months before. The night before that, the three of them had gone to hear Charlebois at Place des Arts, a farewell treat for her. She dressed carefully that night too, and when his wife put on her old down jacket over her dress, he suggested that she might wear her good coat instead. 'It's *cold*,' his wife said stubbornly. 'It's still *cold* out there at night.' She knew that he was comparing the two of them and that he wanted them equally dressed-up.

'Leave her alone,' she said. 'My vanity will probably cost me pneumonia.'

He sat in the middle, as usual, and when Charlebois sang, 'Pourquoi va-tu si loin?' she wanted to touch his knee, but she didn't dare. All that was over. It had been for a long, long time. The next day, when he missed the turn-off to the airport and they ended up in a dreary suburb before he could turn around, his wife said from the back seat, laughing, 'You see, he doesn't want you to go,' It was all right if *she* said it, so they all laughed.

In grade three, we graduated from pencils to pens with steel nibs. They fitted into long wooden holders that were lacquered in bright primary colours. We wiped the points with felt pen-wipers that we made during art lessons the first week. Penwipers are as obsolete as ice-picks now, I guess. The sharp steel nibs were wonderful for carving names and initials into wooden desks. If you were caught 'desecrating the furniture' (I can still hear the voice of Mrs Albee, my 3B teacher), you were sent to the principal to be paddled. The paddle hung on a hook beside the principal's desk and had 'BOARD OF EDUCATION' stencilled across it. I don't believe that it was ever really used on the girls (he had easier ways to make us cry), but I remember many a boy returning red-faced and defiant, easing himself carefully into his seat. The boys were very naughty. They held our heads down in the drinking fountains, dipped our braids in the inkwells, tied our dresses to the backs of our seats, put rubber dog turds at the door of the girls' cloakroom, They made us cry. Still, secretly and carefully, we carved their initials and names into our desks: 'AC + SF', 'JM + PM'—Tom or Dick or Harry. Then we stuck a finger in the inkwell and rubbed over the new incision, to make it look old. We were always covered in ink, all of us, for one reason or another. Now, my daughter comes home with letters and initials up and down her arms. She stands at the sink, scrubbing them off with the nailbrush, because she wants to wear a short-sleeved shirt tomorrow. And the littlest girls stand in the schoolyard with their skipping ropes, chanting the same old rhymes:

> *First comes love,*
> *Then comes marriage,*
> *Then comes baby in the*
> *Bay-by carriage*

(Yet well over half the kids in that school have parents who are single or married again.) Faster and faster they skip, until the boys jump in and spoil it all.

'I don't know why I like him,' my daughter says to me about the predominant set of initials. 'He's not *nice*. There are lots of boys much nicer than he is.'

'Niceness doesn't have much to do with it,' I tell her. (He should probably get a 'HIT THE ROAD' on the top of *his* cupcake, but I'll bet you a dollar, it will be a 'LOVE ME'.)

She sees him before he sees her. He is sitting by the fountain, dressed in the old English policeman's cape that they found one day in an antique shop. She has a cape as well and she is glad that she didn't bring it. They are made of real felt, lovely and warm, and belonged to the Eastbourne Constabulary of maybe fifty years ago. She smiles to think that he has worn it today.

He has not seen her; she can still leave. Once he turns around and looks in her direction, she will be hooked. All he will have to do, then, is reel her in. My mouth hurts, just thinking about it. I cannot give her such a painful metaphor; I will have to think up something else. Right now, I want to play soothsayer and call out to her, 'Beware, beware. Walk away. Run. Leave well enough alone. You're cured.' She stands there at the edge of the huge square, hesitating. He turns, sees her and waves.

It was so nice that they could all be friends. Everybody said so, although a few people—mostly women—told her privately that, really, they couldn't understand how his wife could bear to have her around. After all that had happened; after all that she'd been through. 'Maybe I'm a kind of reminder,' she would say smiling, sipping her drink. 'Something like a *memento mori*. I can't remember my high school Latin, but let's say a *memento perditi*, a "remember you could lose him again". But that's pretty cynical. I actually think that we like one another. When he's not around, we have a lot of fun together, go to galleries and window-shop, go out to tea. After all, he's made his choice, we all know that. It might be more to the point to ask why *I* put up with it, but frankly, I don't think that I could give you an answer.'

'And when the three of you are together?'

'We have a fairly good time. We tend to talk too much and we tease him a lot—back one another up, because we both know him so well. He protests, but actually, he loves it.'

'Did you really all live together?'

'Briefly.'

This was where she usually changed the subject or got up to find another drink. If she were feeling bitter or witty, or both, she would sometimes reply, 'Oh, yes, but I think we did it more for the sound of the thing than anything else.'

Her companion would shake her head, puzzled.

'Ménage à trois. It sounds so nice, so civilized and sophisticated. Quite different from "bigamy" or "screwing two women".'And then, if she really wanted to be shocking, she would add, 'Although, after a while, it sounded more like "ménage à twat" to me.' And then, it really was time to change the subject.

She bought a handbook of French-Canadian words and phrases at Classics the afternoon before, and she has brought it with her to show him. Walking along St Catherines Street, she sees in the window of a restaurant: PAIN DORÉ. 'Golden pain' is the first thing that comes to her; then, 'golden bread'. She stops to look it up. 'Canada: *Pain doré*. France: *Pain perdu*. French Toast'.

Of course. But, in her present state of mind, she likes her first interpretation better—'golden pain'. The real thing. Or what about 'pain perdu'? That was pretty good too. Pain forever lost.

They both liked fooling around with words. They had gone on a trip to Rome together, just the two of them, in the early days of their relationship. They sat in the Forum, eating bread and sausage, and reading to each other out of the phrase book.

'I have no appetite. I get indigestion.'

'Oh oon dee-stoor-boh dee stoh-mah'-koh.'

' "Oh lah feb'ray". I have fever.'

'Mee sahng'gwee-nah eel nah'soh.'

She flipped the pages.

'Guess this one? "Kwell oo-oh'moh me say'gway dahp-pehr-toot-toh".'

They were both laughing so hard that they could barely speak.

'I like the dahp-pehr-toot-toh,' he said. 'Something like, "where do I find a trumpet player"?'

'No. It means "everywhere". That man is following me everywhere".'

'Maybe we'd better stick to *veni, vidi, vici.*'

Later that day, she discovered that a *letto metrimoniale* was a 'double bed.' But she didn't show him that one, as he was still officially matrimonio to someone else.

Once, after he had gone back to his wife, but they were all still in Montréal, they had been in a bar on Mountain Street, where a girl whom he and his wife had known from years past came up to them and said hello. She asked what they had been doing. No mention was made of the long break-up, or of his time with her, or of their reconciliation—of course not. She sat there feeling as if she had been erased, as easily as one erases a name from a blackboard. Rubbed out, the way sometimes the boys in her grade three class had been made to sand down their names and initials, until they disappeared. It was as though her time with him hadn't meant anything, as though, in their official history, she was not going to be mentioned, not even as a footnote. They would change the dates and stretch things, and pretty soon, there would be no gaps—all their time past would be accounted for. She did not blame them—in their place, she would probably have done the same—but she hated them for doing it. They did this thing in front of her, knowing that she would not publicly contradict them. She was not the sort to make scenes in public places.

('He's not even *nice*,' my daughter says to me, puzzled. 'He's mean to us and he's mean to the little kids. There are a lot of boys who are nicer than he is.'

'Niceness doesn't seem to have much to do with it,' I say.)

'Bonjour là,' she says, 'I'm sorry that I'm late.' He looks at his watch. 'Actually, you're two minutes early.' They do not kiss, but as he stands up, they lean a little towards each other and then straighten up. He gives her a big smile (reels her in, reels her in); he is genuinely pleased to see her.

'Before I forget, I have an invitation for you. We would like you to come to dinner tomorrow night, if you're free.' We. We would like. 'I can't,' she says. 'There is an official banquet. But I'm free in the afternoon—or can arrange to be. There are a lot of papers being given. Everyone will think that I'm somewhere else. Maybe Sheila would like to go to the Hundertwasser exhibition and out to tea at that Hungarian tearoom. I'll call her tonight, shall I?' They have begun walking; she has forgotten how long his legs are, how fast he walks. In the French-Canadian handbook, she has marked a page to show him. 'Look,' she will say over lunch, 'In France, you are "un homme grand et efflanqué." Over here, you are "un grand slaque". I like that. My mother would have called you "a long drink of water".'

They will have ordered a carafe of white wine.

'Are you still taking French lessons?' he asks.

'Oh yes, at the Alliance Française. But there is no chance to speak it. And you?'

'Both of us. We'll be ready when the revolution comes.'

(Canada: *casser*. France: *rompre*, to break up). They make polite conversation and wait for the food to come.

The winter before, living around the corner from them in an old apartment building, seeing them two or three times a week, she met a woman at a bus stop whose face had frozen two weeks before. They had to take her to Emergency. 'It's when your face feels really warm that you're in trouble,' she said through her thick woollen scarf. 'That's the frostbite beginning. You'd better wrap up more.'

We used to come in from sledding, in my New York State childhood, and our mother would stick our feet in pans of luke-warm water. There was so much to put on and take off then; leggings (another obsolete word), and mittens, which hung on elastics threaded through your coatsleeves, and black galoshes, with nasty black metal fasteners which became full of packed snow and hurt your fingers to unfasten. Out here, on the British Columbia coast, winter is easier and gentler. We have had one week of snow this year—in January—and *that* was unusual. School was dismissed early on the second snowy day, for fear that the bus wouldn't make the hills. My daughter and I put on long underwear, underneath our jeans, and took pieces of heavy plastic sheeting off the woodpile and slid down all the steep drive-ways that belong to the weekend and summer people. Then, we came home, soaked and laughing, and had cocoa. It had started to snow again, and the world outside our cottage looked as though it were full of chicken feathers. I told my daughter about a won-derful sled that my sister and I owned when we were children. An old sled, fixed up by our grandfather, repainted by him, a nice fire-engine red. It was called a 'Flexible Flyer' and it could really steer. I told her how some steep streets in our town would be blocked off by the police when the heavy snows came, and then, the children would be allowed to go sledding at night. I told her about the big boys, who would jump on back, just as we got going, and zig-zag us dangerously down the hill, trying to steer us into garbage cans that had been put out at the curb, until Somebody's Mother, hearing all the screams and commotion, would come to her front door, apron still on from doing the dinner dishes, and tell them to leave the little kids alone, that they ought to be ashamed of themselves, big boys like that. I tell her about snowballs with lumps of coal in them, but also about maple syrup heated and poured on fresh snow; about skating at Recreation Park to: 'I'm Looking Over a Four Leaf Clover That I Overlooked Before'. She likes to hear stories about my youth. I watch her as she listens and drinks her cocoa, the cat asleep on her lap. She is twelve years old and teetering on the edge. Never again will she be as free as she is now.

After the woman at the bus stop on Côte Saint-Luc told her about her face freezing and thawing again, she thought of how she seemed to have put her heart in some freezing solution, some freezer drawer, and she trembled at the thought of how much it was going to hurt if she ever let it thaw out again. 'The pain was terrible,' the woman said, 'and then, it itched so. And then, it peeled. I'd bundle up more, if I were you.' On particularly snowy, slippery days, cars sped through red lights, their drivers unable to brake, horns honking wildly. The buses were full of the smell of wet wool and fur.

When I went away to college for the first time, my mother gave me her, by now, standard lecture on promiscuity, but, this time, she added a codicil on drinking. If I had to accept a drink at a dance or a party, if I really felt I had to, I was to take a token sip or two, and then pour the rest into a nearby potted palm.

'A potted palm! A potted palm!' How I laughed at her! I shrieked with contemptuous laughter. My mother had me quite late and I realized that she was still back in the early twenties sometime, repeating something that *her* mother must have said to her. But it was all right. I went to a nice college and the boys that I was introduced to on weekends or on blind dates were nice boys. They went elsewhere for their sex.

In Rome, they had walked down stone steps to the river, and she had taken his picture by the Tiber. There was graffiti everywhere and the smell of pee.

'Let Rome in Tiber melt,' she said.

'What's that?'

'Oh, just the words of another great lover, Marc Antony.'

(Angelo loved Sophia. Roman girls were_____. Well, she didn't know what the word meant, but she could guess.)

The ides of February are come. Aye, Madam, but not yet gone. I could take the butter out of the cupboard and put it nearer the stove. It is very cold today and we have no central heating. If the butter stays over there in the cupboard, it won't mix well. I could even make the cupcakes in a little while, and leave the girls to ice and decorate them. I could go out and chop wood. All this sitting down isn't good for me; I need some exercise. I could write a letter to my old mother, or to one of my other daughters. I could get the garbage ready to take down to the Solid Waste Disposal Area (the Dump). I could wash the kitchen floor. It really isn't wise to begin something as important as this story on the ides of the month. I will turn the candy hearts over, shuffle them like cards, draw one; see if I can find an answer. I select a yellow one, chosen at random, and turn it up. 'DON'T BE A DRIP', it says.

When they have finished their lunch, he will suggest that they walk around for a while, down towards Old Montréal, and have a drink at the Hotel Nelson. She has never been inside there, and readily agrees. The sidewalk cafés are all shut up and they are the only people, except for the barmaid, in the bar of the hotel. They sit by the dusty windows and order a beer. He tells her that it was from this hotel that the news about Pierre Laporte was announced. But she doesn't want to talk about past history of any kind. A silence falls upon them. She looks at his long, fine hands on the table.

'You're looking good,' he says. 'That's a real nice skirt.'

'Oh, I got it at a sale,' she lies. In fact, once she knew that she was coming to this conference, she searched and searched for just the right outfit to meet him in, something stylish yet demure. When they lived together, he was always telling her to button up her blouse. So she knew just what to look for. She wanted to look good; she wanted to proclaim by the way that she was dressed, 'Well, *I'm* all right!'

'I have to be home by three-thirty,' he says, glancing at his watch. 'Did Sheila tell you we have a puppy?'

'She may have mentioned it, I don't remember.'

'Well, we do. I promised that I wouldn't stay away from the little fella too long. He's only six weeks old.'

'What happens when the strike ends?'

'Oh, it won't end for a while. And he'll be older then. And Sheila's only substituting, you know. She doesn't work every day.'

She knows that she is supposed to ask what kind of puppy it is, what's its name, all the appropriate things. After all, he has enquired about her children. But instead, she makes patterns with the damp rings on the table.

'Tell me that you miss me?' she says. There is no answer and she does not look up.

Finally, he says, 'Why do you want to torture me?'

She pulls out the French-Canadian handbook and they start going through it. Some of the swear words, 'Les Sacres', have not been translated, and he, who was born here, tells her, more or less, what they mean in English.

'It's interesting how the Québécois, perhaps all Catholics?, use church words as sexual metaphors. We don't have any equivalent to that in English.'

'Well, they just combine the two most taboo things. The church doesn't have the same power in the Protestant world.'

They look at the difference between 'parking' in Canada and France.

' "Se peloter dans une voiture et dans une endroit isolé", as opposed to "faire du parking".'

'Simplification,' he says. 'Actually, can you imagine some French guy asking a girl if she wants to "te peloter dans ma voiture et dans un endroit isolé"? I can't believe that he would really say that. He probably just goes up and grabs her ass.'

They stand on the corner of Notre Dame and Place Jacques Cartier and wait for the light to change. Just as they step off the curb, the light turns red and he pulls her back. 'Arrêtez,' says the signal. Suddenly, she runs right into the middle of the traffic (there really isn't much traffic); she, who is always so cautious about crossing streets; she, who was told last year that she could never become 'une vraie Montréalaise' until she learned to ignore the lights. Some horns blare, but she makes it safely to the other side.

'Tell me that you miss me!' she calls to him. 'Just say it. Just admit it.' He stands on the other side of the street, a tall, handsome, loose-limbed man, 'un grand slaque, un homme grand et efflanqué', her ex-lover, her love, grinning, shaking his head.

'Tell me that you miss me or I'll walk away forever!' Again, he shakes his head and smiles, so she turns her back on him and begins to walk in the direction of the Métro.

'I miss you, you bitch! Tabarnac! I miss you!' She stops.

Then, remembering how Sally Bowles/Liza Minelli said goodbye to her Christopher Isherwood/Michael York boyfriend in *Cabaret*, she reaches her right hand over her left shoulder and, wishing that she had Minelli's green fingernails, she waves good-bye.

And she doesn't look back. In my story, that is. She doesn't look back in my story.

W.D. VALGARDSON

A Matter of Balance

He was sitting on a cedar log, resting, absentmindedly plucking pieces from its thick layer of moss, when he first saw them. They were standing on the narrow bridge above the waterfall. When they realized he had noticed them, they laughed, looked at each other, then turned their backs. In a moment, the short, dark-haired one turned around to stare at him again. His companion flicked a cigarette into the creek.

Bikers, he thought with a mixture of contempt and fear. He had seen others like them, often a dozen at a time, muscling their way along the road. These two had their hair chopped off just above the shoulders and, from where he sat, it looked greasy for it hung in tangled strands. They both had strips of red cloth tied around their heads. The dark-haired boy, he thought, then corrected himself, man, not boy, for he had to be in his middle twenties, was so short and stocky that he might have been formed from an old-fashioned beer keg. They both wore black leather vests, jeans, and heavy boots.

He was sorry that they were there but he considered their presence only a momentary annoyance. They had probably parked their bikes at the pull-off below the waterfall, walked up for god knows what reason—he could not imagine them being interested in the scenery—and would shortly leave again. He would be happy to see them go. He was still only able to work part time and had carefully arranged his schedule so that his Wednesdays were free. He didn't want anything to interfere with the one day he had completely to himself.

The tall blond man turned, leaned against the railing and stared up at Harold. He jabbed his companion with his elbow and laughed. Then he raised his right hand, pointed two fingers like he would a pistol, and pretended to shoot.

The action, childish as it was, unsettled Harold and he felt his stomach knot with anxiety. He wished that he had been on the other side of the bridge and could simply have picked up his pack and walked back to his station wagon. The only way across the river, however, was the bridge and he had no desire to try to force his way past them. They reminded him of kids from his public school days who used to block the sidewalk, daring anyone to try to get by. He had been in grade two at the time and had not yet learned about fear. When he had attempted to ignore them and go around, they had shifted with him to the boulevard, then to the road and, finally, to the back lane. As his mother was washing off his scrapes and bruises and trying to get blood off his shirt, he had kept asking her why, why did they do it? Beyond saying that they were bad boys and that she would speak to the principal, she had no answers. Only later, when he was much older, had he understood that their anger was not personal and, so, could not be reasoned with.

Every Wednesday for the last six months, he had hiked to the end of this trail and then used his rope to lower himself to the river bank. Before the winter rains began and flooded the gorge, he wanted to do as much sniping as possible. The previous week, he had discovered a crack in the bedrock that looked promising but, before he had a chance to get out all the gravel, the day had started to fade and he had been forced to leave. The gorge was no place to spend the night. Even at noon, the light was filtered to a pale grey. He dressed warmly, wearing a cotton shirt, then a wool shirt and, finally, a wool jack-shirt; yet, within a few hours he was always shaking with cold. As strenuous as the panning was, it could not keep out the chill. The air was so damp that when he took a handful of rotting cedar and squeezed it, red water ran like blood between his fingers. On the tree trunks, hundreds of mushrooms grew. At first, because of their small size and dark grey colour, he thought they were slugs, but then he pried one loose with his fingernail and discovered its bright yellow gills.

Although he had been nowhere near the bottom of the crack, he had found a few flakes of gold which he meticulously picked out of his pan with tweezers. Panning in the provincial parks was illegal so he always went right to the end of the path, then worked his way along the river for another hundred yards. Recently, he had started taking as much as half-an-ounce of dust and small nuggets out of the river in a day and he wondered if someone had found out, but he immediately dismissed the idea. Only Conklin knew. When they met each Thursday he always showed Conklin his latest find. As far as his friends and colleagues were aware, he spent his days off hiking, getting himself back into shape after having been ill for over a year.

As he studied the two men below, he told himself he was letting his imagination run away with him again and to get it under control. There was no good in borrowing trouble. He stood up, swung his pack onto his shoulders and, being careful not to look like he was running away, resumed his hike.

From this point on, the trail was a series of switchbacks. If the two on the bridge were planning on following him and stealing his equipment or wallet, they would probably give up after a short distance and wait for easier prey. Unless they were in good condition, the steep climb would leave them gasping for breath.

Large cedars pressed close to the path, blocking out the light. Old man's beard hung from the branches. The ground was a tangle of sword fern, salal, and Oregon grape. In a bit of open space, an arbutus twisted toward the sun. Its bark, deep earth-red, hung in shreds. Here and there, the new pale green bark was visible. That was the way he felt, like a snake or an arbutus, shedding his old skin for a new, better one. The previous year, when nothing else had seemed to work, he had taken his pack and hiked from sunrise to sunset, exhausting himself so completely that he could not stay awake. The sniping, looking for gold in cracks, under rocks, among the roots of trees, had come when he had started to feel better.

At the next bend he stopped and hid behind a rotting stump. In a couple of minutes his pursuers—he told himself not to be foolish, not to be paranoid—appeared. They were walking surprisingly fast. If the trail had been even slightly less steep, they would have been running.

He wished there were a cutoff that would allow him to circle back. He could, he realized, use his equipment, if necessary, to lower himself to the river but to do so, he would need to gain enough of a lead to have time to untie and uncoil the rope, to set it around a tree, to climb down, and then to pull his rope down after him so that it could not be taken away or cut. He then would be faced with the problem of finding a route up. He had to be back by seven. It was the agreed upon time. Since their mother had been killed, the children became upset if he were even a few minutes late.

He looked at his watch. It was ten o'clock. It was a two-hour hike to the end of the trail, but he could hike out in an hour and a half. That did not leave him much time. First, he wanted to clean out the crack and, if possible, begin undercutting a large rock that sat in the centre of the river. Undercutting was dangerous. It would require that he move rocks and logs to divert the shallow water to either side of where he was going to work. Then he would need more logs to prop up the rock. He didn't want to get the work partly done and have half a ton of stone roll onto him. The nuggets that might be clustered around the base were worth some risk but there was no sense in taking more chances than necessary.

Ahead, through a gap in the trees, he saw the railway trestle. The two behind him would, he told himself, stop there. Hardly anyone went further. The trestle was an inexplicable focal point.

Every weekend dozens of people hiked to it, then dared each other to cross over the gorge. Many, terrified of heights, balked after the first few steps and stood, rigid, unable to force themselves to go any further.

That, he reassured himself, was what those two were coming for. They would cross the trestle and scare each other by rough-housing like a couple of adolescents.

He had hoped, unreasonably, that there would be hikers or a railway crew on the tracks. Normally, it was a relief when there was no one there. Hikers were inclined to talk about their experiences and, in the past, he had been afraid that if he were frequently seen on the same trail his weekly visits might come to the attention of a park warden. To avoid that, he had deliberately arranged to come when the park was empty.

He did not stop but crossed over the tracks and entered the forest on the far side. The path dwindled to a narrow line of crushed ferns. The trees were shagged with wind-blown moss and deadfall was everywhere. It was old forest and, in all the times he had come, he had never seen a bird or animal. As a child he had dreamed of living in the forest. In his dreams, his hunting had always been rewarded with game. The discrepancy between what he had hoped for and reality still astounded him.

While he was able to see the railway tracks he stopped and waited. His legs had begun to tire and cramp. He stretched them, then kneaded his right calf with his thumb and forefinger. Always before he had valued the silence and the isolation. Now, however, as he watched the two bikers look up and down the roadbed then cross to the path, Harold felt the forest close around him like a trap.

He hurried away. Even as he fled he reassured himself that they had done nothing. Anyone was free to hike wherever he wanted. If he just stopped, they would catch up and pass him by without paying any attention to him.

He kept his eyes on the path. He had no intention of tripping over a vine or slipping on a log. His fear, he chided himself, was not rational. If a mountie suddenly appeared and asked him what was the matter, what could he say? That he hadn't liked the way they had looked at him earlier? That they had threatened him? And how was that, sir? He could hear the question. And the answer? The blond one pointed his finger at me. Any mountie would think him mad.

The moss was so thick that his feet made no sound. There was only the creak of his pack, the harsh sound of his breathing. He would, he decided, abandon his plans, and when he got to the end of the granite ridge that ran along on his left, he would double back through the narrow pass on its far side. People don't assault other people without good reason, he told himself, but it did no good. His panic fluttered like dry leaves in a rising wind.

He wished that he had brought a hunting knife. It would have made him feel better to have had a weapon. His mind scurried over the contents of the pack as he tried to determine what he could use in a fight. The only possibility was his rack of chock nuts. It wasn't much. A dozen aluminum wedges, even clipped together on a nylon sling, would not be very effective.

As he came to the end of the ridge he turned abruptly to the left. The pass was nearly level and, unlike the area around it, contained only a few, scattered trees. There were, he remembered, circles of stone where people had made campfires. One day he had poked about and discovered used condoms, some plastic sandwich bags, and four or five beer bottles. A broken beer bottle, he thought, would serve as a weapon. He was just beginning to search for one when he saw a movement at the far end of the pass.

He became absolutely still. He felt so weak that he thought he was going to fall down. He craned his neck for a better look. If there were two of them, he could circle back the other way. In a moment, he realized that there was only one. That meant the other was on the path he had just left. He spun on his heel and ran back to the fork. No more than a quarter of a mile away the path ended. At that point, there was nothing to do but return the way he had come or descend to the river. In either case, he was trapped. His mouth, he realized, was so dry he could not swallow.

Behind him, he heard someone ask a question that sounded like 'Where did he go?' and a muffled reply but he could not be sure of the words. The ground was nearly level. He was running when he burst out onto an area where the rock fell from the side of the trail like a frozen set of rapids. There were few places here for trees to root. Leaves and pine needles were swept from the pale green lichen by the winter rains. Rather than continue to what he knew was a dead end, he clambered down the slope. He had not explored this area. In the back of his mind was the hope that the rough rock continued all the way to the river. By the time they found out he was no longer on the path, he could have climbed the other cliff. All at once, he stopped. The rough, black rock turned into sixty feet of smooth slab.

There was no time to go back. He glanced over his shoulder, then at the slab. It was, he realized, deceptive. It angled down toward the river then stopped at a ragged edge. No steeper than a roof at the outset, it curved just enough that every few feet the angle increased. Patches of lichen and the smooth texture of the stone guaranteed that anyone who ventured out on it would be engaged in a test of balance.

There was a chance, because of his friction boots, that he could work his way onto the steepest part of the slope. If the two behind him were not pursuing him, they would pass by and he would never see them again. If they were, for whatever reason, meaning him some harm, they would have great difficulty reaching him.

Quickly, he unzipped the right hand pocket of his pack and pulled out a section of three-millimetre rope. He tied a figure eight knot in both ends, wrapped the rope around his left hand, then crept down to a small evergreen. Ten feet to the right, in a completely exposed area, there was a gnarled bush. Here and there, stunted trees, their trunks nearly as hard as the rock itself, protruded from cracks.

There was little room for error. If he began to slide, it would be difficult to stop before he went over the edge. At this part of the river, the fall would not be great, but height would not make any difference. Even a twenty-foot fall onto the scattered boulders of the river bed would certainly be fatal. He leaned out, brushed away some dust that had collected on the rock, then took his first step.

Above him someone whistled sharply. It startled him but he kept his eyes fixed on the surface of the rock. He fitted the toe of his boot onto a small nubbin, then his other toe onto a seam of cracked quartz. The greatest danger was that, for even a split second, he would allow himself to be distracted. For his next move, he chose a pebbled area no bigger than a silver dollar. From there, he moved to a depression that was only noticeable because of its slight shadow. He had crossed more difficult areas than this but always with the security of a harness and rope and a belayer he could trust. A fall in those circumstances meant no more than some scraped skin and injured pride.

When he was within two feet of the bush he felt a nearly overwhelming urge to lunge forward. He forced himself to stay where he was. On the rock there could be no impetuous moves. Patience, above all else, was to be valued. There seemed to be no place for him to put his foot. He scanned the surface. Just below him there was a hairline crack. If he pressed down hard on it, it would hold him long enough for him to step to the side and up and catch hold of the bush.

Slowly, he pirouetted on his left foot, then brought his right foot behind it. He took a deep breath, forced the air out of his lungs, then in one fluid movement, stepped down, up and across. Even as his hand grasped the wooden stem, he felt his feet begin to slide.

While he unwrapped the three-millimetre rope from his arm, he sat with his legs on either side of the stem. He fitted a loop of rope around an exposed root, then slipped the second loop around his wrist. Unless the root gave way, the most he was going to fall was a couple of feet.

Only then did he allow himself to look back. There was still no sign of anyone. The area of tumbled rock ran on for a fair distance and, he realized, would take awhile to search. Realizing this, he cursed himself for not taking a chance and running back the way he had come.

He hooked his pack to the bush, took out the sling with the hardware on it, then eased himself out onto the steepest section of slab he could reach. Here he crouched, with his back to the trail, his hands splayed against the rock.

There was a sharp whistle above him. It was immediately answered from some distance back toward the trestle. With that, he realized that they had split up. One had blocked the trail while the other had done the searching.

He looked back again. Thirty feet behind him was the dark-haired biker. His blond companion was swinging down from the left. Both of them, Harold could see, were tired. He had, he thought with a distant kind of pleasure, given them a good run for their money. If they had been carrying packs, he would have outdistanced them.

They both stopped at the rough edge, some ten feet apart, looked at each other and smirked.

'Did you want something?' he asked. He had meant to make it a casual question, even offhand, as though he had no idea they had followed him, but panic sharpened his voice.

They both laughed as if at a joke.

'What do you want?' He was no longer sure that what he had planned would work. The blond-haired man had a small leather purse attached to his belt. He unsnapped it and took out a bone-handled clasp knife. He pried out a wide blade.

'Are you crazy?' Harold cried. 'What's the matter with you? I don't even know you.'

They both grinned foolishly and studied their boots. They

looked, he thought wildly, like two little boys caught in the middle of a practical joke.

Panic made him feel like he was going to throw up. 'Are you nuts?' he shouted. 'Are you crazy or something?'

Their answer was to start down the slab, one on each side of him. Their first steps were confident, easy. The surface of the rock was granular and bare at the edge and provided plenty of friction. He could see that neither was experienced. They both came down sideways, leaning into the rock, one hand pressed to the surface. He gripped the nylon sling in his right hand and concentrated on keeping his balance.

The dark-haired one was closest. He was coming down between the tree and the shrub, taking little steps, moving his left foot down, then his right foot, then his left, dangerously pressing all his weight onto the edge of his boot and, even more dangerously, leaning backwards, throwing off his centre of balance. Suddenly, a piece of lichen peeled away and his left foot slid out from under him. Instead of responding by bending out from the rock and pressing down with his toes, he panicked. He was sliding faster and faster. His body was rigid, his face contorted with fear, his eyes, instead of searching for a place he could stop his slide, were desperately fixed on the safe area he had just left behind. He made no sound. When he was finally even with Harold, he reached out his hand as though expecting it to be taken. There was, Harold saw, on the back of the hand, a tattoo of a heart pierced by a knife. A red and blue snake wound up the arm and disappeared beneath the sleeve. It was only by luck that his one foot struck a piece of root and he stopped. He was no more than a foot from the edge.

The blond man had come at an angle, picking his way along by fitting his knife blade into a crack. Just before his companion had lost control, the blond man had started to work his way across an area where there were no cracks. He seemed frozen into place.

'Why?' Harold shouted at him.

The sound seemed to wake the blond man from a stupor. He turned his head slowly to look at Harold. He squinted and formed his mouth into a small circle, then drew his chin down and ran his tongue along his lower lip. For a moment, Harold thought the biker was going to turn and leave.

'Get me out of here,' his companion cried. Fear made his voice seem as young as a child's.

The blond man shook his head, then half-snarled, stood up, and tried to walk across the intervening space. It was as though momentum and will held him upright; then Harold swung the nylon sling over his head, lunged forward, and struck his opponent on the upper arm. The blow was not powerful and, normally, it would have been swept aside. But here, as they both teetered on the steep surface, it was enough to knock them both off balance.

As the blond man skidded down the rock, he jabbed at it with his knife, trying to find an opening. Six feet from the edge, he managed to drive the blade into a crack. The knife held. He jammed the tips of his fingers into the crack.

Harold had slipped, fallen, then been caught by the rope around his wrist. He pulled himself back to the shrub and knelt with his knee against the stem.

'Help us up,' the dark-haired man begged. He looked like he was on the verge of weeping.

Harold loosened the rope, then untied it. Carefully, giving his entire attention to the task, he retraced his original route. Once at the evergreen, he knew he was safe. His sides were soaked with sweat and he could smell his own fear, bitter as stale tobacco. The two men never stopped watching him.

When Harold reached the top of the slab, the blond man called, in a plaintive voice, 'For God's sake, don't leave us here.'

Fear had softened their eyes and mouths but he knew it was only temporary. If he drew them to safety, they would return to what they had been.

'Pull us up,' the dark-haired man whined. His red head-band

had come off and was tangled in his hair.

Around them, the forest was silent. Not a bird called, not an animal moved. The moss that covered the rock and soil, the moss that clung thickly to the tree trunks, the moss that hung in long strands from the branches, deadened everything, muted it, until there were no sharp lines, no certainties. The silence pressed upon them. Harold had, for a moment, a mad image of all three of them staying exactly as they were, growing slowly covered in moss and small ferns until they were indistinguishable from the logs and rocks except for their glittering eyes.

'Tell somebody about us,' the dark-haired man asked.

The words tugged at him like little, black hooks. He looked down. Their faces were bleached white with fear. He could tell someone, a park warden, perhaps, but then what would happen? If he had been certain they would be sent to prison he might have dared tell somebody, but he knew that would not happen. If charges were laid he would have to testify. They would discover his name and address. And, from then on, he would live in fear. Afraid to leave his house. Afraid to go to sleep at night. Afraid for his children. And what if they denied everything, turned it all around? He had the necessary equipment to rescue them and had refused. What if one of them had fallen by the time someone came? He could be charged with manslaughter and the children would be left without mother or father. No matter how he tried to keep Conklin out of it, he would become involved. Harold knew how people thought. His short stay in hospital for depression, his weekly visits to a psychiatrist to siphon off pain and, automatically, he was crazy.

'You bastard,' the blond man screamed. 'You bastard. Get us out of here.' He kept shifting his feet about, trying to find a purchase where there was none. 'If you don't, our friends will come. They'll get us out. Then we'll start looking for you. There's thousands of us. We'll find you.'

The screaming startled him for a moment but then he thought about how soon the little warmth from the sun would disappear, of how the fog would drift down with the darkness, of how the cold would creep into everything, of how few people came this way.

'No,' he said. He wondered if his wife had screamed like that. Six of her fingernails had been broken. *Unto the third generation*, Conklin had said. His children and his grandchildren, should he have any, would feel the effects. Alone on a dark parking lot, desperately fighting for her life, and he had been sitting in his study, reading. 'Help never comes when it is needed most.'

Then with real regret for the way things were but which couldn't be changed, he hefted his pack so that it settled firmly between his shoulders and returned the way he had come.

GUY VANDERHAEGHE

Man Descending

It is six-thirty; my wife returns home from work. I am shaving when I hear her key scratching at the lock. I keep the door of our apartment locked at all times. The building has been burgled twice since we moved in and I don't like surprises. My caution annoys my wife; she sees it as proof of a reluctance to approach life with the open-armed camaraderie she expected in a spouse. I can tell that this bit of faithlessness on my part has made her unhappy. Her heels click down our uncarpeted hallway with a lively resonance. So I lock the door of the bathroom to forestall her.

I do this because the state of the bathroom (and my state) will only make her unhappier. I note that my dead cigarette butt has left a liverish stain of nicotine on the edge of the sink and that it has deposited droppings of ash in the basin. The glass of Scotch standing on the toilet tank is not empty. I have been oiling myself all afternoon in expectation of the New Year's party that I would rather not attend. Since Scotch is regarded as a fine social lubricant, I have attempted, to the best of my ability, to get lubricated. Somehow I feel it hasn't worked.

My wife is rattling the door now. 'Ed, are you in there?'

'None other,' I reply, furiously slicing great swaths in the lather on my cheeks.

'Goddamn it, Ed,' Victoria says angrily. 'I asked you. I asked you *please* to be done in there before I get home. I have to get ready for the party. I told Helen we'd be there by eight.'

'I didn't realize it was so late,' I explain lamely. I can imagine the stance she has assumed on the other side of the door. My wife is a social worker and has to deal with people like me every day. Irresponsible people. By now she has crossed her arms across her breasts and inclined her head with its shining helmet of dark hair ever so slightly to one side. Her mouth has puckered like a drawstring purse, and she has planted her legs defiantly and solidly apart, signifying that she will not be moved.

'Ed, how long are you going to be in there?'

I know that tone of voice. Words can never mask its meaning. It is always interrogative, and it always implies that my grievous faults of character could be remedied. *So why don't I make the effort?*

'Five minutes,' I call cheerfully.

Victoria goes away. Her heels are brisk on the hardwood.

My thoughts turn to the party and then naturally to civil servants, since almost all of Victoria's friends are people with whom she works. Civil servants inevitably lead me to think of mandarins, and then Asiatics in general. I settle on Mongols and begin to carefully carve the lather off my face, intent on leaving myself with a shaving-cream Fu Manchu. I do quite a handsome job. I slit my eyes.

'Mirror, mirror on the wall,' I whisper. 'Who's the fiercest of them all?'

From the back of my throat I produce a sepulchral tone of reply. 'You Genghis Ed, Terror of the World! You who raise cenotaphs of skulls! You who banquet off the backs of your enemies!' I imagine myself sweeping out of Central Asia on a shaggy pony, hard-bitten from years in the saddle, turning almond eyes to fabulous cities that lie pliant under my pitiless gaze.

Victoria is back at the bathroom door. 'Ed!'

'Yes, dear?' I answer meekly.

'Ed, explain something to me,' she demands.

'Anything, lollipop,' I reply. This assures her that I have been alerted to danger. It is now a fair fight and she does not have to labour under the feeling that she has sprung upon her quarry from ambush.

'Don't get sarcastic. It's not called for.'

I drain my glass of Scotch, rinse it under the tap, and stick a toothbrush in it, rendering it innocuous. The butt is flicked into the toilet, and the nicotine stain scrubbed out with my thumb. 'I apologize,' I say, hunting madly in the medicine cabinet for mouthwash to disguise my alcoholic breath.

'Ed, you have nothing to do all day. Absolutely nothing. Why couldn't you be done in there before I got home?'

I rinse my mouth. Then I spot my full, white Fu Manchu and begin scraping. 'Well, dear, it's like this,' I say. 'You know how I sweat. And I do get nervous about these little affairs. So I cut the time a little fine. I admit that. But one doesn't want to appear at these affairs too damp. I like to think that my deodorant's power is peaking at my entrance. I'm sure you see—'

'Shut up and get out of there,' Victoria says tiredly.

A last cursory inspection of the bathroom and I spring open the door and present my wife with my best I'm-a-harmless-idiot-don't-hit-me smile. Since I've been unemployed I practise my smiles in the mirror whenever time hangs heavy on my hands. I have one for every occasion. This particular one is a faithful reproduction, Art imitating Life. The other day, while out taking a walk, I saw a large black Labrador taking a crap on somebody's doorstep. We established instant rapport. He grinned hugely at me while his body trembled with exertion. His smile was a perfect blend of physical relief, mischievousness, and apology for his indiscretion. A perfectly suitable smile for my present situation.

'Squeaky, pretty-pink clean,' I announce to my wife.

'Being married to an adolescent is a bore,' Victoria says, pushing past me into the bathroom. 'Make me a drink. I need it.'

I hurry to comply and return in time to see my wife lowering her delightful bottom into a tub of scalding hot, soapy water and ascending wreaths of steam. She lies back and her breasts flatten; she toys with the tap with delicate ivory toes.

'Christ,' she murmurs, stunned by the heat.

I sit down on the toilet seat and fondle my drink, rotating the transparent cylinder and its amber contents in my hand. Then I abruptly hand Victoria her glass and as an opening gambit ask, 'How's Howard?'

My wife does not flinch, but only sighs luxuriantly, steeping herself in the rich heat. I interpret this as hardness of heart. I read in her face the lineaments of a practised and practising adulteress. For some time now I've suspected that Howard, a grave and unctuously dignified psychologist who works for the provincial Department of Social Services, is her lover. My wife has taken to working late and several times when I have phoned her office, disguising my voice and playing the irate beneficiary of the government's largesse, Howard has answered. When we meet socially, Howard treats me with the barely concealed contempt that is due an unsuspecting cuckold.

'Howard? Oh, he's fine.' Victoria answers blandly, sipping at her drink. Her body seems to elongate under the water, and for a moment I feel justified in describing her as statuesque.

'I like Howard,' I say. 'We should have him over for dinner some evening.'

My wife laughs. 'Howard doesn't like you,' she says.

'Oh?' I feign surprise. 'Why?'

'You know why. Because you're always pestering him to diagnose you. He's not stupid, you know. He knows you're laughing up your sleeve at him. You're transparent, Ed. When you don't like someone you belittle their work. I've seen you do it a thousand times.'

'I refuse,' I say, 'to respond to innuendo.'

This conversation troubles my wife. She begins to splash around in the tub. She cannot go too far in her defence of Howard.

'He's not a bad sort,' she says. 'A little stuffy, I grant you, but sometimes stuffiness is preferable to complete irresponsibility. You, on the other hand, seem to have the greatest contempt for anyone whose behaviour even remotely approaches sanity.'

I know my wife is now angling the conversation toward the question of employment. There are two avenues open for examination. She may concentrate on the past, studded as it is with a series of unmitigated disasters, or on the future. On the whole I feel the past is safer ground, at least from my point of view. She knows that I lied about why I was fired from my last job, and six months later still hasn't got the truth out of me.

Actually, I was shown the door because of 'habitual unco-operativeness'. I was employed in an adult extension program. For the life of me I couldn't master the terminology, and this created a rather unfavourable impression. All that talk about 'terminal learners', 'life skills', etc., completely unnerved me. Whenever I was sure I understood what a word meant, someone decided it had become charged with nasty connotations and invented a new 'value-free term'. The place was a goddamn madhouse and I acted accordingly.

I have to admit, though, that there was one thing I liked about the job. That was answering the phone whenever the office was deserted, which it frequently was since everyone was always running out into the community 'identifying needs'. I greeted every caller with a breezy 'College Of Knowledge. Mr Know-It-All here!' Rather juvenile, I admit, but very satisfying. And I was rather sorry I got the boot before I got to meet a real, live, flesh-and-blood terminal learner. Evidently there were thousands of them out in the community and they were a bad thing. At one meeting in which we were trying to decide what should be done about them, I suggested, using a bit of Pentagon jargon I had picked up on the late-night news, that if we ever laid hands on any of them or their ilk, we should have them 'terminated with extreme prejudice'.

'By the way,' my wife asks nonchalantly, 'were you out looking today?'

'Harry Wells called,' I lie. 'He thinks he might have something for me in a couple of months.'

My wife stirs uneasily in the tub and creates little swells that radiate from her body like a disquieting aura.

'That's funny,' she says tartly. 'I called Harry today about finding work for you. He didn't foresee anything in the future.'

'He must have meant the immediate future.'

'He didn't mention talking to you.'

'That's funny.'

Victoria suddenly stands up. Venus rising from the bath. Captive water sluices between her breasts, slides down her thighs.

'Damn it, Ed! When are you going to begin to tell the truth? I'm sick of all this.' She fumbles blindly for a towel as her eyes pin me. 'Just remember,' she adds, 'behave yourself tonight. Lay off my friends.'

I am rendered speechless by her fiery beauty, by this many-times-thwarted love that twists and turns in search of a worthy object. Meekly, I promise.

I drive to the party, my headlights rending the veil of thickly falling, shimmering snow. The city crews have not yet removed the Christmas decorations; strings of lights garland the street lamps, and rosy Santa Clauses salute with good cheer our wintry silence. My wife's stubborn profile makes her disappointment in me palpable. She does not understand that I am a man descending. I can't blame her because it took me years to realize that fact myself.

Revelation comes in so many guises. A couple of years ago I was paging through one of those gossipy newspapers that fill the news racks at supermarkets. They are designed to shock and titillate, but occasionally they run a factual space-filler. One of these was certainly designed to assure mothers that precocious children were no blessing, and since most women are the mothers of very ordinary children, it was a bit of comfort among gloomy predictions about San Francisco toppling into the sea or Martians making off with tots from parked baby carriages.

It seems that in eighteenth-century Germany there was an infant prodigy. At nine months he was constructing intelligible sentences; at a year and a half he was reading the Bible; at three he was teaching himself Greek and Latin. At four he was dead, likely crushed to death by expectations that he was destined to bear headier and more manifold fruits in the future.

This little news item terrified me. I admit it. It was not because this child's brief passage was in any way extraordinary. On the contrary, it was because it followed such a familiar pattern, a pattern I hadn't until then realized existed. Well, that's not entirely true. I had sensed the pattern, I knew it was there, but I hadn't really *felt* it.

His life, like every other life, could be graphed: an ascent that rises to a peak, pauses at a particular node, and then descends. Only the gradient changes in any particular case; this child's was steeper than most, his descent swifter. We all ripen. We are all bound by the same ineluctable law, the same mathematical certainty.

I was twenty-five then; I could put this out of my mind. I am thirty now, still young I admit, but I sense my feet are on the down slope. I know now that I have begun the inevitable descent, the leisurely glissade which will finally topple me at the bottom of my own graph. A man descending is propelled by inertia; the only initiative left him is whether or not he decides to enjoy the passing scene.

Now, my wife is a hopeful woman. She looks forward to the future, but the same impulse that makes me lock our apartment door keeps me in fear of it. So we proceed in tandem, her shoulders tugging expectantly forward, my heels digging in, resisting. Victoria thinks I have ability; she expects me, like some arid desert plant that shows no promise, to suddenly blossom before her wondering eyes. She believes I can choose to be what she expects. I am intent only on maintaining my balance.

Helen and Everett's house is a blaze of light, their windows sturdy squares of brightness. I park the car. My wife evidently decides we shall make our entry as a couple, atoms resolutely linked. She takes my arm. Our host and hostess greet us at the door. Helen and Victoria kiss, and Everett, who distrusts me, clasps my hand manfully and forgivingly, in a holiday mood. We are led into the living-room. I'm surprised that it is already full. There are people everywhere, sitting and drinking, even a few reclining on the carpet. I know almost no one. The unfamiliar faces swim unsteadily for a moment, and I begin to realize that I am quite drunk. Most of the people are young, and, like my wife, public servants

I spot Howard in a corner, propped against the wall. He sports a thick, rich beard. Physically he is totally unlike me, tall and thin. For this reason I cannot imagine Victoria in his arms. My powers of invention are stretched to the breaking-point by the attempt to believe that she might be unfaithful to my body type. I think of myself as bearish and cuddly. Sex with Howard, I surmise, would be athletic and vigorous.

Someone, I don't know who, proffers a glass and I take it. This is a mistake. It is Everett's party punch, a hot cider pungent with cloves. However, I dutifully drink it. Victoria leaves my side and I am free to hunt for some more acceptable libation. I find a bottle of Scotch in the kitchen and pour myself a stiff shot, which I sample. Appreciating its honest taste (it is obviously liquor; I hate intoxicants that disguise their purpose with palatability), I carry it back to the living-room.

A very pretty, matronly young woman sidles up to me. She is one of those kind people who move through parties like wraiths, intent on making late arrivals comfortable. We talk desultorily about the party, agreeing it is wonderful and expressing admiration for our host and hostess. The young woman, who is called Ann, admits to being a lawyer. I admit to being a naval architect. She asks me what I am doing on the prairies if I am a naval architect. This is a difficult question. I know nothing about naval architects and cannot even guess what they might be doing on the prairies.

'Perspectives,' I say darkly.

She looks at me curiously and then dips away, heading for an errant husband. Several minutes later I am sure they are talking about me, so I duck back to the kitchen and pour myself another Scotch.

Helen finds me in her kitchen. She is hunting for olives.

'Ed,' she asks, 'have you seen a jar of olives?' She shows me how big with her hands. Someone has turned on the stereo and I sense a slight vibration in the floor, which means people are dancing in the living-room.

'No,' I reply. 'I can't see anything. I'm loaded,' I confess.

Helen looks at me doubtfully. Helen and Everett don't really approve of drinking—that's why they discourage consumption by serving hot cider at parties. She smiles weakly and gives up olives in favour of employment. 'How's the job search?' she asks politely while she rummages in the fridge.

'Nothing yet.'

'Everett and I have our ears cocked,' she says. 'If we hear of anything you'll be the first to know.' Then she hurries out of the kitchen carrying a jar of gherkins.

'Hey, you silly bitch,' I yell, 'those aren't olives, those are *gherkins*!'

I wander unsteadily back to the living-room. Someone has put a waltz on the stereo and my wife and Howard are revolving slowly and serenely in the limited available space. I notice that he has insinuated his leg between my wife's thighs. I take a good belt and appraise them. They make a handsome couple. I salute them with my glass but they do not see, and so my world-weary and cavalier gesture is lost on them.

A man and a woman at my left shoulder are talking about Chile and Chilean refugees. It seems that she is in charge of some and is having problems with them. They're divided by old political enmities; they won't learn English; one of them insists on driving without a valid operator's licence. Their voices, earnest and shrill, blend and separate, separate and blend. I watch my wife, skilfully led, glide and turn, turn and glide. Howard's face floats above her head, an impassive mask of content.

The wall clock above the sofa tells me it is only ten o'clock. One year is separated from the next by two hours. However, they pass quickly because I have the great good fortune to get involved in a political argument. I know nothing about politics, but then neither do any of the people I am arguing with. I've always found that a really lively argument depends on the ignorance of the combatants. The more ignorant the disputants, the more heated the debate. This one warms nicely. In no time several people have denounced me as a neo-fascist. Their lack of objectivity pleases me no end. I stand beaming and swaying on my feet. Occasionally I retreat to the kitchen to fill my glass and they follow, hurling statistics and analogies at my back.

It is only at twelve o'clock that I realize the extent of the animosity I have created by this performance. One woman genuinely hates me. She refuses a friendly New Year's buss. I plead that politics should not stand in the way of fraternity.

'You must have learned all this stupid, egotistical individualism from Ayn Rand,' she blurts out.

'Who?'

'The writer. Ayn Rand.'

'I thought you were referring to the corporation,' I say.

She calls me an ass hole and marches away. Even in my drunken stupor I perceive that her unfriendly judgement is shared by all people within hearing distance. I find myself talking loudly and violently, attempting to justify myself. Helen is wending her way across the living-room toward me. She takes me by the elbow.

'Ed,' she says, 'you look a little the worse for wear. I have some coffee in the kitchen.'

Obediently I allow myself to be led away. Helen pours me a cup of coffee and sits me down in the breakfast nook. I am genuinely contrite and embarrassed.

'Look, Helen,' I say, 'I apologize. I had too much to drink. I'd better go. Will you tell Victoria I'm ready to leave?'

'Victoria went out to get some ice,' she says uneasily.

'How the hell can she get ice? She doesn't drive.'

'She went with Howard.'

'Oh . . . okay. I'll wait.'

Helen leaves me alone to ponder my sins. But I don't dwell on my sins; I dwell on Victoria's and Howard's. I feel my head, searching for the nascent bumps of cuckoldry. It is an unpleasant joke. Finally I get up, fortify myself with another drink, find my coat and boots, and go outside to wait for the young lovers. Snow is still falling in an unsettling blur. The New Year greets us with a storm.

I do not have long to wait. A car creeps cautiously up the street, its headlights gleaming. It stops at the far curb. I hear car doors slamming and then laughter. Howard and Victoria run lightly across the road. He seems to be chasing her, at least that is the impression I receive from her high-pitched squeals of delight. They start up the walk before they notice me. I stand, or imagine I stand, perfectly immobile and menacing.

'Hi, Howie,' I say. 'How's tricks?'

'Ed,' Howard says, pausing. He sends me a curt nod.

'We went for ice,' Victoria explains. She holds up the bag for proof.

'Is that right, Howie?' I ask, turning my attention to the homebreaker. I am uncertain whether I am creating this scene merely to discomfort Howard, whom I don't like, or because I am jealous. Perhaps a bit of both.

'The name is Howard, Ed.'

'The name is Edward, Howard.'

Howard coughs and shuffles his feet. He is smiling faintly. 'Well, Ed,' he says, 'what's the problem?'

'The problem, Howie, is my wife. The problem is cuckoldry. Likewise the incredible amount of hostility I feel toward you this minute. Now, you're the psychologist, Howie, what's the answer to my hostility?'

Howard shrugs. The smile which appears frozen on his face is wrenched askew with anger.

'No answer? Well, here's my prescription. I'm sure I'd feel much better if I bopped your beanie, Bozo,' I say. Then I begin to do something very stupid. In this kind of weather I'm taking off my coat.

'Stop this,' Victoria says. 'Ed, stop it right now!'

Under this threat of violence Howard puffs himself up. He seems to expand in the night; he becomes protective and paternal. Even his voice deepens; it plumbs the lower registers. 'I'll take care of this, Victoria,' he says gruffly.

'Quit acting like children,' she storms. 'Stop it!'

Poor Victoria. Two wilful men, rutting stags in the stilly night.

Somehow my right arm seems to have got tangled in my coat sleeve. Since I'm drunk, my attempt to extricate myself occupies all my attention. Suddenly the left side of my face goes numb and I find myself flat on my back. Howie towers over me.

'You son of a bitch,' I mumble, '*that* is not cricket.' I try to kick him in the family jewels from where I lie. I am unsuccessful.

Howard is suddenly the perfect gentleman. He graciously allows me to get to my feet. Then he ungraciously knocks me down again. This time the force of his blow spins me around and I make a one-point landing on my nose. Howie is proving more than I bargained for. At this point I find myself wishing I had a pipe wrench in my pocket.

'Had enough?' Howie asks. The rooster crowing on the dunghill.

I hear Victoria. 'Of course he's had enough. What's the matter with you? He's drunk. Do you want to kill him?'

'The thought had entered my mind.'

'Just you let me get my arm loose, you son of a bitch,' I say. 'We'll see who kills who.' I *have* had enough, but of course I can't admit it.

'Be my guest.'

Somehow I tear off my coat. Howard is standing waiting, bouncing up on his toes, weaving his head. I feel slightly dizzy trying to focus on his frenetic motion. 'Come on,' Howard urges me. 'Come on.'

I lower my head and charge at his midriff. A punch on the back of the neck pops my tongue out of my mouth like a released spring. I pitch head first into the snow. A knee digs into my back, pinning me, and punches begin to rain down on the back of my head. The best I can hope for in a moment of lucidity is that Howard will break a hand on my skull.

My wife saves me. I hear her screaming and, resourceful girl that she is, she hauls Howie off my back by the hair. He curses her; she shouts; they argue. I lie on the snow and pant.

I hear the front door open, and I see my host silhouetted in the door-frame.

'Jesus Christ,' Everett yells, 'what's going on out here?'

I roll on my back in time to see Howard beating a retreat to his car. My tigress has put him on the run. He is definitely piqued. The car roars into life and swerves into the street. I get to my feet and yell insults at his tail-lights.

'Victoria, is that you?' Everett asks uncertainly.

She sobs a yes.

'Come on in. You're upset.'

She shakes her head no.

'Do you want to talk to Helen?'

'No.'

Everett goes back into the house nonplussed. It strikes me what a remarkable couple we are.

'Thank you,' I say, trying to shake the snow off my sweater. 'In five years of marriage you've never done anything nicer. I appreciate it.'

'Shut up.'

'Have you seen my coat?' I begin to stumble around searching for my traitorous garment.

'Here.' She helps me into it. I check my pockets. 'I suspect I've lost the car keys,' I say.

'I'm not surprised.' Victoria has calmed down and is drying her eyes on her coat sleeves. 'A good thing too, you're too drunk to drive. We'll walk to Albert Street. They run buses late on New Year's Eve for drunks like you.'

I fall into step with her. I'm shivering with cold but I know better than to complain. I light a cigarette and wince when the smoke sears a cut on the inside of my mouth. I gingerly test a loosened tooth with my tongue.

'You were very brave,' I say. I am so touched by her act of loyalty I take her hand. She does not refuse it.

'It doesn't mean anything.'

'It seems to me you made some kind of decision back there.'

'A perfect stranger might have done the same.'

I allow that this is true.

'I don't regret anything,' Victoria says. 'I don't regret what happened between Howard and me; I don't regret helping you.'

'Tibetan women often have two husbands,' I say.

'What is that supposed to mean?' she asks, stopping under a street-light.

'I won't interfere any more.'

'I don't think you understand,' she says, resuming walking. We enter a deserted street, silent and white. No cars have passed here in hours, the snow is untracked.

'It's New Year's Eve,' I say hopefully, 'a night for resolutions.'

'You can't change, Ed.' Her loss of faith in me shocks me.

I recover my balance. 'I could,' I maintain. 'I feel ready now. I think I've learned something. Honestly.'

'Ed,' she says, shaking her head.

'I resolve,' I say solemnly, 'to find a job.'

'Ed, no.'

'I resolve to tell the truth.'

Victoria actually reaches up and attempts to stifle my words with her mittened hands. I struggle. I realize that, unaccountably, I am crying. 'I resolve to treat you differently,' I manage to say. But as I say it, I know that I am not capable of any of this. I am a man descending and I should not make promises that I cannot keep, not to her—of all people.

'Ed,' she says firmly, 'I think that's enough. There's no point any more.'

She is right. We walk on silently. Injuries so old could likely not be healed. Not by me. The snow seems to fall faster and faster.

HELEN WEINZWEIG

What's Happened to Ravel's Bolero?

Sylvia sipped her martini from the plastic bathroom tumbler, not taking her eyes off the light patches of paint on the wall opposite. Her teeth chattered; she put the tumbler down on the bare floor. Richard said, 'They haven't put the heat on yet.' He poured himself another martini from the glass jar into a paper cup he held in his other hand. Some of the liquid spilled down the side of the jar, onto his bare thigh. Sylvia leaned over and licked his skin. He laughed like a boy and spilled a bit more. They were undressed and sat close together at the far end of the sofa. She picked up her drink. 'Are you going back to your wife?' she asked. He lifted the glass jar and held it in the air and said, 'Cheers.' This time he gulped from the bottle. He began to undress her the moment she came through the door: he could never wait. She kicked off her shoes. On the wall opposite were two square patches of light gray paint. 'The pictures, the ones I gave you?' she asked. 'My sons came up in the station wagon over the week-end and took everything they could carry.' Sylvia sipped from the tumbler. Her teeth chattered. He put his robe around her shoulders.

Richard lay stretched out the full length of the sofa, his long white legs muscular for his age. On the wall opposite, over the table where they often ate, there were two square patches of light gray paint. She got on top of him. 'Are you going to sleep with your wife?' Sylvia wanted to know. In the darkening room she could not make out his expression. When she sat up the juices drained out of her on to the cushion, but she knew the stain would be absorbed by the rough brown cloth; even now she had to look closely to see an unevenness of color in the middle cushion. He stood up and she put her face into the soft flesh of his belly; she smelled their sweat on his skin. Sylvia thought her purse felt heavier with the weight of the articles she had taken. She smiled up at him. Together they got up and started towards the bedroom.

Sylvia sipped from the plastic tumbler. The rugs were rolled up, her clothes were all over the bare floor, one shoe near the window, her dress in a heap. The rough brown cloth would absorb his ejaculation which dripped out of her when she sat up. Richard was wearing the wool tartan bathrobe she had given him that first Christmas. She had never seen him in house slippers. 'What's wrong?' she asked immediately. 'I think I'm catching a cold,' Richard said. She could not find her other shoe. Her teeth chattered; she put the tumbler down on the bare floor. He gulped from the bottle. This time when she came in, having let herself into the apartment with a key she kept separate in a red leather case, she had to seek him out. He was in the kitchen; in front of him on the counter were a bottle of gin and a bottle of vermouth. He was wearing the bathrobe she had given him that first Christmas. He couldn't find anything to mix the martinis in; he opened and banged shut the cupboard doors. The cupboards were empty. The first desperate clutching, followed by sticky stuff seeping out of her all over the middle cushion when she sat up, but the rough brown synthetic material dried quickly. She stared at the empty hi-fi cabinet. 'What's wrong?' Sylvia asked when she found him in the kitchen. 'I've been asleep,' Richard said, 'I took the day off; I don't feel well.' His wife will have the sofa cleaned, Sylvia thought. He was pale and kept his face averted. 'The movers are coming in the morning,' Richard said. He could never wait to make love to her. She put the palm of her hand against his forehead: it was hot. She got down on all fours and searched for the other shoe under the sofa. He looked at her finally and then away again. He couldn't find what he wanted in the empty cupboards and banged each door shut. Sylvia watched him consider an almost empty olive jar. He dumped a half dozen olives on the counter. She brought out the ice cubes. 'What's wrong?' Sylvia kept asking. 'I've been transferred to New York. I'll be working out of Head Office.' (His familiar bony face with the deep line down each cheek.) When he saw that she was not going to make a scene, he turned to face her. His brown eyes were clouded over. Side by side on the sofa, undressed, they drank martinis. He could never wait to make love to her. Across the room, against the wall opposite, at the oak table where they used to eat, she observed there was one chair and one place setting on the table in front of the chair. While he was under the shower she started to pick up her clothes. She couldn't find the other shoe.

Richard gulped the martini straight from the glass jar. 'Does your wife still love you?' Sylvia asked. He moved to the end of the sofa, farthest from her, because the middle cushion was wet. (But the rough brown cloth would absorb the moisture.) Her teeth chattered; she put down the empty tumbler on the bare floor. He looked at her and away again. Together they got up and started towards the bedroom. She stopped at the corner to the little hall to look at the empty hi-fi cabinet. The second time, in his bed, was to be for her satisfaction. On top of the dresser were his wrist watch, wallet, keys and a Texaco bill. The dresser drawers were empty. He got under the covers, his feet were cold, as were hers, the heat had not come on yet in the apartment even though it was the middle of October. Together they got up and started towards the bedroom. She stopped to look at the hi-fi cabinet. The shelves were empty, the record compartments were empty. 'What happened to Ravel's *Bolero?*' Sylvia asked. 'Darling, I'm sorry, but my sons cleared out everything they could carry. I didn't dare say anything,' Richard said. She turned and went first into the bathroom. She stretched out in the bed. She watched him go into the bathroom. When he returned she arched her back while he placed a towel under her. The second time, in the bed, where they could move more freely, was to be for her satisfaction. On top of the dresser were his wrist watch, wallet, keys and a Texaco bill. She picked up the bill and asked, 'Is this where you live on Long Island?' He snatched the paper out of her hand.

Sylvia waited until he came out of the bathroom. 'Will I see you again?' she asked. 'We had to come to the end of the road some time. This is it,' Richard told her. Over the dresser where the mirror used to hang was an oblong patch of light gray paint in contrast with the darker paint. Richard snatched the bill out of her hand. She watched him go into the bathroom. Blowing his nose and shuffling in his slippers Richard looked old. The bedroom was at the back of the building and was quiet, unlike the living room which echoed the constant noise of traffic on Avenue Road. She lay down on the towel. The second time was to be for her pleasure. 'How old is your wife,' Sylvia asked. 'Same age as I am,' Richard replied. He pulled the towel from under her and wiped his groin. All the same, their love-making was not entirely successful. She began to dress, picking up her garments one by one from the bare floor. He lay with his eyes shut. The dresser drawers were empty. She arched her back while he placed a towel under her. 'Do you have twin beds or a double bed in your house on Long Island?' Sylvia wanted to know. In reply Richard said, 'She is not like you in bed: she hasn't your energy.' The elevators were still, everyone having gone out or decided to stay in for the evening. She had not been satisfied. His feet were cold, but his face when he kissed her was hot. He snatched the bill out of her hand. 'It's a big promotion,' he said later, 'vice-president in charge of personnel. 82,000 employees, all over the world. I will have to live up to the job.' He had small teeth that didn't suit his large features. She watched him go into the bathroom. On the oak table where they used to eat was a place setting for one. She couldn't find her other shoe. The dresser drawers were empty.

Sylvia pulled the drapes in the living room and lit the lamps. The sofa cushions were reversible. She began to pick up her clothes. On the oak table was set out a plate, a linen napkin in a sterling silver ring, a knife, fork and spoon, and sterling silver salt and pepper shakers. They went towards the bedroom. Where the mirror had hung opposite the bed there was an oblong patch of light gray paint on the wall. She would wait to comb her hair when he came out of the shower. 'My sons took the records.' She knew he referred to Ravel's *Bolero* which she had bought him for his birthday. Yet their love-making was not entirely successful. The dresser drawers were empty. 'Where are my things?' Sylvia asked. 'Darling, I'm sorry, The incinerator. I had no choice,' His wrist watch, wallet and keys were on top of the dresser. She picked up the Texaco bill with his name and address imprinted in carbon from a credit card. 'Is this where you live on Long Island?' she asked. Richard snatched the paper out of her hand; he put it in his wallet in front of the bills. He put the watch on his wrist and the keys in his pocket.

Sylvia let herself into the apartment with a key she kept separate in a red leather case. At first she thought he was out. Then she found him in the kitchen, looking for something in the cupboards. She saw the cupboards were empty. When she came in, he pulled his bathrobe together over his bare chest, tightening the sash. He looked at her then away again. 'What's wrong?' Sylvia asked. He kept his face averted. 'The movers are coming in the morning,' Richard replied. She brought out the ice cubes. He gulped from the bottle. 'Cheers,' he said, holding up the glass jar. When he saw that she was not going to make a scene he turned towards her. 'I think I'm catching a cold,' he said. His brown eyes were clouded over. They moved more freely in the bed. Before she went into the bathroom, she covered him with a blanket. The first thing his wife will do will be to have the sofa cleaned, Sylvia reflected. She noticed her purse where she had left it on the oak table where they sometimes ate. When he saw she was not going to make a scene, Richard began to undress her: he couldn't wait to make love to her. Some of the liquid spilled down the side of the jar onto his bare thigh. Sylvia bent over and licked his skin. He laughed like a boy. He snatched the bill out of her hand. Blowing his nose and shuffling in his slippers Richard looked old. She kicked off her shoes and one landed near the windows. 'Listen,' Richard said, 'if you ever get to New York . . .'

He took off his robe and put it around his shoulders. Her teeth chattered. When she sat up the juices drained out of her onto the middle cushion, but the rough brown cloth absorbed the spill. His narrow white body was in sharp contrast with the dark cloth; she would forever remember the shape of him, she thought to herself. The bedroom was at the back of the building and was quiet. It faced the little gardens of the new condominiums on Oriole Road. She lay down on the towel and pulled the sheet up to her chin. He was apologetic. 'My wife told my sons to start moving me back home. They left me with one towel.' He never waited: he began to undress her the moment she came into the apartment. Their love-making was not entirely successful. He pulled the towel from under her and wiped his groin. 'Hungry?' Richard asked. 'We'll have to go out to eat. Let's go down to Pierre's. You'd like that, eh?' She began to dress. The evening traffic sounded loud in the living room. She went and stood outside the bathroom door to make sure he was still under the shower. She noticed her purse where she had left it on the oak table and picked up the sterling silver napkin ring and the sterling silver salt and pepper shakers and put them in her purse. She snapped the clasp shut. She went down on all fours to look for her other shoe under the sofa. When he strode back into the living room he was fully dressed. He looked distinguished in his dark blue suit, white shirt and dark blue tie with small flecks of red in it. His brown eyes were clear. 'You must be hungry,' he said, pulling on his cuffs, 'we'll go down to Pierre's. You'd like that, Sylvia, eh?' She thought her purse felt heavier with the weight of the silver.

Sylvia remembered she hadn't combed her hair. When he came out of the shower she went into the bathroom and locked the door. She watched him go into the bathroom, admiring his long, lean back and small waist. He came back with a towel. 'Does your wife still love you?' He stroked her legs and kissed her breasts. He held her and said, 'I have no choice. They're a very conservative company; a family firm run by family men. No private telephones.' She began to dress. She got down on all fours to look for her shoe under the sofa. The evening traffic was loud in the living room. She stood outside the bathroom door to make sure he was still under the shower. She snapped the clasp shut. He held the door open. 'Will you write?' she asked. 'No promises,' he replied, stepping backwards. 'You're safe with me,' she said. 'No promises,' he repeated. Blowing his nose and shuffling in his slippers he looked old. He held the door open for her. He was distinguished in his dark blue suit. The smell of his shaving cream and cologne was familiar. Sylvia was abstracted and silent. She shifted her purse to her other hand. Now that he knew she would not make a scene he smiled down at her.

Notes

MARGARET ATWOOD. Born in Ottawa in 1939, Margaret Atwood was educated at the University of Toronto and Harvard University and lives in Toronto. She has become one of Canada's best-known writers—distinguished in poetry, fiction, and criticism—and has an international reputation.

Atwood's first book of poems, *The Circle Game* (1966), won a Governor General's Award. Since then she has published ten other collections, including *The Journals of Susanna Moodie* (1970), *Power Politics* (1973), *Interlunar* (1984), and *Selected Poems* (1976). She is the editor of *The New Oxford Book of Canadian Verse in English* (1982). Her novels are *The Edible Woman* (1969), *Surfacing* (1972), *Lady Oracle* (1976), *Life Before Man* (1979), *Bodily Harm* (1981), and *The Handmaid's Tale* (1985). Her short fiction has been collected in *Dancing Girls* (1977), *Murder in the Dark* (1983), and *Bluebeard's Egg* (1983). In criticism Atwood is the author of the influential and controversial *Survival: A Thematic Guide to Canadian Literature* (1972) and of *Second Words: Selected Critical Prose* (1982).

One reason for Atwood's popularity as a writer of fiction can be found in her imaginative explorations of the nuances of late twentieth-century society, as in 'The Salt Garden', reprinted here from *Bluebeard's Egg*.

SANDRA BIRDSELL (b. 1942) grew up in rural Manitoba and now lives in Winnipeg. She began publishing her short stories in 'little magazines'—particularly those in western Canada such as *Grain, Capilano Review, NeWest Review*, and *Prairie Fire*—and became an active member of the Manitoba Writers' Guild for a number of years. Her first collection, *Night Travellers* (1982), consists of a series of linked stories set in the fictitious Manitoba town of Agassiz. Her story about illness, age, and death, 'Niagara Falls', is reprinted here from *Ladies of the House* (1984), which contains stories from rural Manitoba and others that explore the (often gritty) working class life of Winnipeg.

Besides short stories Sandra Birdsell has written film scripts for the National Film Board, including dramatizations of her own work, and plays for Winnipeg theatres. She won a National Magazine Award for fiction, and in 1984 received the Gerald Lampert Award, administered by the League of Canadian Poets and given in alternate years for poetry and prose fiction.

NEIL BISSOONDATH was born in 1955 in Trinidad and now lives in Toronto. He comes from a literary family. His grandfather Seepersad Naipaul was a journalist on the *Trinidad Guardian* for most of his working life and published a collection of short stories in Trinidad in 1943. (An expanded version of this book appeared in London in 1976 as *The Adventures of Gurudeva and Other Stories*.) Two of Seepersad Naipaul's sons became well-known writers: V.S. Naipaul and Shiva Naipaul, who died suddenly at the age of forty in August 1985.

Neil Bissoondath immigrated to Canada in 1973, partly on the advice of his uncle V.S. Naipaul. He studied French at York University, Toronto, and after graduation taught in a language school in that city. His stories have been broadcast on the CBC's 'Anthology' and published in *Saturday Night*. 'There Are a Lot of Ways to Die'—a story that links the world of Trinidad and Toronto—is reprinted from his first book, *Digging Up the Mountains* (1985), which contain stories set in Trinidad, Canada, Central America, and Japan.

BARRY CALLAGHAN, the son of Morley Callaghan, was born in 1937 in Toronto, where he still lives, and educated at St Michael's College, University of Toronto. Since the mid-1960s he has taught contemporary literature at Atkinson College, York University. He has had a parallel and very active career in journalism as a writer and commentator on radio and television and as a contributor to such magazines as *Toronto Life* and *Saturday Night*. For a half-dozen years in the late 1960s he edited and wrote extensively for a lively, wide-ranging, and frequently controversial weekly book page in the Toronto *Telegram*. He is publisher and editor of the literary quarterly 'Exile', and under the imprint Exile Editions also publishes books, with an emphasis on imaginative literature and the visual arts.

Barry Callaghan's stories have appeared in *Saturday Night, Exile, The Ontario Review*, and frequently in the English magazine *Punch*. Notable for their literary sophistication and for the sympathy with which he writes about the gamblers, whores, gays, and other non-conformists, they have been collected in *The Black Queen Stories* (1983), from which the title story is reprinted here. Callaghan is also a poet, the author of a complex and ambitious long poem, *The Hogg Poems and Drawings* (1978), and of *As Close as We Came*, a collection that appeared in 1983. He edited an anthology of Canadian love poems in English and French, *Lords of Winter and of Love* (1983), and gathered together

The Lost and Found Stories of Morley Callaghan (1985). He has also edited a major anthology for publication in 1986: *Alchemists in Winter: Canadian Poetry in French and English*.

MATT COHEN was born in 1942 in Kingston, Ont., and grew up in Ottawa. He now lives in Toronto, but spends some of his time on a farm he owns near Verona, north of Kingston. He began his career as a writer of fiction with *Korsoniloff* (1969). His second novel, *Johnny Crackle Sings* (1971), has the Ottawa Valley as its setting. In the next few years Cohen published five ambitious novels; three of them, beginning with *The Disinherited* in 1974, take place in the fictitious eastern Ontario town of Salem. In 1984 he published *The Spanish Doctor*, a major historical novel. His short stories have been collected in several books, from *Columbus and the Fat Lady* (1972) to *Café Le Dog* (1983). Cohen has been active in the literary community as an editor of fiction for Coach House Press, as a member of the Writer's Union, and in other ways.

As a writer Cohen has been both an innovator and the author of fiction that occupies the traditional middle ground. 'The Sins of Tomas Benares', reprinted here from *Café Le Dog*, explores aspects of the Old World and the New in a downtown Toronto neighborhood. At the same time it is a family saga, written within the confines of a short story.

MAVIS GALLANT (b. 1922). Born in Montreal and educated in seventeen different public, private, and convent schools in Canada and the United States, Mavis Gallant worked briefly for the National Film Board and then on the Montreal *Standard* (a weekly newspaper that was a competitor of the *Star Weekly*; both papers are now gone). She left Montreal in 1950 and has lived in Paris ever since. She returned to Canada in 1983-4 to be writer-in-residence at the University of Toronto.

Gallant has published two novels—*Green Water, Green Sky* (1959) and *A Fairly Good Time* (1970)—and five collections of short stories. Almost all her stories first appeared in *The New Yorker*, to which she began contributing in 1951. ('The Chosen Husband', reprinted here, was first published in *The New Yorker* in April 1985.) Her short-story collections are: *The Other Paris* (1956), *My Heart Is Broken* (1959), *The Pegnitz Junction* (1973), *From the Fifteenth District* (1979), and *Home Truths* (1981), which won a Governor General's Award. (An American edition of this collection of her Canadian stories was published in 1985 to highly favourable reviews.) Her latest collection is *Overhead in a Balloon: Stories of Paris* (1985). A selection of Gallant's stories, *The End of the World and Other Stories*, edited by Robert Weaver, was published in the New Canadian Library in 1974.

Mavis Gallant has also written much distinguished non-fiction. *The New Yorker* published (in September 1968) her two-part account of the student riots in Paris in the spring of 1968—'The Events in May: A Paris Notebook'—and a long essay that served as the introduction to *The Affair of Gabrielle Russier* (1971), about a thirty-year-old teacher of languages in Marseilles who had a love affair with a sixteen-year-old male student and later killed herself.

Issue 28 (1978) of *Canadian Fiction Magazine* was devoted to Gallant and her work.

KATHERINE GOVIER was born in 1948 in Edmonton and studied at the University of Alberta, where she was encouraged as a young writer by Rudy Wiebe and Dorothy Livesay. In 1971 she received an M.A. from York University, Toronto, where she now lives, teaching one course in creative writing at York. She has written articles for the Toronto *Globe & Mail*, the Toronto *Star*, *Saturday Night*, and *Toronto Life*, and has won two national journalism awards.

Govier has published two novels, *Random Descent* (1979) and *Going Through the Motions* (1982). Her short stories appeared with increasing frequency in the late 1970s and 1980s in a variety of Canadian magazines. Many of them are set in Toronto, and they often deal with people trying to come to terms with the world of the Yuppie Generation. Her story 'The Dragon', reprinted here, was included in her first collection, *Fables of Brunswick Avenue*, published in 1985 in the Penguin Short Fiction series.

W.P. KINSELLA was born in 1935 in Edmonton, Alta. He worked as a civil servant, a life-insurance salesman, a cab driver, and as the manager of a pizza parlour before really beginning his literary career after enrolling in the creative writing department at the University of Victoria in Victoria, B.C. Later he attended the Writer's Workshop at the University of Iowa. He taught for several years at the University of Calgary, and now lives as a full-time writer in White Rock, B.C. Kinsella has written four books of Indian stories, beginning with *Dance Me Outside* in 1977. In 1980 he published a collection of baseball stories, *Shoeless Joe Jackson Comes to Iowa*, and in 1982 a novel, *Shoeless Joe*, which won the Houghton Mifflin Literary Fellowship and the 'Books in Canada' First Novel Award. Both *Shoeless Joe* and *Dance Me Outside* have been optioned for film productions, and a second baseball novel, *The Iowa Baseball Confederacy*, is to be published in 1986.

In 'The Thrill of the Grass' and his other baseball stories Kinsella makes exuberant use of the traditions, myths, and present-day issues that enliven a sport that has attracted so many fiction writers in Canada and the United States. This story was broadcast on the CBC radio program 'Anthology' and the CBC stereo program 'Storyline' and later became the title story of a second collection of baseball stories, published in the Penguin Short Fiction series in 1984.

NORMAN LEVINE (b. 1923). In *Canada Made Me* Norman Levine has described how he grew up in the Jewish community in Ottawa's Lower Town. He served in the RCAF during the Second World War and afterwards studied at McGill University. He went to England in the late 1940s and lived there—for much of the time in St. Ives, Cornwall—until his return to Canada in 1980. He now lives in Toronto. He has been a full-time writer for most of his adult life.

Levine published a collection of poetry, *The Tight-Rope Walker*, in 1950 and a war novel, *The Angled Road*, two years later. In the mid 1950s he began to work on a book that would combine autobiographical material with an investigation of Canadian society from the underside in the manner of Henry Miller and George Orwell. That book became *Canada Made Me*, published in England and the United States in 1958; but because of its disenchanted view of life in this country, there was no Canadian edition until 1979.

Levine published a second novel, *From a Seaside Town*, in 1970; but he is best known, as a writer of fiction, for his short stories. Among his collections are *One Way Ticket* (1961), *Thin Ice* (1979), and *Champagne Barn* (1984). Many of his stories have been broadcast by the CBC and the BBC, and have been translated and published throughout Europe. His translators in West Germany were the distinguished novelist Heinrich Böll and his wife.

Norman Levine's 'Django, Karfunkelstein, & Roses', a story about memory and the deceptions that memory plays on us, was commissioned for broadcast in November 1984 during the celebration of the 30th anniversary of the CBC radio series 'Anthology'. It has since been published in *The Canadian Forum* and will be appearing in the Autumn 1985 issue of the English monthly *Encounter* and will be broadcast on BBC Radio 3.

JOYCE MARSHALL was born in 1913 in Montreal and educated at McGill University; but her career as a writer, editor, and translator has taken place in Toronto. Her first novel, *Presently Tomorrow* (1946), was set in the Eastern Townships of Quebec in the early 1930s, and a second novel, *Lovers and Strangers* (1957), took place in Toronto in the late 1940s.

Among Marshall's translations are *Word from New France: The Selected Letters of Marie de l'Incarnation*, for which she wrote an important historical introduction, and *No Passport: A Discovery of Canada*, by the late Quebec travel writer Eugène Cloutier. Her translations of three books by Gabrielle Roy—*The Road Past Altamont, Windflower*, and *Enchanted Summer*—involved her in a close collaboration with that author; she was awarded the Canada Council Translation Prize in 1976 for her translation of *Enchanted Summer*.

Marshall's only collection of short stories, *A Private Place* (1975), brought together seven finely crafted stories written between the early 1950s and the 1970s. 'My Refugee', a remembrance of the war years, is one of several new stories. It has been broadcast on the CBC's 'Anthology' series, and was included in *83: Best Canadian Stories*, edited by David Helwig and Sandra Martin, the short-story annual published by Oberon Press. Another of Marshall's recent stories, 'Avis de Vente', won the Silver award for fiction in the 1985 National Magazine Awards.

ALICE MUNRO (b. 1931) lives in Clinton in southwestern Ontario not far from Lake Huron and from another southwestern Ontario town, Wingham, where she was born and grew up. She attended the University of Western Ontario in London, and then lived for a number of years in Vancouver and Victoria, B.C., where her first husband owned a bookstore.

Munro began writing stories while she was at university. Her early stories were published in such magazines as *Chatelaine*, *The Canadian Forum*, *The Montrealer*, and *The Tamarack Review*. Her first collection, *Dance of the Happy Shades*, appeared in 1968 and won a Governor General's award; her first novel, *Lives of Girls and Women* (1971), won the Canadian Booksellers' Award in 1972. Three more collections of stories have been published: *Something I've Been Meaning to Tell You* (1974), *Who Do You Think You Are?* (1978), and *The Moons of Jupiter* (1982). *Who Do You Think You Are?* won a Governor General's Award and was a runner-up for the Booker Prize in the United Kingdom. Most of her recent stories first appeared in *The New Yorker*; one or two long stories and a memoir of her father were published in the New York literary quarterly *Grand Street*. 'Miles City, Montana', an exploration of family life, was published in *The New Yorker* in January 1985, and will be included in a new collection of stories, tentatively called *The Progress of Love*, to be published by Macmillan of Canada in the fall of 1986.

Several of Munro's stories have been dramatized for television: 'Boys and Girls', a production by Atlantis Films, Toronto, won an Academy Award in 1984. Alice Munro was the first Canadian winner, in 1978, of the Canada-Australia Prize.

LEON ROOKE was born in 1934 in North Carolina and educated there. He served in the U.S. Army in Alaska from 1958 to 1960, and taught English and creative writing in several American universities before moving to Victoria, B.C., in 1969. In 1981 he won the Canada-Australia literary prize, and in 1984-5 he was writer-in-residence at the University of Toronto. With the writer John Metcalf he edited *The New Press Anthology: Best Canadian Short Fiction #1* in 1984, to begin what is intended to be an annual collection of unpublished short stories and the editors' choices of the best stories of the year from the literary magazines.

Rooke himself has been a prolific contributor of stories to literary magazines in Canada and the United States, and since 1968 has published almost a dozen books—both novels and short-story collections. His novels include *Fat Woman* (1980) and *Shakespeare's Dog* (1983), which won a Governor General's Award. His short-story collections include *The Broad Back of the Angel* (1977), *The Birth Control King of the Upper Volta* (1982), *Sing Me No Love Songs, I'll Say You No Prayers* (1984), and *A Bolt of White Cloth* (also 1984). (Imaginative book titles are a Leon Rooke trademark.)

Critics have described Rooke as a 'post-realistic' and a 'post-modernist' writer. His fiction is notable for its moments of magic and illusion, and for its portraits of strong, exuberant women—characteristics that are well displayed in the title story of *A Bolt of White Cloth*, reprinted here

CAROL SHIELDS was born in 1935 in Oak Park, Illinois, and now lives in Winnipeg. She is married to a professor of civil engineering and she herself has taught at the universities of Ottawa, British Columbia, and Manitoba.

In the past dozen years Carol Shields has published poetry, short stories, literary criticism, and novels. She has written for the stage, and her radio play 'Women Waiting'—a prize winner in the CBC's literary competition in 1983—has been broadcast twice on 'Morningside'. Her first novel, *Small Ceremonies* (1976), won the Canadian Authors' Association Award for the best novel of the year. Her other novels are *The Box Garden* (1977), *Happenstance* (1980), and *A Fairly Conventional Woman* (1982).

Shields' cool-eyed character study, 'Mrs. Turner Cutting the Grass', the story reprinted here, was first published in *Arts Manitoba*, and received the Gold Award for fiction in the National Magazine Awards for 1985. It is included in the first collection of stories, *Various Miracles* (1985).

ELIZABETH SPENCER was born in 1921 in Carrollton, Mississippi and attended Bellhaven College in Jackson and Vanderbilt University. She worked as a teacher and journalist before beginning a distinguished career as novelist and short-story writer. Since 1958 she and her husband have lived in Montreal.

Spencer has published five novels, two novellas, and two collections of short stories. Her early novels, beginning with *Fire in the Morning* in 1948, belong to the magnificent literary tradition of the American South. In 1956 she went to Italy on a Guggenheim Fellowship, and her two novellas, *The Light in the Piazza* (1960) and *Knights and Dragons* (1965), are about Americans living in Italy. *The Light in the Piazza* was filmed in 1962, starring Olivia de Havilland, and

Knights and Dragons was reprinted in a major collection of her short fiction, *The Stories of Elizabeth Spencer* (1981), which has a Foreword by a fellow writer from Mississippi, Eudora Welty. Spencer has published only a few stories set in Canada, but like all her fiction they are notable for moments of intuitive insight and a sense of self-discovery. 'Madonna' first appeared in *84 Best Canadian Stories* (Oberon Press), the short-story annual edited by David Helwig and Sandra Martin.

AUDREY THOMAS was born in 1935 in Binghamton, N.Y., and educated at Smith College in the U.S. and St Andrews University in Scotland. She and her ex-husband immigrated to Canada in 1959, though in the mid-sixties she lived for three years in Ghana, where her husband was teaching at the time. The United States, Canada, and West Africa have all provided settings for her fiction. In recent years she has combined her own writing with periods of teaching at the University of Victoria and the University of British Columbia. In the academic year 1985–86 she was writer-in-residence at the Centre of Canadian Studies at the University of Edinburgh in the annual exchange program of Canadian and Scottish writers that is supported by the Canada Council and the Scottish Arts Council.

Thomas's first book, published in 1967, was a collection of short stories, *Ten Green Bottles*. Her other fiction includes novels (*Mrs. Blood*; *Blown Figures*), two related novellas published in one volume (*Munchmeyer* and *Prospero on the Island*), and two more collections of stories, *Real Mothers* and *Two in the Bush and Other Stories*, both published in 1981. One critic has written of Audrey Thomas's stories that 'the complex emotions and ideas explored never strain the capacities of the form', and this is the case with 'Crossing the Rubicon', which is reprinted from *Real Mothers*.

W.D. VALGARDSON (b. 1939) grew up in Gimli, a town in the Interlake District of Manitoba not far from Winnipeg, whose inhabitants are mostly of Icelandic descent. He was educated at United College in Winnipeg, the University of Manitoba, and the University of Iowa, where—like W.P. Kinsella and a number of other Canadian writers—he was enrolled in the university's influential Writer's Workshop. Valgardson has published three collections of short stories: *Bloodflowers* (1973), *God is Not a Fish Inspector* (1975), and *Red Dust* (1978). He is also the author of a book of poetry, *In the Gutting Shed* (1978), and a novel *Gentle Sinners*, which won the 'Books in Canada' First Novel Award for 1980. *Gentle Sinners* and several of Valgardon's short stories have been filmed for television.

Much of Valgardson's fiction deals with situations in which poverty, isolation, and the kind of random violence depicted in 'A Matter of Violence' are commonplace. This story won first prize in the fiction section of the CBC literary competition in 1980.

GUY VANDERHAEGHE was born in 1951 in Esterhazy, Sask. He studied history at the University of Saskatchewan, where he wrote an M.A. thesis about the novelist John Buchan. He has worked as a teacher, archivist, and researcher, and is now a full-time writer living in Saskatoon.

Vanderhaeghe began writing short stories in the late 1970s, influenced—as the critic David Staines has noted—by such prairie novelists as Margaret Laurence, Sinclair Ross, and Robert Kroetsch. Other major influences have been Alice Munro and certain writers from the American South for their treatment of small-town life. Vanderhaeghe's stories were published widely in Canadian literary magazines, and in 1980 his story 'The Watcher' won the annual contributor's prize awarded by *Canadian Fiction Magazine*. Twelve of his stories appeared in the collection *Man Descending* (1982), which won a Governor General's Award. *The Trouble with Heroes*, a second collection of stories, was published in 1983.

Ed, who appears in 'Man Descending', the story reprinted here, is also the protagonist of Vanderhaeghe's first novel, *My Present Age*, a black comedy published in 1984.

HELEN WEINZWEIG (b. 1915) came to Canada from Poland at the age of nine. She attended high school in Toronto, but had to give up her schooling during the Depression to go to work as a stenographer and later as a receptionist and a sales-person. She married the musician and composer John Weinzweig in 1940. They live in Toronto. She did not publish her first novel *Passing Ceremony* until she was 57. Her second novel, *Basic Black with Pearls*, appeared in 1980 and won the City of Toronto Book Award in 1981. Both books are short novels—the longer of the two, *Basic Black with Pearls*, is only 135 pages; fantastical, perceptive, comic, and pathetic in turn, they are the work of a writer who has read widely in European and North American fiction.

Helen Weinzweig's short stories, so far uncollected, have been published in *Jewish Dialog*, *The Tamarack Review*, *Saturday Night*, *The Canadian Forum*, and other magazines, and broadcast by the CBC. 'What Happened to Ravel's Bolero', which has the qualities found in Helen Weinzweig's longer fiction, first appeared in *The Fiddlehead* in April 1982.
